PROGRAMMING: AN INTRODUCTION TO COMPUTER LANGUAGES AND TECHNIQUES

PROGRAMMING: an introduction to computer languages and techniques

WARD DOUGLAS MAURER

University of California, Berkeley

Department of Electrical Engineering and Computer Sciences

HOLDEN-DAY, INC.

San Francisco, Cambridge, London, Amsterdam

TO CAROL

PREFACE

The word **programming,** without any qualifying adjective, refers to the construction of programs for an electronic digital computer. The number of programmers currently working in the United States on a full time basis has been estimated at over 100,000. This book is an introduction to the basic techniques of programming in an algebraic language and in machine language. It is intended for use in an intermediate course on programming at the junior, senior, or graduate level; in exceptional situations, it may be used at the sophomore level. Students should have done well in high school mathematics, but such courses as accounting, elementary statistics, and calculus are not necessary in order to use this book, since it contains no numerical analysis and no discussion of business languages or operations research. However, familiarity with some algebraic programming language, such as ALGOL, FORTRAN, JOVIAL, MAD, or NELIAC, is assumed, and the student should also be acquainted with the binary number system and should know how to read and construct a flowchart.

In addition to learning the fundamentals of programming, the student should be given the opportunity to program a computer himself. Any algebraic language, and any machine language, may be used for this purpose. The principles of machine language programming are broad enough in scope to apply to any digital computer. The operations manual and the assembler manual of the given computer should be used as texts, and material from these manuals learned, either in this course or in a prerequisite course; a book describing the particular machine language being studied may also be helpful. For use under the quarter system, the first eleven chapters may be covered in ten weeks, as is done in the author's own course. For use under a semester system, the first two weeks may be given over to a review of programming in an algebraic language, and the last week may be used for review, allowing a pace of one chapter per week. In order to provide a means of illustrating some of the principles, a machine language has been invented for the purposes of this book. This is *not* to be used in class assignments after the first few weeks; if a program is assigned, it should be written in either the algebraic language or the machine language which is actually under study. A full discussion of "textbook machine language" is given in Appendix A. There is also a summary of those features of FORTRAN which the reader must know in order to understand some of the examples, in Appendix B; and a summary of the binary number system in Appendix C.

If machine language is being taught concurrently, the instructor may find it necessary to take some material out of sequence. In particular, a certain amount of discussion of input-output on the computer to which the student has access will be necessary in order to write and check out machine language programs. Material from sections 6-1, 6-2, 10-1 through 11-3, and 11-8, together with Appendix D on checkout, may be used for this purpose; this material does not depend on anything beyond section 3-2. In this case, problems dealing with the specific machine language being studied should be constructed and assigned.

The flavor of a programming course is quite different from that of, say, either a chemistry course or a calculus course. Computer program checkout imposes a discipline which is fully as strict as anything found in chemistry; every statement in a program must be right, or the program will not produce correct results, except rarely by accident. And yet, in the broader sense, programming is much less an exact science than either chemistry or calculus. If there is one way to write a program, there are a hundred ways. Two students asked to solve the same problem independently will never write the same program. Also, as is painfully evident from the various data processing glossaries, many objects and concepts in programming still have more than one name, depending on the make and model of the computer involved, and the best we can do is to learn the two or three commonest names. Almost any flat statement which can be made about programming, including several in this book, will have exceptions; the reader is exhorted to take nothing on faith, but to refer for final arbitration in any situation to the appropriate computer manual.

One important issue which must be faced in teaching machine language is that of reference to equipment manufactured by specific companies. Previous books on machine language programming have confined themselves to a single make and model or a single series; they have thereby not only limited (and dated) their applicability, but have been unable to present a general conception of programming in machine language. We, however, make reference to over a dozen specific, currently available computers by make and model. Almost all discussion of specific computers is confined to the sections in smaller type that are scattered throughout the book; each of these sections is associated with a concept, such as floating point, shifting, double precision, subroutine calling instructions, card readers, macro-assembly, or standard tape formats, and describes the approach taken by each of several computers. Such a catholicity of approach forces the student to become aware of a broader range of machine language techniques than if he confined himself to any one computer, no matter how powerful. Too many IBM 360 programmers have never heard of indirect addressing; too many CDC 6600 programmers would not know how to make use of skip instructions; too many IBM 7094 programmers are unaware of how the presence of a two-way rather than a three-way comparison instruction affects binary searching, all because these features are nonexistent on the corresponding computers.

In most cases, we have used the popular abbreviation for a computer rather than its full name. The manufacturers of computers mentioned in this way are as follows:

Control Data Corporation	CDC
Digital Equipment Corporation	DEC
General Electric	GE
International Business Machines	IBM
Radio Corporation of America	RCA
Scientific Data Systems	SDS

Some manufacturers, such as Burroughs, Honeywell, and Philco, do not use mnemonics. The name UNIVAC is a special case; it stands for Universal Automatic Computer, and gave its name to the UNIVAC Corporation, which no longer exists; UNIVAC computers are presently made by the UNIVAC Division of Remington Rand.

Among computer model names, the IBM 700 series includes the IBM 704, 709, 7090, 7094, 7040, and 7044; the IBM 1400 series includes the IBM 1401, 1410, 1440, and 1460; and the "IBM 360" is actually the IBM System/360. The Digital Equipment Corporation uses a separate mnemonic, PDP (Programmed Data Processor) for its computers, which are known as the PDP-1, PDP-6, etc. Most of the other model numbers are self-explanatory. The following computer models are "paired," in that they are very similar to each other, and most references in this book to one member of the pair will also apply to the other:

CDC 1604 and CDC 3600
CDC 6400 and CDC 6600

GE 625 and GE 635
Honeywell 800 and Honeywell 8200
IBM 360 and RCA Spectra 70
SDS 930 and SDS 940
UNIVAC 1107 and UNIVAC 1108

For example, the SDS 940 is a modification for time-sharing of the SDS 930; the UNIVAC 1108 is an improvement on the UNIVAC 1107. Thus the data and instruction word formats and most of the instructions are basically the same.

There is still a certain amount of disagreement among people associated with computers as to which are the most important concepts. In keeping with the use of this book as an undergraduate text, we have emphasized that material which is by now well established. This means that most of the concepts in computing which have become important in 1965 or thereafter receive only passing mention or no mention at all. Our own solution to this problem has been to present the newer material in a graduate course on programming. The only major exception to this policy is Chapter 12, which is an introduction to the mathematical theory of computer instructions; this is a revision, for textbook use, of an article which appeared in the April 1966 issue of the Journal of the Association for Computing Machinery.

The author is deeply grateful to the many people who have helped in the preparation of this book. Stoughton Bell, Butler Lampson, and Douglass Williams read the entire manuscript and suggested numerous modifications. Donald Deuel, Butler Lampson, and Robert Morris used the manuscript in the aforementioned programming course and have given me the benefit of their experience with it. Several students, including Subramani Arunkumar, Stephen Fine, Anne-Louise Guichard, Karl Malbrain, and V. K. Premchand, have corrected errors in the programming examples. Janet DeLaney, Icole Brown, and Jacqueline Wilson contributed to the typing effort. Special thanks must go to Lotfi A. Zadeh, my department chairman, for an unlimited fund of encouragement. Finally, this book would not have been possible without the understanding and forbearance of my many teachers: Joel Erdwinn, David Ferguson, Hugh Grover, Marvin Minsky, Owen Mock, Seymour Papert, John Rhodes, Douglas Ross, Bernard Rudin, and Mrs. Russell Shull.

WARD DOUGLAS MAURER

Berkeley, 1967

CONTENTS

Chapter 1

MACHINE LANGUAGE

1-1 Languages

The word **language,** when used as a technical term in programming, refers to a collection of rules which specify how a certain set of symbols may be combined to form meaningful statements. Thus we may speak of the FORTRAN *language,* or the ALGOL *language.* (Languages in the nontechnical sense, such as English, are called in programming *natural languages.*) There are several dozen different types of languages that computers may use. Of these, three are especially important:

(1) **Algebraic languages,** which permit the programmer to use algebraic statements such as Z = A + B + C ; many other types of statements are usually acceptable, and a mechanism is usually present which handles various kinds of data. ALGOL, FORTRAN, JOVIAL, MAD, and NELIAC are examples of algebraic languages.

(2) **Machine languages** or **assembly languages,** of which each specific type of computer has at least one; these specify instructions to a computer in its own instruction format. ASCENT, AUTOCODER, FAP, MAP, and SLEUTH are examples of machine languages. A sample machine language, used throughout this book, is defined in Appendix A.

(3) **Business languages,** in which statements are written as sentences, usually in English; the analogue of Z = A + B + C, for example, might be ADD A AND B AND C GIVING Z. COBOL and FACT are examples of business languages.

In an algebraic language, a calculation according to a formula such as

$$k = \frac{ij - i + j}{n}$$

for specific values of *i, j,* and *n,* may be made by means of an *algebraic statement* such as

$$K = (I*J - I + J)/N$$

In machine language, every *operation* (such as addition, subtraction, etc.) must be specified separately in order. The operations in this case are the following:

1. Take I.
2. Multiply by J.
3. Subtract I.
4. Add J.
5. Divide by N.
6. Call the result K.

Each of these machine operations has an **operation code.** The operation codes vary from one computer to another; each computer has its own set of operations which it may perform, called its instruction set. No two instruction sets, for different types of computers, are alike. However, most computers have a mechanism (macro-assembly, described in Chapter 7) by which they can accept an operation code that may be arbitrarily specified (within limits). We may therefore use a standard collection of operation codes, with the assurance that these codes would be acceptable to most computers using a macro-assembly facility. In machine language, each operation code is represented by an abbreviation, or **mnemonic.** For the above example, the operation codes and their mnemonics are as follows:

Take	LD
Add	AD
Subtract	SU
Multiply by	MU
Divide by	DI
Call the result	ST

The machine language code corresponding to the algebraic statement given above is then given by listing each operation code, together with the variable to which it applies:

LD	I
MU	J
SU	I
AD	J
DI	N
ST	K

Operations such as these are also called **instructions** (or **commands,** or **orders**).

1-2 Temporary Symbols

Some algebraic expressions may not be given as a series of operations in as simple a manner as the one given above. For example, let us take

$$z = ad + bc$$

We cannot say: Take *a;* multiply by *d;* add the product of *b* and *c;* call the result *z.* The expression must be *completely* presented as a series of operations; the statement "add the product of *b* and *c*" is not acceptable. However, this expression may be given as follows:

1. Take A.
2. Multiply by D.
3. Call the result T.
4. Take B.
5. Multiply by C.
6. Add T.
7. Call the result Z.

Using the mnemonics given for these operation codes in the previous example, this expression would appear as

```
LD    A
MU    D
ST    T
LD    B
MU    C
AD    T
ST    Z
```

The symbol T is a **temporary symbol.** It has no part in the final value of the expression, but serves only as an aid to calculation. Its name must be chosen in such a way that it does not coincide with the name of any symbol used in the calculation.

Using temporary symbols, we may decompose any algebraic expression consisting of variables and arithmetic operators into a series of operations as above. For a more complex example, let us take

$$Z = A*(B + C) + (A*D - B*C*E)*F - E*E$$

This expression is decomposed into operations as follows:

```
LD   B    (Take B.)
AD   C    (Add C, forming B + C.)
MU   A    (Multiply by A.)
ST   T    (Call the result T; T = A*(B + C).)
LD   B    (Take B.)
MU   C    (Multiply by C.)
MU   E    (Multiply by E.)
ST   U    (Call the result U; U = B*C*E.)
LD   A    (Take A.)
MU   D    (Multiply by D, forming A*D.)
SU   U    (Subtract U, forming A*D − B*C*E.)
MU   F    (Multiply by F.)
AD   T    (Add T, forming the whole expression except the last term.)
ST   T    (Now call this result T.)
LD   E    (Take E.)
MU   E    (Multiply by E.)
ST   U    (Call this result U.)
LD   T    (Take T.)
SU   U    (Subtract U; the result is the entire expression.)
ST   Z    (Call the result Z.)
```

This machine language code uses two temporary symbols, T and U. Both T and U are used twice; this is perfectly legal, as long as the separate uses of a symbol are not conflicting. Alternatively, we could have used four temporary symbols; or Z itself could have been used as a temporary symbol. Note that when we treat A*D − B*C*E, we calculate the *second* expression first; then we calculate the first expression and subtract the second. What happens when we do not do this is evident at the end of the code, where we calculated E*E after the remainder of the expression; this necessitated more operations than were strictly necessary.

1-3   Registers and Memory

Most computers have an **accumulator** or its equivalent. The word "accumulator" is borrowed from the terminology of the desk calculator, where it refers to the row of dials in which the sum is accumulated. Addition in a desk calculator consists of adding the number entered on the calculator's keyboard to the present contents of the accumulator. Similarly, an operation such as "Add Y," or AD   Y   in our machine language, is performed by adding the value of Y to the computer's accumulator. In either case, the result is left in the accumulator, ready to be used in subsequent operations.

The places where the values of the variables (such as X and Y) are kept in a computer, are collectively called **memory,** or sometimes **storage.** An ordinary electromechanical desk calculator usually has no memory, and cannot perform calculations such as $z = ad + bc$ unless at least one partial result is "remembered" somewhere else—either by the person using the calculator, or on a piece of scratch paper. (Electronic desk calculators with small amounts of memory do exist.)

Each place in which a value may be kept is called a **word,** or a **location,** or a **cell.** The words of the memory are numbered from 0 through n-1, where n is the total number of words, or the **memory size.** The number, in this numbering scheme, which corresponds to a given word is called its **address.** Any word in memory may be referenced by its address. Thus we may write

$$\text{SU} \quad 5$$

in machine language; this causes *the number which is now contained in cell number 5* to be subtracted from the accumulator. Normally, it is not necessary to use addresses in this way. However, if we write

$$\text{SU} \quad \text{I}$$

we actually assume that the address of a cell containing the variable I is represented by the symbol I, for the purposes of this machine language program; here I is the **symbolic address** of the given cell.

The instructions AD, SU, MU, and DI designate that the contents of the accumulator are to be modified by the contents of the cell whose address appears with it. We may symbolize this as follows: Let the contents of the accumulator be denoted by $C(AC)$; let the value of Y, or the contents of the cell Y, be denoted by $C(Y)$; then

AD	Y	sets	$C(AC)$	equal to	$C(AC) + C(Y)$
SU	Y	sets	$C(AC)$	equal to	$C(AC) - C(Y)$
MU	Y	sets	$C(AC)$	equal to	$C(AC) * C(Y)$
DI	Y	sets	$C(AC)$	equal to	$C(AC) / C(Y)$

The operation LD   Y   sets $C(AC)$ equal to $C(Y)$; the number in Y passes directly to the accumulator. This operation is called **loading** the accumulator from the cell Y. The operation ST   Y   sets $C(Y)$ equal to $C(AC)$; the number in the accumulator passes directly to Y. This operation is called **storing** the accumulator in the cell Y. The sequence "Take A" and "Add B" corresponds to loading the accumulator with A and adding B to it; if the accumulator is now stored at C, this is equivalent to "Call the result C." The operations discussed above leave their results in the accumulator, except for ST. Some computers have special arithmetic operations which leave the result in memory. In the case of addition, we would speak of **add to memory** or **add to storage.** The operations of "Add" and "Add to memory" may be compared as follows:

$$
\begin{array}{llllll}
\text{"Add"} & \text{sets} & C(AC) & \text{equal to} & C(AC) + C(Y) \\
\text{"Add to memory"} & \text{sets} & C(Y) & \text{equal to} & C(AC) + C(Y)
\end{array}
$$

The accumulator is a special case of the concept of a **register.** There are many types of registers, each with its own set of instructions. Some registers are very simple and can only be loaded and stored. Others perform functions which will be introduced in Chapter 2, such as indexing. Still others are capable of a large variety of functions. It is quite possible for a computer to have no registers at all; in this case, most instructions involve more than one variable. Thus AD   X,Y,Z might be an instruction to add X to Y and call the result Z. We speak of a **single-address, double-address,** or **triple-address** computer, depending on whether most instructions reference one, two, or three variables.

On the other hand, a computer may also have more than one accumulator. In this case, the accumulators are often called **arithmetic registers,** and are themselves numbered; an arithmetic register number or its symbolic equivalent appears in the machine language. Thus LD   A1,X might be an instruction to load "accumulator" number 1 from cell X. Sometimes registers have not only register numbers but addresses as well, so that they may be used as if they were words in memory; we then speak of the registers as being **addressable.** In any event, it is common practice to include the registers in the term "memory"; that part of the memory which consists of words with addresses is then called **main memory.**

The memory size of a computer refers to the total number of locations, each of which has an address. On most computers, each such location is called a word; but there are some exceptions. On the IBM 360, each location is called a *byte;* a group of four bytes is called a word. On the IBM 1400 series and the Honeywell 200 series, each location is called a *character;* the term "word" on these machines refers to a group of adjacent characters with a word mark in the leftmost character. We speak of computers with *word addressing, byte addressing,* or *character addressing.* The CDC 3100 and the Honeywell 8200 have two separate addressing schemes, one for words and one for characters.

1-4   Representation of Integers

The accumulator of a desk calculator cannot contain an arbitrary integer; such an integer must be less than 10^n, where n is the number of dials in the accumulator. Some computers are constructed along similar lines; each word, whether in a register or in main memory, consists of a certain number of decimal digits. Other computers, however, express each integer as a certain number of *binary* digits, or **bits** (the word "bit" is a contraction of "binary digit"). That is, all words are expressed in the binary number system. Such computers are called **binary computers,** in contrast to **decimal computers.** A few computers, such as the IBM 360 and the UNIVAC III, may be considered, in different contexts, as either binary or decimal. (A review of number systems can be found in Appendix C.)

The value of an integer contained in a word of a binary computer must be less than 2^n, where n is the number of bits in the word. The size of the memory is determined by the number of bits (or decimal digits, for a decimal computer) in a word, and by the number of words in the memory. Thus a binary computer may have 16384 thirty-six-bit words; its memory size is then $16384 \cdot 36 = 589824$ bits. A decimal computer may have 8000 10-digit words; its memory size is $8000 \cdot 10 = 80000$ decimal digits. Ten bits are roughly equivalent to three (actually, $10 \log_{10} 2 \cong 3.0103$) decimal digits.

The IBM 700 series, the UNIVAC 1105 and 1108, and many other computers have 36-bit words; the CDC 1604, CDC 3600, and Honeywell 800 have 48-bit words; the CDC 6600 has 60-bit words; the SDS 930 has 24-bit words; the CDC 160 has 12-bit words. Among decimal machines, the IBM 7070 has 10-digit words. The Honeywell 200 and IBM 1400 series effectively have 1-digit words, and each number is expressed in more than one word. The word is actually 8 binary digits, of which 1 bit is used for parity, 1 bit is used as a word mark—for numbers, to denote the highest order digit—and 6 bits may be used to express any character, including numbers as well as digits. The IBM 360 has 32-bit words, but addresses refer to the four 8-bit fields or **bytes** of each word. If a word in this computer has address a, the next word has address $a + 4$.

The number of words in the memory of a binary computer is almost always a power of two—usually 4096, 8192, 16384, 32768, 65536, 131072, or 262144. For convenience these are usually referred to as 4K, 8K, 16K, 32K, 64K, 128K, and 256K respectively; the letter K is an abbreviation of "times 1024." The number of words in the memory of a decimal computer is often a multiple of 1000, such as 4000, 8000, 16000, etc.; these are also referred to as 4K, 8K, 16K, etc., where the letter K now means "times 1000." Thus "4K 12-bit words" means 4096; "4K 12-digit words" or "4K characters" means 4000.

In practice, if a word in a binary computer contains n bits, these bits are used to express all integers between -2^{n-1} and 2^{n-1} (exclusive), rather than all integers between 0 and 2^n. Negative numbers may be represented in various ways.

In a **signed-magnitude** representation, the left-most bit of the word denotes the sign of the integer. A zero is used to denote positive numbers, and a one to denote negative numbers. In order for the computer to add two integers, it must first determine their signs and add or subtract accordingly. Thus, to add two positive numbers, their magnitudes are added; to add a positive and a negative number, the smaller of the two is subtracted from the larger, and the result has the sign of the larger. Changing the value of the sign bit converts a number into its negative.

In a **one's complement** representation, a number is converted into its negative by changing the values of *all* its bits. Thus, for a 36-bit word,

$$000000000000000000000000000000001001 \quad \text{denotes} \quad 9$$
$$111111111111111111111111111111110110 \quad \text{denotes} \quad -9$$

The value of the left-most bit is still a valid indication of whether a number is positive or negative.

In both signed-magnitude and one's complement representations, taking the number zero and converting it into its negative produces "minus zero," a configuration of bits which does not represent any actual integer. If one variable has the value minus zero and another has the value zero, the computer does not ordinarily consider them to be equal. In some computers, great care is taken to ensure that minus zero does not occur as the result of addition or subtraction; thus subtracting -5 from -5 will give zero, whereas on other computers it may give minus zero.

In a **two's complement** representation, there is no minus zero. A number is here converted into its negative by changing the values of all its bits, as in the one's complement representation, *and then adding 1*. Applying this process to zero gives zero again.

> The IBM 700 series have signed-magnitude representations; the CDC 6600 and the UNIVAC 1108 are one's complement machines; the Philco 2000, the SDS 930, and the GE 625 are two's complement machines. Among decimal computers, the IBM 7070 employs a sign digit, and the IBM 1400 series employ "low-order overpunching," a term borrowed from the representation of a number on a card with a 12 (plus) or an 11 (minus) punch over the digit of lowest order.
> The terms "one's complement" and "two's complement" are the binary analogues of "9's complement" and "10's complement," respectively. The 9's complement of a decimal integer is the integer obtained by subtracting each digit from 9; the 10's complement is the 9's complement plus one. These terms are used frequently when working with desk calculators.

1-5 Floating Point

One of the most important properties of a computer is its ability to handle types of data other than integers. The arithmetic instructions we have introduced assume that the numbers in the accumulator and in memory that are to be combined are integers. But a computer may have other instructions, which treat these numbers as codes of various kinds. The most common of these is **floating point,** used for the manipulation of real numbers.

Floating point is another name for what is sometimes called "scientific notation." In chemistry we are taught to use numbers such as 6×10^{23}, rather than 600,000,000,000,000,000,000,000. In general, a decimal number is in **scientific notation** if it is expressed as some number n, with $1 \leq n < 10$, times an integral power of 10. Thus 555 would be expressed as 5.55×10^2. Such a convention has the advantage that very large numbers and very small fractions are easier to write down. In computing, we use floating point because it allows us to express numbers which cannot fit into a computer word in any other way. For example, a word of 48 bits cannot express any integer greater than 2^{48}, or about 10^{15}, in absolute value; this is much less than the number quoted above.

Floating point as used on a binary machine is constructed around the number 2, rather than 10. A floating point number consists of a number n, with $1/2 \leq n < 1$, times an integral power of 2. The number n is the **fractional part** or the **coefficient** of the floating point number; the power of 2 involved is the **exponent** or the **characteristic.** The convention $1/2 \leq n < 1$ is chosen rather than $1 \leq n < 2$ because it simplifies the circuitry of the computer. The fractional part of the number is expressed as a *binary fraction,* which is the analogue of a decimal fraction in the binary number system. A binary number with x bits to the right of the **binary point** (which is the analogue of the decimal point) signifies that the binary integer expressed by these bits is to be divided by 2^x to give a fraction. A binary fraction n with x bits, for which $1/2 \leq n < 1$, consists of a binary point followed by x bits, of which the first is always 1.

The exponent of a floating point number may be either positive or negative; the number itself may also be positive or negative. On most computers, the same convention (signed magnitude, one's complement, or two's complement) is used for negative floating point numbers as for negative integers. The exponent, however, is usually **biased,** that is, forced to be positive by the addition of a large positive number to every exponent; this number is called the **bias.** If the exponent contains y bits, exclusive of the sign bit, then $x + y + 1$ is equal to the number of bits per word; and the bias consists of a one bit followed by $y - 1$ zero bits.

Most short-word-length (36 or fewer bit) computers use 1 bit for the sign and 8 bits for the exponent; long-word-length (48 or more bit) computers use 1 bit for the sign and 11 bits for the exponent. The remainder of the word in each case is used for the fraction. The exponent is almost always in two's complement; on the CDC 6600, it is in one's complement. Also on this machine the binary point is at the *right* of the coefficient rather than the left. The IBM 360 uses hexadecimal floating point, rather than binary floating point; its 32-bit word is considered to be divided into eight 4-bit groups, or hexadecimal (base 16) digits, of which the first two are reserved for the sign and the exponent and the other six are used by the fraction n, which satisfies $1/16 \leq n < 1$. The 48-bit word of the Honeywell 800 is handled similarly.

Floating point numbers are manipulated by *floating point instructions*. We introduce four floating point instructions into our machine language:

Floating add Y	FA	Y
Floating subtract Y	FS	Y
Floating multiply by Y	FM	Y
Floating divide by Y	FD	Y

These operations assume that the accumulator contains a floating point number; they add, subtract, multiply by, or divide by a floating point word in memory and leave the result in the accumulator. The internal circuitry of the computer is much more complex for floating point operations than for integer, or **fixed point,** operations. Loading and storing are the same for floating point numbers as for integers, but the programmer must be careful not to fall into the error of using a fixed point add instruction instead of a floating point add, or vice versa.

Sometimes the floating point instructions will initially produce a fraction n that is outside the normal characteristic range (usually $1/2 \leq n < 1$). If the fraction is *smaller* than normal, it may be represented in a memory word in floating point format, but with fewer than the normal number of significant bits. Such a number is said to be unnormalized. In general, a floating point number in which the fraction is in its normal characteristic range is called **normalized.** Sometimes the floating point operations of a computer are so constructed that they will always produce a normalized result. More commonly, a normalized result is produced only if both floating point numbers which are to be combined are normalized. Some computers have a separate instruction which normalizes a floating point number, without performing any other operations on it; others have two sets of floating point instructions, only one of which always produces a normalized result.

Floating point instructions almost always produce a fraction which has more bits than will fit into the fractional part of a floating point word. Therefore, this fraction may be **rounded.** The usual process of rounding a decimal fraction to y digits consists of removing all the extra digits and adding 1 to digit y (with carry if necessary) if digit $y+1$ is 5 or more.

In the case of a binary fraction, if bit $y+1$ is a one, then 1 is added to bit y in the rounding process. Some floating point instructions round the result; others do not. If the result is not rounded, the extra bits are often left in a separate register. Some computers have a special instruction which rounds the floating point number in the accumulator, using this extra-bit information, without performing any other operations on it.

Some computers, such as the SDS 930 and the IBM 1400 series, have no floating point instructions. They do, however, have standard floating point formats, together with special routines that operate on data in these formats. If a computer has more than one arithmetic register, these registers are generally used for both fixed and floating point numbers, except on the IBM 360, which has separate floating point registers.

1-6   Double Precision

An integer which is contained in a single memory word must be absolutely less than a certain maximum value. However, the computer can still treat integers which are larger than this value. All that is needed is for each such integer to be stored in more than one memory word. The most common multiple-word format for integers is known as **double precision.**

A double precision integer is stored in two memory words; the maximum value of a double precision integer is roughly the square of the maximum value of an ordinary, **single precision** integer. A double precision floating point number is stored in two memory words; the first word is a single precision floating point number, and the second word serves as "extra decimal places" or "extra binary places" for the fractional part of the floating point number. In addition, the second word may also have an exponent, which is redundant. Double precision integers and floating point numbers are added, subtracted, multiplied, and divided either by special routines or by a separate set of double precision instructions.

Two registers are needed to hold a double precision integer or floating point number. In computers with more than one arithmetic register, two adjacent registers are usually used; a double precision operation which specifies register 6 will involve registers 6 and 7. Where there is only one accumulator, there is usually one other register which handles the right half of a double precision number. We shall call this register a **quotient register,** although many computers have different names for it.

The quotient register may have several other functions which are not connected with double precision. In integer multiplication, for example, the result is automatically a double precision integer, since multiplying two x-bit numbers gives a $2x$-bit number. This integer will be kept in the accumulator and the quotient register. In most cases, the integer will be small enough to fit into the quotient register, and the accumulator will be zero. In integer division, the dividend is very often assumed to be a double precision integer (since division is the reverse of multiplication); this is divided by a single precision divisor to obtain a single precision quotient and a single precision remainder, one of which is left in the accumulator and the other in the quotient register. If the dividend is originally single precision, it should be placed in the quotient register *and the accumulator should be cleared,* or set to zero, before dividing. For a negative dividend, the accumulator should be set to minus zero (on two's complement machines, −1).

The quotient register is also used in single precision floating point. All the floating point instructions are capable of producing a result that is at least double precision. This number is left, in some assumed format, in the accumulator and the quotient register. Ordinarily, the part of this number in the accumulator may be used as an ordinary single precision floating point number, since that part of the fraction which is contained in the quotient register consists of the least significant bits.

The IBM 700 series has a **multiplier-quotient register,** or MQ register. This register also contains the multiplier; i.e., to perform multiplication, one integer is loaded into the MQ, this is multiplied by the other integer, and the result, if it is still a single precision integer, is left in the MQ. The CDC 1604 has a quotient register; the multiplier is placed in the accumulator. The UNIVAC 1108 uses two adjacent A registers (arithmetic registers) in place of the accumulator and quotient register for all double precision work. The CDC 6600 has no integer multiplication or division.

Double precision floating point instructions are much more common than double precision integer instructions; they are found on the IBM 360, where floating point instructions reference "short" and "long" (single and double precision) operands, and on the IBM 7094 and UNIVAC 1108 (though not on the IBM 709 and UNIVAC 1107). The CDC 6600 has a 60-bit word, which may be used, in most applications, as if it were a double precision word.

Routines which perform operations such as double precision addition assume a wide variety of formats. Sometimes an entire word is taken by the exponent and another word by the fraction.

Double precision is a special case of **multiple precision,** in which possibly more than two words are used to store a number. The Honeywell 200 and IBM 1400 series arithmetic operations effectively handle multiple precision to any level. Since there is one character per word, an integer with x digits requires x words, the left-most of which contains a word mark (that is, the word mark bit is set to one in this word and to zero in all other words of the number). The add and subtract instructions act on any two numbers in this format, possibly of different lengths. Multiply and divide instructions, which are available optionally at extra cost, also act on any two such numbers.

We introduce two instructions for the quotient register:

Load quotient register   LQ
Store quotient register   SQ

In adding two positive double precision integers, the lower halves of the integers are added first. This operation may produce an integer which is larger than a computer word. In fact, if the left-most bit of each of these words (exclusive of the sign bit) is a 1, their sum will **overflow** the left-hand end of the word. The upper halves are now added, and their sum is incremented by 1 if overflow occurred when adding the lower halves; this operation is called *carrying,* and works much the same as it does in pencil-and-paper addition.

1-7 Masking and Logical Operations

Clearing a register, or a memory word, means setting all its bits to zero; clearing a bit means setting it to zero. **Setting** a bit usually means setting it to one. In many situations we find it necessary to clear or set certain bits of a register or a memory word, ordinarily because we are interested only in those remaining. This process is called **masking.**

As an example, suppose that the accumulator contains 24 bits, and that we would like to clear all but the right-most six of these bits. We may do this by means of a **masking instruction,** whose address is a special word called a **mask** which contains zeroes in the bits we wish to clear, and ones elsewhere. This process is illustrated as follows:

Contents of accumulator	010110001111101011010110
Contents of mask	000000000000000000111111
Result after masking	000000000000000000010110

A part of a word such as the right-most six bits in this example is called a **field** of a word. When a word is coded in one of various ways, it is broken up into fields, and each field has a special significance. For example, a 48-bit word might be broken up into a 1-bit sign field, an 11-bit exponent field, and a 36-bit fractional part field, for the purposes of floating point. Masking instructions allow the various fields of a word to be treated separately. For example, we can take two floating point numbers and mask them so that only their exponents remain. We can then subtract one from the other; if the result is zero, this means that the original two floating point numbers had the same exponent.

Masking instructions are of various types. Some use one-bits, instead of zeroes, in the positions at which bits are to be cleared; some set the bits indicated by the mask, rather than clearing them. Masking instructions are interesting from a theoretical point of view, because they are identical with the so-called **logical (or Boolean) operations.** In fact, we may notice in the above example that each bit of the result after masking depends only on the corresponding bits of the initial contents of the accumulator and the contents of the mask word. The result bit may be determined by reference to the following table:

		Initial contents of accumulator	
		0	1
Mask	0	0	0
	1	0	1

This is exactly the truth table for the "and" function in logic, with 0 and 1 interpreted as "false" and "true" respectively. Hence this masking operation is usually referred to as a **logical AND.** The **logical OR** and the **exclusive OR** use the following tables:

LOGICAL OR	Mask	Initial contents of accumulator		EXCLUSIVE OR	Mask	Initial contents of accumulator	
		0	1			0	1
	0	0	1		0	0	1
	1	1	1		1	1	0

We introduce into our machine language three logical operations, which are analogous to the arithmetic operations—that is, they perform the given logical operation on the contents of the accumulator and the memory word, leaving the result in the accumulator:

Logical AND	AND Y
Logical OR	OR Y
Logical exclusive OR	XOR Y

The logical OR is useful for combining separate fields into a single word. The exclusive OR is often used to find out if two words are equal; if they are equal the result will be zero. Subtracting one of the words from the other also works, but on many computers this is a slower instruction.

The IBM 1400 series has no logical operations. The CDC 1604 has a logical OR (Selective Set), a logical "and-not" (Selective Clear), and a third masking operation called Selective Substitute, which performs a Selective Clear followed by a Selective Set. This computer also has masked arithmetic instructions, with the mask contained in the quotient register. On the SDS 930, logical OR and logical AND are called Merge and Extract, respectively. The IBM 700 series has a logical OR and a logical AND to storage, analogous to the "add to memory" instruction. On the UNIVAC 1108, the result of a logical operation involving arithmetic register n is left in register $n+1$. The PDP-6 has sixteen families of logical operations, to correspond with the sixteen possible binary operations on the variables "true" and "false."

1-8 Shifting

The operation of **shifting** an accumulator is somewhat like shifting the carriage of a desk calculator. The effect is to multiply or divide by some power of 2 (or 10, for a desk calculator or a decimal computer). The operations are not completely logically identical, because when the carriage—which contains the accumulator—of a desk calculator is shifted, the entire accumulator still remains. Shifting an accumulator in a computer is more like transferring the numbers on the dials, from each dial to its neighbor on the left or on the right. For a **left shift,** the right-most digits or bits are filled with zeroes, and the left-most digits or bits disappear. For a **right shift,** the reverse is true.

In practice, there are several other types of shifting; the type described above is called **logical shifting.** Logical shifting does not always correspond to multiplication or division, particularly when negative numbers are involved. In a signed-magnitude representation, a left shift (logical) of a small negative number would produce a positive number, since the sign bit would be lost. This difficulty may be circumvented by not shifting the sign bit at all; such a shift is called an **arithmetic shift.** In a one's complement representation, the left-most digits or bits should be filled with zeroes for positive numbers and ones for negative numbers in an arithmetic right shift, and similarly with the right-most digits or bits for an arithmetic left shift. Such instructions are sometimes called **sign-extending shifts,** because the bit which is used as a filler is exactly the sign bit, which is zero for positive numbers and one for negative numbers.

A third type of shifting is called **rotation** or **circular shift,** in which the extra digits or bits are *not* lost, but rather cycle to the other side of the accumulator. A circular shift of 18 bits in a 36-bit register, for example, exchanges the left and right halves of the register.

The number of bits or digits to shift is called the **shift count.** The shift count itself (and *not* the address of a word containing the shift count) is almost always written at the right of the shift operation code. This shift count usually must be positive. Some computers, however, allow a negative count; a left shift with a negative count is equivalent to a right shift with a positive count.

Shifting is most commonly performed in accumulators or arithmetic registers, although some computers allow other kinds of registers to be shifted; one computer features a shift of an arbitrary memory word by one bit. Some shift instructions involve two arithmetic registers, or the accumulator and the quotient register, which are treated as if they were one long (double length) register and shifted. Bits from the right-hand end of the accumulator enter the left-hand end of the quotient register, for a right shift, and vice versa for a left shift. Such shifts are called **double shifts,** and may be logical, arithmetic, or circular. Sign extension takes place in a double shift in the same manner as for a single shift. In a signed-magnitude representation, both registers have sign bits, and neither sign bit may be involved in the shift, but the sign of the quotient register may be set equal to the sign of the accumulator.

We introduce the following shift instructions:

Left shift accumulator (logical)	LSL
Right shift accumulator (logical)	RSL
Left shift accumulator (arithmetic)	LSA
Right shift accumulator (arithmetic)	RSA
Left shift accumulator (circular)	LSC
Right shift accumulator (circular)	RSC
Left shift double (logical)	LDL
Right shift double (logical)	RDL
Left shift double (arithmetic)	LDA
Right shift double (arithmetic)	RDA
Left shift double (circular)	LDC
Right shift double (circular)	RDC

Shifting and masking are often combined in working with parts, or fields, of words. If a field in the middle of a word contains an integer, it is often necessary not only to mask out the other fields, but to shift this field to the right-hand end of the word, so that it is properly positioned for arithmetic operations. A field at the right-hand end of a word is said to be **right justified;** a field at the left-hand end of a word is **left justified.** For example, suppose that a word X is broken up into fields as follows:

P	Q	R	S
7 bits	11 bits	8 bits	10 bits

The P field is left justified and the S field is right justified. To bring the S field into the accumulator, with all other bits zero, we would perform the following instructions:

```
LD    X
AND   SMASK
```

where SMASK is the octal word 000000001777. To bring the Q field into the accumulator, right justified, with all other bits zero, we would perform:

```
LD    X
RSL   18
AND   QMASK
```

where QMASK is the octal word 000000003777. The RSL instruction may here, of course, be replaced by any right shift.

1-9   Character Codes

A computer manipulates letters of the alphabet by giving each letter a constant integer code. The digits 0 through 9, considered as symbols, and the punctuation symbols, as well as the blank, are also given codes. The collection of all these codes is called the **character code** of the given computer. Digits are known as **numeric characters;** letters of the alphabet are known as **alphabetic characters;** and all other characters, except the blank, are called **special characters.** A character is **alphanumeric** (or **alphameric**) if it is either alphabetic or numeric.

Each character is contained in a word or a field of a word. If the words in a computer are long, several characters may fit into one word. The number of bits per character depends on the number of allowable characters, but it is usually 5, 6, 7, or 8, corresponding to a maximum of 32, 64, 128, or 256 characters, respectively. The character codes are then non-negative integers less than this maximum. For example, if there are six bits per character, and 36 bits in a computer word, then each word may contain six characters. (This, incidentally, is the source of the requirement, in some algebraic languages, that no symbol may contain more than six characters; each such symbol is probably kept in a single 36-bit word by the program which processes such a language.) In general, if there are n bits per character and d bits per word, then each word may contain d/n characters. The number n, and the character code itself, depend on the particular type of computer. Almost all computers have one character code; a few have two.

The IBM 700 series and many other computers use BCD character code. This stands for Binary Coded Decimal, so called because it was originally applied as a code for numeric digits. The UNIVAC 1107 and 1108 use FIELDATA code, which, like BCD, is a 6-bit code. The IBM 360 uses EBCDIC, an 8-bit code which is an extension of BCD. The SDS 930 uses ASCII (American Standard Code for Information Interchange), an 8-bit code which has been adopted as a standard for communication between computers. A 5-bit code cannot represent more than 32 characters; in order to represent all the letters and digits $(26 + 10 = 36)$ the codes must include *shift* codes, analogous to the case shift on a typewriter. Such codes are sometimes used for transmission of characters by a teletype. The IBM 7070 uses a 2-digit code, which is theoretically capable of representing 100 characters.

Just as some computers—but not all—have instructions which manipulate floating point numbers, so some computers have instructions which act on character codes in their fields of a word. On those which do not, each character in a word must be loaded into a register by loading its entire word, shifting, and masking. We shall assume, in our machine language, that this is the case.

The UNIVAC III, the IBM 7070, and the PDP-6 have instructions which load or store an accumulator from an arbitrary field of a word. The UNIVAC 1108 has instructions which perform any of a large class of functions on any *character* of a word, but not on any field smaller than a character. On the IBM 360, various instructions act on bytes (8 bits), half-words (16 bits), words (32 bits), and double words (64 bits).

A set of consecutive characters is called a **string.** A word (in the nontechnical, layman's sense) is a string; a sentence is also a string, because the blank, or space, is a character. A string of non-blank characters is sometimes called a **symbol,** although in some contexts the word "symbol" is defined more strictly; this and other matters concerning character strings are further discussed in Chapter 8. A string of x characters may be contained in a computer word of more than x characters in several ways. If the last character of the string is the right-most character in the word, the character string is **right justified;** if the first character of the string is the left-most character in the word, the string is **left justified.** In either case, if the remaining bits in the computer word are zero, the word is said to be **zero-filled;** if the remaining characters are blank characters, the word is **blank-filled.** On some computers zero-filling and blank-filling are equivalent; this is true if the character code for a blank character is zero.

PROBLEMS

1. Write machine language instructions to perform the following operations on integer variables:
   (a) M = N1*N2 + N3 − N4
   (b) COST = TUITN + ROOM + BOARD + BOOKS + ENTERT + MISC
   (c) P = W²
   (d) Y = A1*B1 + A2*B2 + A3*B3
   (e) K = (A*F − C*E)/(A*D − B*C)
   (f) X = (A*B*C)/(D*E*F)

2. In some machine languages, constants may be referred to by prefixing them with the symbol = ; thus LD   =5 means "Take 5" and SU   =6 means "Subtract 6." Using this convention, write machine language instructions to perform the following operations on integer variables:
   (a) AVERAG = (U + V + W)/3
   (b) NUMBER = 1000*THOUSD + 100*HUNDSD + 10*TENSD + UNITSD
   (c) DIFF = ((X + 2)² − X²)/2

3. (a) Given the three operations on integer variables
       X1 = A
       X2 = A + B
       X3 = A + B + C

   write a series of *six* machine language instructions which performs all of these operations.

   (b) Given the operation on integer variables
       POLY = X⁴ + 23X³ − 17X² + 26X − 1

   write a series of *nine* machine language instructions which performs this operation.

   (c) The formula for the area of a triangle is A = ½ B*H, where B is the base and H is the height. Assuming that all the variables are integers, what is the difference between computing this area according to the first and the second series of machine language instructions given below? (For the use of = , see problem 2 above.)

LD	B
DI	=2
MU	H
ST	A

LD	B
MU	H
DI	=2
ST	A

4. (a) How is the number −12 represented in 24-bit signed magnitude?
   (b) How is the number −26 represented in 36-bit one's complement?
   (c) How is the number −100 represented in 9-bit two's complement?

(d) What does the binary number 111111001010 represent in 12-bit signed magnitude? one's complement? two's complement?

5. (a) Using the definition of two's complement given in the text, show that, if the b-bit two's complement representation of the integer n is treated as an unsigned integer, the result is the integer n mod 2^b. (For arbitrary integers n and m, the integer n mod m is that integer i with $0 \leq i < m$ such that $n - i$ is a multiple of m.) Thus show that two two's complement integers may be added by treating them as unsigned integers and adding them without carry from the highest order bit.

(b) Show that two one's complement integers may be added by treating them as unsigned integers and adding them with *end-around carry:* If the result of the highest order bit addition produces a carry, then 1 is added to the result. Also show that the unsigned integer corresponding to the b-bit one's complement integer n is equal to n mod $(2^b - 1)$.

6. (a) Consider the problem of adding two double precision integers on a one's complement machine with n-bit registers. Assume that the double precision numbers are treated as $2n$-bit one's complement integers. Try to describe a method of adding such integers. What difficulty arises? (Hint: What happens if the sum has all one bits in the n positions of the low order word?)

(b) Now consider the problem of adding two integers, each of which is considered as a two-digit integer in a number system whose base is $2^n - 1$, on a one's complement machine. Does this representation make it easier to add two such numbers? Give an algorithm for doing so. (Hint: See Problem 5b.)

(c) Let $n = 36$. What is the representation of 2^{48} in the number system described in part (b) above?

7. The octal number system has digits 0, 1, 2, 3, 4, 5, 6, and 7; each octal digit is equivalent to three binary digits or bits. In the following problems, all numbers are given in octal.

(a) What is the result of a logical AND applied to 037466213524 and 325536403507?

(b) What is the result of a logical exclusive OR applied to 203655 and 330412?

(c) What is the result of a logical OR applied to 2635243541130045 and 3102530341145277?

(d) What is the result of shifting a 36-bit register containing the number 372553601345 circularly right by 12 bits?

(e) What is the result of shifting a 24-bit register containing the number 44527361 logically left by 9 bits?

(f) What is the result of shifting a 12-bit register containing the number 3264 circularly left by 7 bits?

(g) In a binary fraction, the first bit is the "halves position," the next bit the "fourths position," the next bit the "eighths position," and so on. The binary fraction .10101 is thus equal to $1/2 + 1/8 + 1/32$, or $21/32$. What is the value of the endless binary fraction .10101010. . .?

(h) How would the fraction of problem (g) above be represented as an octal fraction?

(i) A floating point number on the UNIVAC 1107 consists of one bit for the sign, 8 bits for the biased exponent, and 27 bits for the fraction. The octal number 207400000000 thus represents the decimal number 64. What is the representation of the decimal fraction 3.1?

8. The hexadecimal number system has digits 0, 1, 2, 3, 4, 5, 6, 7, 8, 9, A, B, C, D, E, and F; each hexadecimal digit is equivalent to four binary digits. In the following problems, all numbers are given in hexadecimal.

(a) What is the result of a logical AND applied to AB549210 and 0A6F337E?

(b) What is the result of a logical exclusive OR applied to 5381 and C4CA?

(c) What is the result of a logical OR applied to 8D426A1B37CF09E5 and 936F82A0417CED5B?

(d) What is the result of shifting a 32-bit register containing the number AC5920BF logically left by 12 bits?

(e) What is the result of shifting a 64-bit register containing the number 94CD6273FAAAA43A arithmetically right by 20 bits?

(f) What is the result of shifting a 20-bit register containing the number 69DA3 circularly right by 9 bits?

(g) What is the value of the endless binary fraction .001001. . .?

(h) How may this fraction be represented as an endless hexadecimal fraction?

(i) A floating point number on the IBM 360 consists of one bit for the sign, seven bits for the biased hexadecimal exponent, which is a power of 16, and either 24 or 56 bits for the hexadecimal fraction. Thus 42800000, or 4280000000000000, represents the decimal number 128. What is the representation of the decimal fraction 1/15?

9. The following problems are to be done using the DPC code of the CDC 6400 and 6600, given below. (DPC means "display code"; this is a 6-bit code, and 48 of the possible 64 characters are used. We use two octal integers to stand for each 6-bit quantity.)

Idle	00	P	20	5	40
A	01	Q	21	6	41
B	02	R	22	7	42
C	03	S	23	8	43
D	04	T	24	9	44
E	05	U	25	+	45
F	06	V	26	−	46

G	07	W	27	*	47
H	10	X	30	/	50
I	11	Y	31	(	51
J	12	Z	32	)	52
K	13	0	33	$	53
L	14	1	34	=	54
M	15	2	35	Blank	55
N	16	3	36	,	56
O	17	4	37	.	57

(a) Convert the 20-octal-digit word 20221707220115150522 to DPC.

(b) Convert the 16-octal-digit word 0317152025240522 to DPC.

(c) Convert the 12-octal-digit word 150125220522 to DPC.

(d) What is the octal representation of the character string $12.95?

Chapter 2

THE ASSEMBLER

2-1 The Stored Program

When a computer is performing arithmetic operations on integers, it will normally use one word of memory for each integer. In general, one or more words of memory, or sometimes part of a word, is needed for each variable. For example, some programs manipulate variables which can take only the values 0 and 1 (usually called **logical variables**). If a program has ten logical variables, they can be kept in ten of the bits of a single word (or in the decimal digits of a ten-digit word in a decimal machine). On the other hand, to represent a complex number, for instance, two words are required, one for the real part and one for the imaginary part. To represent a vector in three dimensions with real coefficients, three words are required, one for each coefficient.

A computer also uses one or more words, or part of a word, for each operation, or instruction. The amount of memory which is used for an instruction will be called an **instruction word.** In contrast, ordinary words are sometimes called "data words," although "location" or "cell" is better terminology here. Depending on the type of computer, the instruction word may use one location, more than one location, or part of a location; and in several computers the instruction words for different instructions are of different sizes.

The IBM 700 series, the UNIVAC 1105 and 1108, the SDS 930, and many other computers use one word per instruction. The CDC 1604 uses one half of its 48-bit word, or 24 bits, per instruction (usually referred to as "two instructions per word"). The CDC 6600 uses one fourth of its 60-bit word, or 15 bits, per instruction, although some instructions use 30 bits. The IBM 1400 series uses 1, 2, 4, 5, 7, or 8 characters per instruction. The IBM 360 uses 1, 2, or 3 half words (2, 4, or 6 bytes) per instruction. On the Burroughs B5000, an instruction is called a "syllable," and there are 12 bits per syllable, 4 syllables per word.

An instruction word is a code word, which is broken up into fields. Each instruction word completely specifies one instruction. In order to do this, it must contain several kinds of information. Each of these is coded as an integer and placed in a specific field of the instruction word.

The **operation code** (or **instruction code** or **function code**) is an integer which identifies an instruction by type. It is contained in a field of its own, which may be of different lengths for different instruction words, but is usually given at the *left-hand end* of the instruction word. The number of bits in this field depends on the number of instruction types which the given computer has. A field which is n bits long is capable of holding any positive integer less than 2^n. Thus, if there are 70 different instructions, and the instruction code field is to be of constant length, it must be at least 7 bits long (since $2^6 = 64$ and $2^7 = 128$).

If an instruction involves a data word, the instruction word for this instruction will have an **address field,** which contains the address of that data word. The address field is usually given at the *right-hand end* of the instruction word, and its length depends on the memory size. For binary computers, if the memory contains 2^n words, the address field must be at least n bits long. For decimal computers, if the memory contains 10^n words, the address field must be at least n digits long. This assumes that standard addressing, as opposed to relative and base-register addressing (see §2-8), is used, so that the address field must be capable of containing the address of an arbitrary word in memory. Sometimes a given computer will be available in several memory sizes, with the same instruction word format for each size; in this case, the size of the address field reflects the largest memory size.

> The IBM 700 series has a 15-bit address field, reflecting a maximum memory size of 32K (that is, $32,768 = 2^{15}$ words); the same is true of the CDC 1604 and the UNIVAC 1105. The UNIVAC 1108 has a 16-bit address field; the CDC 6600 has an 18-bit address field. The IBM 1400 series has a 3-digit address field, reflecting a maximum memory size of 1000 characters, except for the IBM 1410, which has a 5-digit address field. In addition, the 1400 series has a complex scheme for handling addresses which may have any value less than 16000, based on the fact that a word in such a machine may contain any letter of the alphabet as well as any digit; thus the address code for 15999 is I9I. Further details are given in the operations manuals for the 1400 series. The address fields of the IBM 360, the UNIVAC III, the Honeywell 800, and the CDC 160 will be taken up in §2-8.

A complete description of the instruction word format or formats of a computer may be found in its **operations manual.** Every computer has an operations manual, which is distributed by the manufacturer. In addition to the instruction word format, the operations manual also contains the data word formats: the representation of integers, the character codes, and any other types of data which the computer is capable of handling directly, such as double precision or floating point. The operations manual also contains a complete description of each instruction.

The idea of keeping coded instruction words, as well as data, in the memory of a computer is called the **stored program concept.** It is the fundamental concept underlying the digital computer. It is due to several people independently, including John von Neumann.

2-2 The Assembly Process

When computers first became available, all the instruction words in a program had to be coded by hand. The result was that most programs were very short; longer programs were too expensive to write. It was not long, however, before someone conceived the idea of writing a program which produced instruction words and data words as output. Such a program is called a **processor.**

Each of the computer languages mentioned in Chapter 1 has a processor associated with it. These processors, which are large and complex programs, accept as input the **source code,** or **source program,** that is, a meaningful collection of statements in the given language as presented to the computer on cards, tape, or otherwise. They produce as output a collection of data and instruction words, called the **object code** or **object program,** which the computer can execute. For an algebraic language, this program is called an **algebraic compiler.** Thus we may speak of a FORTRAN compiler, or an ALGOL compiler. Each computer that can process FORTRAN has its own FORTRAN compiler; sometimes there are several FORTRAN compilers for the same computer, and sometimes a FORTRAN compiler which runs on one computer produces an object program to be executed by a different computer.

The program that processes a given machine language is known as an **assembly program,** or an **assembler.** The input to the assembler consists of a collection of **statements,** which may include machine language instruction and data codes. These statements are treated as strings of characters, including blank characters, and are input to the assembly program in the form of character codes. This process is automatic and takes place in any one of several ways: the source program may be contained on cards and input through a card reader, or on tape and input through a magnetic tape or paper tape unit, or on a drum or disk unit, or it may be typed on a typewriter or Teletype. In any case, the characters of the program become character codes in some fixed location within the computer.

Each statement in character code form is processed by the assembler, and a number coded in data format or instruction word format is produced for it. In order to be able to code a number in instruction word format, for example, the assembler contains a table of all the operation codes of the computer. We have used the word "operation code" in two ways: to denote the mnemonic, such as AD, and to denote the number in the operation code field of the instruction word which identifies this operation. The assembler must keep a table of operation codes in both senses. One is a table of mnemonics, kept in the usual character code format, and the other is a table of integers. If the integer corresponding to AD is 14, for example, the assembler will find AD in its tables whenever it reads a card containing AD, and will assemble an instruction word with an operation code of 14. The assembler does *not* actually add at this point. The instruction word is grouped with all the other instruction words in an object program; then, at a later time, all the instructions comprising this program are executed in their natural order. The processing of data words by the assembler will be discussed in §2-4.

The output of the assembler consists of the assembled collection of data and instruction words as produced by the computer on cards, tape, or otherwise, to represent the object program. If the object program is produced on cards, it is called the **object deck** (or simply the **binary deck,** for a binary computer). This object deck may be presented to the computer at a later time; the computer will then execute the program—that is, perform the instructions, which operate on the data. If the object program is produced on tape, the assembler, after it has finished, may rewind the tape, read the object program, and cause it to be executed; this is called "assemble-and-execute," or "assemble-and-go." The same may happen if the object program is placed by the computer on drum or disk. In addition to the object program, the assembler produces a printer **listing** of all the machine language statements and their associated data and instruction words.

The operation of an algebraic compiler is similar to that of an assembler. The input consists of a collection of statements in the given algebraic language, called the source code. These statements are considered as character strings, just as in an assembler. The internal processes of an algebraic compiler are usually much more complicated than those of an assembler, because a compiler normally produces several instruction words for a single statement. The first example in Chapter 1, for example, requires six instruction words for the given statement. The output consists of an object program which appears to the programmer much like the object program of an assembler, and it may be executed in the same way. The printer listing produced by the compiler contains all the statements of the programmer's source code, and may in addition contain a machine language listing of the instruction words which the compiler produced. Some algebraic compilers, in fact, produce a machine language source program as their initial output, and then turn control over to an assembler to produce the actual object program.

2-3   Control Cards and Pseudo-operations

Every assembler has an **assembler manual,** which is distinct from the operations manual of its computer. The assembler manual contains the complete description of the format of an instruction word and a data word as given in machine language. It usually contains a list of instructions, but usually does *not* describe their operation; this task is performed by the operations manual.

Included in the assembler manual is usually a description of the **control cards** which direct the assembler to exercise one of several options:

(1)   To produce a listing, or not;

(2)   To produce *only* a listing, and not an object program;

(3)   To execute the object program, or not;

(4)   To produce any one of various supplementary listings, or not;

(5)   To produce a symbol table, or not.

These control cards (or control functions, for an assembler called by Teletype input) are normally placed at the beginning of the machine language program, although sometimes a few are placed at the end. Sometimes an assembler runs under the control of a **monitor** or **executive** program, i.e., a program which directs the operation of other programs. This monitor or executive program usually has its own manual, in which the control cards are described.

The assembler manual also describes the **pseudo-operations** which are processed by the assembler. A pseudo-operation (or "pseudo-op") is a mnemonic which appears in the same place as an operation mnemonic in machine language format, but does not correspond to an instruction. Pseudo-operations in assembly languages for different computers are much more likely to resemble each other than are instruction mnemonics. In particular, two pseudo-operations, ORG and END, almost always have the same format and the same mnemonics.

The pseudo-operation ORG stands for "origin." It specifies the location at which the program is to start. Thus if we write ORG   700 , the first instruction or data word after this statement is placed by the assembler into cell 700, that is, the memory word with address 700. Successive words are placed into successive locations. This takes place, of course, in a figurative sense; the words are only associated with their addresses in the object program, and are actually placed there only later, when the object program is loaded and executed.

An ORG statement is ordinarily placed at the *beginning* of a machine language program, although there are situations where it may be placed later. If the program contains no ORG statement, the assembler will assume that the first instruction or data word is to be placed at some fixed location—usually zero, but sometimes a larger address such as 100 or 6000. In some situations, the machine language programmer is advised to omit the ORG statement, since the assembler's choice of a starting location is desired.

The pseudo-operation END *must* be the *last* statement of the machine language program. It signifies to the assembler that there are no more statements in this program. Sometimes the END statement will have a variable field, signifying the address at which the program is to start.

The pseudo-operation END is not to be confused with the place at which the *program* is to end. In the first place, this may not necessarily be the last statement of the program, for any of several reasons; a program may have its instruction statements first, followed by its data statements, so that the program ends at the last instruction statement; or the programmer may decide that the program ends before the last instruction statement, or is capable of ending at more than one place, depending on the computation. The logical end of a program may be signified in various ways. Almost all computers have a *halt* or *stop* instruction, which stops the operation of the computer; this is certainly one way of ending a program. However, on a computer which operates continuously, with several programs being executed sequentially or simultaneously, it is not feasible to halt after the end of any given program. Such computers operate under the control of a monitor or executive program, one of whose features is a standard method of *returning* (that is, returning to the executive program) after execution. Even if a halt instruction exists on such a computer, the programmer should never use it.

Comments about the problem being programmed may be made in machine language as well as in algebraic language code. It is usually possible to put a comment on every card, beyond a special character such as a semicolon, or beyond a specific column, or even after the first blank in the variable field. A special operation code, such as REM (meaning "remark"), is used by some assemblers for more extensive comments; it is even sometimes possible to put a special character in column 1 of a card and use the rest of the card for a comment. If anything, it is even more advisable to include comments with machine language code than with algebraic language code, since without them the code may well be almost unintelligible. One comment per card, or at least comments on 75% of the cards, is not uncommon; one comment every four cards is a desirable minimum.

2-4   Data in Machine Language

Pseudo-operations are also used in machine language to define data. In some algebraic languages it is not necessary to define data. If the statement $R = D/T$ appears, the compiler assumes that there is a variable called R, which is a real number, and is therefore to be stored somewhere in memory in floating point format. This is almost never the case in machine language. Every symbol representing a variable must be *defined,* usually by means of a pseudo-operation.

Machine language code for data is ordinarily kept separate from machine language code for instructions. One way to do this is to write the data codes first, followed by the instruction codes; another way is to code them on separate sheets of paper. The code for variables which are integers or floating point numbers consists in reserving one memory cell for each such number. We introduce a pseudo-operation which reserves n cells:

Reserve n cells   RE n

Thus the machine language code for the algebraic statement $k = (ij - i + j)/n$, including both data and instruction codes, is

I	RE	1
J	RE	1
K	RE	1
N	RE	1
	LD	I
	MU	J
	SU	I
	AD	J
	DI	N
	ST	K

Note that we are now keeping three columns instead of two. These columns are called the **label field,** the **operation field,** and the **variable field.** Fields as used in this sense should be distinguished from fields of a word, although the two concepts arise in similar ways: if the machine language code is keypunched on cards, the columns of these cards may be divided into fields. For data, the label field contains the name of the variable involved. In some machine languages, the operation field must occupy certain fixed card columns, whereas in others it may occupy any columns past the first. Still other machine languages have no label column at all; any symbol followed by a certain special character (usually a colon) is treated as a label.

A memory word can also contain a *constant*. For example, suppose that we replace the algebraic statement above by $k = (ij - i + j)/2$. This necessitates a change in the divide instruction, DI   N . We cannot simply write DI   2 ; as noted earlier, this instruction would divide the contents of the accumulator by *the number in the cell whose address is 2*. Instead of this, we may use a symbol with an arbitrary name, such as L2; then, in the data coding, we may specify that L2 is a memory word containing the number 2. We introduce the pseudo-operation CO (constant) for this purpose, as follows:

$$\text{Constant whose value is } n \qquad \text{CO} \quad n$$

The machine language code for the algebraic statement $k = (ij - i + j)/2$ is then:

I	RE	1
J	RE	1
K	RE	1
L2	CO	2
	LD	I
	MU	J
	SU	I
	AD	J
	DI	L2
	ST	K

The variable field of a statement does not necessarily consist of a single variable name or a constant. It may be an expression, such as I+1. In this case, the value of I is assumed to be its symbolic address. For example, the assembler may position the variable I at the address 30652; if the variable J follows I, i.e., if I and J are given one after the other in the assembly as

I	RE	1
J	RE	1

without any intervening data or instruction statements, then the assembler will position the variable J at address 30653. The value of I+1 is

30652+1 or 30653; that is, it is the same as the value of J. Thus the instruction LD I+1 will have the same effect, in this situation, as LD J . It is important to distinguish the value of the *variable* I, or the contents of the cell I, from the value of the *symbol* I. If the cell I contains 5, we may speak of the "value" of I as being 5 within the context of the program; but this does not mean that we can bring the number 10 into the accumulator by writing

LD I+I

In fact, this instruction is legal, but it would load the accumulator with the contents of the cell whose address is 30652+30652. To load the accumulator with twice the value of the variable I, we might write

LD I
AD I

2-5 Transfers

A **transfer** or **jump** or **branch** instruction in machine language serves the same function that a GO TO or TRANSFER TO statement does in an algebraic language. It specifies an instruction word; the computer performs this instruction and proceeds in sequence from it.

The variable field of a transfer statement in machine language specifies the instruction word to which transfer is made. This may be done by giving this instruction word a label. Thus *instruction statements, as well as data statements, may have labels.* An instruction label is analogous to a statement number in FORTRAN or a statement label in most other algebraic languages. It is the symbolic address of an instruction word, just as a variable name is the symbolic address of a data word. We shall introduce a transfer instruction into our machine language as follows:

Transfer to Y   TR Y

The following statements serve to calculate $A + B + X + Y$ when started at P1, and $C + D + X + Y$ when started at P2. All variables are assumed to be floating point numbers.

Variable A	A	RE	1	Variable A
Variable B	B	RE	1	Variable B
Variable C	C	RE	1	Variable C
Variable D	D	RE	1	Variable D
Variable X	X	RE	1	Variable X
Variable Y	Y	RE	1	Variable Y

Load A	P1	LD	A	
Add B, giving A+B		FA	B	
Transfer		TR	P3	
	P2	LD	C	Load C
		FA	D	Add D, giving C+D
Add X, giving A+B+X	P3	FA	X	Add X, giving C+D+X
Add Y, giving A+B+X+Y		FA	Y	Add Y, giving C+D+X+Y

The comments at the left show how control is passed from one instruction to another when the code is started at P1; the comments at the right show the flow of control when the code is started at P2.

Every computer has a special register called its **location counter** or **instruction counter** or **program counter,** which contains the address of the instruction word being executed (or on some computers, this address plus one). Normally, the location counter is incremented after every instruction, so that instructions are executed in sequence. When the computer executes a transfer instruction with address Y, the location counter is loaded with the number Y. The address Y here is arbitrary; thus we may transfer either forward or backward. Backward transfers are especially useful in iteration, in which a group of statements are executed more than once.

The process of incrementing the location counter depends on the relative size of the memory word and the instruction word. If there is one instruction per word, the location counter is incremented by 1 after each instruction. If there is more than one memory word per instruction, the location counter is incremented by the number of memory words in the given instruction word. When there is more than one instruction per word, there must be an extra internal register of one or two bits that indicates which instruction in a given word is currently being executed. Normally, this register is not accessible to the programmer. Since the address specified in a transfer instruction is the address of a data word, rather than an instruction word, it is conventionally assumed, if there is more than one instruction per word, that the transfer is to the *left-most* instruction in a word. The assembler for such a computer will place any instruction word with a label at the left-hand end of a data word.

The variable field of a transfer instruction may contain an expression, such as P1+5. If the instruction word P1 has address 20112, then P1+5 refers to the instruction word with address 20117. Most assemblers also have a special symbol, usually * but sometimes . or $, which means "the location of this instruction or data word"; thus a transfer to *−1 means a transfer to the immediately preceding *data* word. Again, if there is more than one instruction per word, care must be taken to make sure

that data words, rather than instruction words, are being counted in setting up a transfer to a location such as *+3 or *−2.

Symbols in an assembly may receive values by being given as labels
for instruction or data codes. They may also be given values by the
pseudo-operation EQU, present in almost all machine languages. This
pseudo-operation sets one symbol equal to another, or to the value of an
expression. For example, if a program contains the statement X   EQU
Y , then LD   X   produces the same instruction word as LD   Y . This
pseudo-operation is often used for constants within a program which may
be changed at some later time. If the size of a table is 100, one may
write TBLSZ   EQU   100 , and then use TBLSZ, rather than 100, in
all further places in which the table size is needed—in loading a register,
for example, or in reserving space for the table (in our machine language,
we should say TBL   RE   TBLSZ). If the table size is to be changed,
the assembly code may be updated by changing only the EQU card. In
some assemblers, the symbol = is used or may be used instead of EQU;
in others, this symbol is used as a logical operator.

2-6   Instruction Word Reference

The instructions and the data that comprise a program are both kept
in the same memory, and care must be taken to keep them separate except under carefully controlled conditions. As an extreme example, consider what would happen if we wrote

```
          TR    L1
    L1    CO    1
```

in our machine language. The TR instruction transfers control to L1;
the computer expects to find an instruction word at L1. Since it actually finds a data word, it will try to interpret this as an instruction word. If the address field is contained at the right-hand end of
the instruction word, the operation code field will contain zero, and the
computer will act accordingly. Many computers guard against this situation by specifying that an operation code of zero is either an illegal instruction, causing an interrupt (see Chapter 10), or the code for a halt.
The situation is more complicated if L1 contains characters or a floating
point integer; the results may now be completely unpredictable, because
the contents of the operation code field may be perfectly legal.

This sort of mistake is not very common. However, if a programmer
intermixes his instructions and data—if, for example, he writes

```
          ST    Y
    Y     RE    1
```

—the same results will occur. Here we have assumed that ST   Y   is the last instruction in a section of code. After it is executed, the computer will try to execute the next *word* in sequence, whether it is an instruction word or a data word. If this word is the value of Y, we have the same situation as above. We may, however, write

```
        ST    Y
        TR    P1
   Y    RE    1
```

Because of the transfer, the computer will not try to execute Y as an instruction. In general such situations may be avoided by writing the data codes *before* the instruction codes, or by grouping data code sections after transfer instructions. The situation described here must be distinguished from that which occurs in some algebraic languages, in which instructions and data *can* be mixed; the compiler keeps them separate. Format statements in FORTRAN, VECTOR VALUES statements in MAD, and *array* statements in ALGOL, all of which are data statements, may occur anywhere within a program; the compiler keeps the data given by such a statement in a separate section of memory. Theoretically, an assembler could be constructed to do likewise; however, most assemblers do not, because they would lose flexibility thereby.

A different kind of confusion between instructions and data occurs when the address field of an instruction word refers to another instruction word, rather than to a data word. If the instruction is a load or an arithmetic operation, no harm is usually done except that the accumulator receives a meaningless number, often called "garbage." If the instruction is a store, the situation is more serious, because if the computer subsequently tries to execute this instruction, it will execute a word of garbage.

Sometimes, more commonly on some computers than on others, **instruction word reference,** such as described above, is done on purpose. The following code is meant to be executed more than once. The first time, it calculates $(a + b + c + d)^2$; after that, it calculates $(a + b)^2$. All variables are floating point. The code given here works *only* if the instruction and data word lengths are the same. Starting location is P1. The result is left in the accumulator.

```
   A    RE    1
   B    RE    1
   C    RE    1
   D    RE    1
   T1   RE    1
   P3   LD    P4
```

```
              ST    P1
        P4    LD    B
              FA    C
              FA    D
              TR    P2
        P1    TR    P3
        P2    FA    A
              ST    T1
              MU    T1
```

If this code is executed again, instruction word P1 does not contain TR   P3 ; instead, it contains LD   B .

Instead of storing the complete instruction word, a programmer may store only the address field, the operation code field, or some other field of an instruction word. This is called **address modification** or **operation code modification,** respectively. Address modification is quite common on some computers and is discussed in greater detail in Chapter 3.

2-7 Indexing

Machine language code must also be able to handle subscripted variables. In an algebraic language, a subscripted variable is normally written using parentheses or brackets, such as M(I) or M[I]. If the array M contains 6 integers, a special statement such as INTEGER M(6) or DIMENSION M(6) or *array* M(6) will be given to denote this fact. In machine language, an array containing n integers, or n floating point numbers, is coded as data by reserving n words of memory. Thus in this case we would write

```
              M     RE    6
```

This implies that the words of the array M have consecutive addresses. If M has the address 560, then M(4) has the address 564. The six words from address 560 to address 565 have been reserved, corresponding to subscripts M(0) through M(5). In FORTRAN, the subscript zero is not allowed, and the range in this case would be from M(1) through M(6); M(4) would have the address 563. In MAD, the statement DIMENSION M(6) actually corresponds to reserving 7 words of memory, as the subscript range is from M(0) through M(6). This subject is expanded upon in Chapter 3.

A machine language instruction which refers to the subscripted variable M(I) must refer to both M and I. The name of the array, M, corresponds to an address which is contained in the address field of the instruction. For the subscript I, another field is needed. Theoretically, this could be another address field; but on most computers, this would make the instruction word too long. A better solution is to use an **index register field,** or **tag field.**

An **index register** is a register which can contain the address of any memory word. The number of index registers in a given computer is usually a small integer of the form 2^i-1; that is, 1, 3, 7, or 15. The index register field in the instruction word is capable of containing the number of any index register (that is, 1 for index register 1, etc.) *or* a special code to denote that *no* index register applies to this instruction (usually zero). Thus, if there are 1, 3, 7, or 15 index registers, the tag field is 1, 2, 3, or 4 bits long, respectively; the integers that may appear in the tag field are 0 or 1, 0 through 3, 0 through 7, and 0 through 15, respectively.

When the index register field of an instruction word does not contain zero, the integer contained in the corresponding index register is *added to* (or, in the IBM 700 series, subtracted from) the address given in the address field of the word. This process is called **modification** (specifically, address modification by an index register), and the result is called the **effective address.** It is this address which is actually used, or **referenced,** when the computer executes this instruction, and the instruction is said to **refer to** the word whose address is the effective address of the instruction.

> The UNIVAC 1108 has 15 index registers, 4 of which may be used as arithmetic registers. The IBM 360 has 16 general registers, 15 of which may be used as index registers. The CDC 1604 has six index registers, numbered from 1 to 6; the tag field is three bits long, and a tag value of 7 denotes indirect addressing, described in the next section. The IBM 700 series has three index registers, except for the IBM 7094, which has seven; but in any case the tag field is three bits long, and where there are only three index registers, each one corresponds to a bit of the tag field; some instructions are thus capable of referencing more than one index register. The SDS 930 has one index register. The IBM 1400 series has three index registers which are optional at extra cost; there is no tag field, and the index designation is carried out in the address field using letters of the alphabet in much the same way as addresses themselves are formed. For example, 2X9 stands for 279 with index register 1. The UNIVAC 1105 has no index registers and two address fields. The IBM 7070, a decimal machine, has 99 index registers and a tag field of two digits. The Honeywell 800 has 64 index registers in total, but usually only 8 are allocated to any one program.

We add to our list of machine language codes two instructions, LX (load index register) and SX (store index register). LX   Y,N   will take the contents of memory cell Y and put them in index register N. SX Y,N   will take the contents of index register N and put them in memory cell **Y**. (We note that on some computers these instructions would have been written with Y and N interchanged.) To allow for the tag field of an instruction, we expand the format of our other instructions. Thus AD Y,N   will add the contents of the cell whose address is $Y + C(N)$, where $C(N)$ is the contents of index register number N. The same is true of the other instruction codes. Our new instructions are as follows:

Load index N		LX	Y,N
Store index N		SX	Y,N

Thus, to perform N1 = K(M) + N in machine language, where the array K has dimension 12 and all variables are integers, we would write

N	RE	1
N1	RE	1
M	RE	1
K	RE	12
	LX	M,1
	LD	K,1
	AD	N
	ST	N1

using index register 1.

2-8   Addressing

The index register or tag field is a special case of a **register field.** If a computer has more than one arithmetic register, there will be a register field containing an arithmetic register number. Register fields and address fields are generally distinguished by their size—register fields are normally 1 to 5 bits long, whereas address fields are 12 to 18 bits long. Some computers have two address fields; others have one address field and one register field; still others have one address field and two register fields. Short instruction words may have simply one address field, or two or three register fields.

Among other common fields of an instruction word, we find the **indirect address field,** which is normally one bit long. The instruction LD 5   loads the accumulator with the contents of the cell whose address is 5, and is said to use **direct addressing.** If the indirect address field of this instruction word contained a 1, it would be referred to, in our machine language, as LD*   5 , and would load the accumulator with *the contents of the cell whose address is contained in the cell whose address is 5.* Thus the data and instruction codes

```
X    CO   Y
     LD*  X
```

would produce the same effect as LD   Y . The data code X   CO   Y
may be used to signify that the number contained in cell X is the address
of Y. The instruction word is then said to use **indirect addressing.** Indirect
addressing may be combined with indexing; for example, the instruction
LD*   X,1   adds the contents of index register 1 to the address of X
and considers *that* word as containing the address of a data word to load.

Because the address field of an instruction word is usually at the
right, the address of Y, in this case, will be in the address field, and all
other fields will be zero. Sometimes a computer will treat the data word
at the address given by an indirectly addressed instruction as a code word,
with index and indirect address fields of its own, and act accordingly.
Thus successive indexing and indirect addressing may be carried to any
level. The end result of this process is the effective address of the original
instruction, and the process itself is called the **effective address scheme** of
the given computer.

> The IBM 360, the CDC 6600, and the IBM 1400 series have no
> indirect addressing. The CDC 1604 has indirect addressing but no
> separate indirect addressing field; indirect addressing is indicated by
> an index register field value of 7. Thus indexing *or* indirect addressing
> may take place, but not both. On the UNIVAC 1108, the asterisk for
> indirect addressing is attached to the address in the variable field,
> rather than to the operation code. On the IBM 700 series, the indirect
> address field is two bits long; both bits must be set to 1 for indirect
> addressing to apply. The effective address scheme of these machines
> allows only one level of indirect addressing; the indirect address field
> of the indirectly addressed word is not interrogated. In addition, some
> instructions, such as shifts, cannot be indirectly addressed on these
> machines.

Another type of addressing is known as **immediate addressing.** The
instruction LX   5,1   does not place the number 5 in index register 1.
Instead, it places the contents of cell 5 (the cell whose address is 5) in index
register 1. However, we may visualize another instruction LXI, such that
LXI   5,1   does indeed place the number 5 in index register 1. Here
the number 5 is contained in the address field of this instruction word, and
is transferred from there to the index register. Instructions that operate
in this fashion are said to use immediate addressing. We shall introduce four
instructions which use immediate addressing:

Load accumulator, immediate	LDI	Y
Load index, immediate	LXI	Y,N
Add to accumulator, immediate	ADI	Y
Add to index, immediate	AXI	Y,N

Immediate addressing is often used when a constant occurs in an expression. If we wish to calculate $N + 6$, we load N using direct addressing and add 6 using immediate addressing, if this is possible on the given computer. When an index register is used to count the number of times a process takes place, we may load the index register with this number, if it is a constant, using immediate addressing. Shift instructions, under the usual definition, use immediate addressing as the normal mode; other instructions normally use direct addressing. Most computers do not have an "immediate addressing field"; instructions that use immediate addressing have different operation codes from those that use direct and indirect addressing.

There are various other types of addressing. Some computers, such as the UNIVAC III, the Honeywell 800, and the IBM 360, use **base-register addressing,** which may be illustrated as follows. Suppose that the first instruction of a program consists of loading a **base register** (usually an index register, but sometimes a special register used only for this purpose) with the address of the first word used by the program. Then *every* address which appears later in the program may be calculated by adding the contents of this register to some number which is less than the program length L, i.e., the total number of words in the program. One advantage of base-register addressing is that L is often much smaller than the total number of words in the computer, and thus a smaller number of bits are needed in the address field. Thus, in the IBM 360, only 12 bits are used in the address field, together with the 4-bit tag to specify a base register (in this case, one of the 16 general registers). This allows for a program length of 4096 words. If a given program is longer than this, more than one base register may be used in the same program. Base registers are also used in some time-shared computers, in which the entire memory is divided into **pages** of 2^i words, for some i; such computers, for example, can direct a program which is less than one page long to run in an arbitrary page of memory by changing the values of the base registers. The CDC 160 uses **relative addressing,** in which, for some instructions, the address of the instruction word itself is used as an index. This decreases the size of the address field to 6 bits.

Several computers have special instructions for addressing various fields of a word. On the UNIVAC 1108, halves, thirds, and sixths of a word may be directly accessed. On the UNIVAC III and the PDP-6, any field of any word may be directly accessed, although on the PDP-6 such fields may only be loaded and stored. On the IBM 7030 (STRETCH), any field of less than one word size (64 bits) may be directly accessed even if it overlaps a word boundary.

Besides the types of instruction word fields which we have introduced, there are many miscellaneous types. Some instructions on the IBM 700 series have a **decrement** field, which is as long as an address field and designates a number to be compared with or added to an index register. The UNIVAC 1108 has an index incrementation bit; if this bit is 1, the index register given in this instruction is incremented by the value of its left half. The IBM 1400 series has a one-character field called the *d-character* in some of its instructions, which sometimes serves as part of the operation code and sometimes as a second immediate addess. The SDS 930 and some other computers have a bit in the instruction word format which causes a program interrupt (see Chapter 10). The IBM 360 has a **displacement** field, which, in the base register addressing mechanism of this computer, is what we have called the address field.

2-9   Routines and Subroutines

Among the concepts that are useful in structuring large programs, the **subroutine** is especially important. A program, sometimes called a **routine,** performs a task which may be broken up into smaller tasks, each of which is performed by a subroutine. Often a subroutine will be used, or **called,** more than once. Sometimes the subroutines will themselves have subroutines, so that there are several levels of subroutines. At the lowest level, there will be subroutines which perform very common functions, and which may be called by more than one subroutine at a higher level, as well as more than once in such a routine.

If a program is written entirely in machine language, the entire program, including all the subroutines, is sometimes assembled all at once, producing a single object program which is then executed. Or each subroutine may be assembled separately, producing a collection of object programs which are **loaded,** or brought into the computer, together. Or a few subroutines may be bunched and assembled together, producing a single object program. In general, it is desirable, while a program is under development, to assemble it in pieces that are as small as possible; when a part of the program is changed, only one small piece will then need to be reassembled. The extent to which a program may be broken up into pieces that can be assembled separately depends on the amount of information which must be shared between various parts of the program. Further discussion of this and other matters relating to subroutines is given in Chapter 7.

Many algebraic languages are compatible with machine language in that programs written in these languages may call, and be called by, machine language programs. In this case it is possible to code some of the subroutines of a routine, and possibly even the routine itself, in the algebraic language, and other subroutines in machine language. Sometimes a program will call standard subroutines, whose object decks do not have to be supplied with the program, but are supplied automatically by the executive system of the computer. Among these are the input-output subroutines (see Chapters 10 and 11 for a general discussion of input-output). In scientific calculations, *trigonometric* (and *hyperbolic*) *function subroutines* are used very commonly. Such subroutines normally use the registers; a tangent subroutine, for example, may assume that the angle x, in radians, is given as a floating point number in the accumulator; when the subroutine finishes, tan x will be in the accumulator, also as a floating point number. We say that this routine is **entered with** x in the accumulator, and that it **exits with** or **leaves** tan x in the accumulator. Trigonometric function subroutines almost always work by algebraic approximation; that is, they calculate some algebraic expression in x which approximates tan x to some specified accuracy. Usually the approximation is valid only in a certain range, and the original angle is therefore converted to lie in this range by such identities as tan $(\pi + x) = \tan x$. The same is true of the other so-called **mathematical subroutines:** the logarithm subroutine, the exponential subroutine (for e^x), the square-root subroutine, and so on. The sine routine is a special case; because of the identity cos $x = \sin (\pi/2 + x)$, the sine routine is very often presented as a routine which can be started at either of two places, one to calculate the cosine and the other to calculate the sine.

We introduce two instructions in our machine language for subroutine handling:

Call subroutine Y	CA	Y
Return from subroutine	RT	

The instruction CA   Y   transfers control to the subroutine Y, and at the same time stores in another location the **return address,** which is the address at which the computer is to continue after the subroutine is finished—that is, the address of the next instruction after the CA   Y . The instruction RT transfers control to the return address, which it takes from the place at which the CA   Y   instruction left it. It is logically the last statement in the subroutine.

There are three widely used ways of handling return addresses. The return address may be left in an index register; the return statement is then a transfer to an address indexed by this register. A call statement which operates in this way is called an **index linkage.** Or the return address may be left in memory, immediately preceding the first instruction word of the subroutine; the return statement is then a transfer to the instruction word in whose address field the return address was placed, sometimes with indirect addressing. A call statement which works in this way is called a **memory linkage.** Or the machine may have a special register for subroutine return addresses, which contains a proper return address after *every* transfer instruction. In this case, the first instruction of the subroutine will store this register so that transfer may be made later to the proper return address.

Memory linkage instructions differ widely. In the CDC 1604, which has two instructions per word, the return address is stored in the address field of the left half of the first word of a subroutine; the first instruction of the subroutine is contained in the right half of this same word. In the CDC 6600, which has two long instructions per word, the return address is stored in the address field of the left half, and the operation code for a jump is stored in the operation code field of the left half; but the first instruction of the subroutine is in the next data word. In such a case, the return must be made without indirect addressing, since indirect addressing would assume that the return address would be *right* justified within the word. In the UNIVAC 1108 and the PDP-6, both of which have one instruction per word, return should be made with indirect addressing, since it is faster; both of these computers also have index linkage instructions. The IBM 1400 series uses its B register for the return address after every branch. In the IBM 700 series, which has an index linkage (TSX), the negative (two's complement) of the return address is placed in the index register, since index register values are subtracted rather than added to form an effective address. The Honeywell 800 has two *sequence registers* (i.e., location counters), one in use and one standby at any given time; the status may be exchanged by an instruction.

PROBLEMS

1. A certain computer has two instruction code formats. In the first format, the left-most 5 bits constitute the operation code field, whereas in the second format the left-most 8 bits constitute the operation code field. An instruction word is in the second format if and only if the left-most 2 bits are both equal to zero. How many possible operation codes can this machine have?

2. The instruction words which an assembler produces are assumed to be in sequential addresses in memory unless otherwise specified. Therefore, the assembler has a variable which contains the current address. Each time the assembler processes a new instruction on a card, the value of this variable is increased by 1, for a computer with one instruction word per data word.

   (a) How should this procedure be modified if there are two instruction words per data word ("two instructions per word")?

   (b) How should it be modified if there are several words per instruction, the number of words depending on the instruction?

   (c) How should it be modified if there are 1, 2, or 3 half-words per instruction, where a word contains 32 bits, a byte contains 8 bits, and each byte has an address?

3. Suppose that a computer which accepts our machine language has one instruction word per data word. The following program is written:

```
              ORG   770
       START  LD    A
              AD    B
              ST    T
              LD    A
              SU    B
              MU    T
              ST    Y
```

(a) What algebraic statement does this program perform?

(b) What is the address of the instruction word ST   Y ?

4. Suppose that a computer which accepts our machine language has two instructions per word. The following program is written:

```
                ORG    1320
        U       RE     1
        V       RE     1
        START   LD     U
                AD     V
                MU     U
                AD     V
                MU     V
                SU     U
```

(a) What quantity is left in the accumulator at the end?

(b) What is the address of the instruction word SU   U ?

(c) What is the address of the data word V?

5. Suppose that machine language code is to be written to transfer to P1, P2,
P3, P4, P5, P6, P7, P8, P9, or P10, depending on whether a variable called
SWITCH is set to 1, 2, 3, 4, 5, 6, 7, 8, 9, or 10, respectively.

(a) Show how this can be done using an instruction TZ such that TZ   Y
transfers to Y if the accumulator is zero, and otherwise proceeds to the next
instruction in sequence.

(b) Show how this can be done in another way, using an indexed transfer
instruction.

6. The following program uses the instruction TZ of problem 5 above. It is
assumed that A contains some small integer.

```
        A       RE     1
        B       RE     1
        C       RE     1
        L1      CO     1
        START   LD     A
                ST     B
                ST     C
        P1      LD     C
                SU     L1
                TZ     P2
                ST     C
                MU     B
                ST     B
                TR     P1
        P2      LD     B
```

What quantity is left in the accumulator at the end? (Note: This problem and the next problem are examples of *loops*. For more on loops, see §3-2.)

7. The following program, which contains an error, was written to calculate the first n Fibonacci numbers and to place them in locations F+1 through $F + n$, where $n < 100$. (The Fibonacci numbers F_i are defined by $F_1 = 1$, $F_2 = 2$, $F_i = F_{i-1} + F_{i-2}$, $i \geq 3$.) This program uses the instruction TZ of problem 5 above; it is assumed that N contains the integer n.

```
COUNT RE    1
N     RE    1
F     RE    100
L1    CO    1
P1    LD    L1
      ST    F+1
      AD    L1
      ST    F+2
      LXI   3,1
      LD    N
      ST    COUNT
P2    LD    F-2,1
      AD    F-1,1
      ST    F,1
      AXI   1,1
      LD    COUNT
      SU    L1
      TZ    P2
P3    (next instruction)
```

(a) Find the error and correct it.

(b) Assume that n is a multiple of 2. Can you change this program so that it runs faster (takes a smaller total number of steps)? How many steps have been eliminated? (Note: The new program may contain more instruction words than the old program.)

8. The UNIVAC 1107 is a binary computer with a 36-bit instruction word (one instruction word per data word). Bits in the word are numbered from 0 at the left to 35 at the right. The instruction format is as follows:

Bits 0–5	F field (operation code field)
Bits 6–9	J field
Bits 10–13	A field
Bits 14–17	B field
Bit 18	Index incrementation field
Bit 19	Indirect address field
Bits 20–35	U field (address field)

The operation codes for some of the instructions are as follows:

SA   (Store accumulator)   01
SX   (Store index register)   06
LA   (Load accumulator)   10
LX   (Load index register)   27
AA   (Add to accumulator)   14
AX   (Add to index register)   24
MSI (Multiply single integer)   31

An instruction is given in machine language as

F,J   A,U,B

If the indirect address field is 1, an asterisk precedes the U field; if the index incrementation field is 1, an asterisk precedes the B field. Any field which is missing is presumed to be zero.

In a certain assembly, the following symbols are used, with values as given in octal:

SYMBOL	VALUE
X	102451
Y	102452
Z	102453
TBL	102454
N1	103076
N2	103077
LH	2
RH	1
C1	10
C2	11
C3	12
C4	13
C5	14
C6	15

Express the codes for the following machine language instructions as 12-octal-digit numbers. (Hint: The J, A, and B fields should first be written in binary.)

(a) SA,LH   2,N1
(b) LX   9,0,9
(c) MSI,C4 3,TBL,7
(d) AA,3   0,*Y
(e) LA,C6   14,TBL,*6
(f) SX,RH   5,2,5
(g) AX,12   2,*N2,*11

How might the following instruction words, given as 12-octal-digit numbers, be expressed in this machine language using the symbols given?

   (h) 245120302451
   (i) 310027102454
   (j) 060200102452
   (k) 014462502454
   (l) 277420010001
   (m) 144340102453
   (n) 106375703077

9. Suppose that a computer accepts our machine language except for the subroutine call and return instructions, CA and RT. Show how subroutine
   calling and return might be done on such a computer. Allow for the possibility that the same subroutine may be called more than once within a routine.

Chapter 3

ARRAYS

3-1   Real and Integer Arrays

A real number—that is, a floating point number—occupies one word of memory. A **real array** or a **floating point array** is a set of memory words, each of which contains a floating point number, with addresses in sequence. An **integer array** is a set of memory words, each of which contains a (single precision) integer, with addresses in sequence. In either case, the **length** of the array is the number of words. A real or integer array of length n, whose name is X, is given in machine language by reserving n words for it, as in our instruction

$$\text{X} \qquad \text{RE} \qquad n$$

If the symbolic address of X is x, the array will consist of words whose addresses range from x to $x+n-1$. Each word of the array is at location $x+i$, where $0 \leq i \leq n-1$. The number i is called the **index** of the word at $x+i$, and the elements of the array are said to be **indexed** from 0 to $n-1$. In an algebraic language, we would write $X(I)$ for the word at $x+i$.*

Elements of an array may be indexed in other ways. If the range of the index is from 0 to n, an extra element must be reserved for the array; that is, we would write in our machine language

$$\text{X} \qquad \text{RE} \qquad n+1$$

If the range of the index is from 1 to n, which is the most common method in practice (in fact, *all* arrays in FORTRAN II are indexed this way), then only n elements need to be reserved, and the array is "offset" by 1. The element which would be referred to as $X(4)$ in an algebraic language is found at $x+3$, not at $x+4$, if the array is indexed from 1 to n.

Index registers are used to access elements of an array whenever the index is variable. If the array is indexed from 0 to $n-1$ or from 0 to n,

* Except on the IBM 360 and RCA Spectra 70. See §1-4.

the word at location $x+i$ may be referenced by an instruction whose address field contains x and whose index register field contains r, where the index register r contains the number i. If the array is indexed from 1 to n, the address field should contain $x-1$, rather than x. These differences between indexing an array from 0 to $n-1$ and from 1 to n give rise to a large number of machine language programming errors; a machine language programmer should always keep in mind the type of indexing he is using before starting to write code. One way in which the problems of offsetting may be avoided is to index all arrays from 0 to n even though only the values from 1 to n are to be used. The extra word may now be used for other purposes.

In the algebraic language PL–I, and in some specialized situations in machine language, an array may be indexed from m to n. In this case, the array is "offset" by m; the number of reserved locations is $n-m+1$. For example, an array X indexed from -5 to 5 uses 11 storage locations, which would be referred to in an algebraic language as $X(-5)$ through $X(5)$. If the address of $X(-5)$ is x, then the address of $X(3)$, for example, is $x+8$. To use $X(I)$ in a calculation, the number I appears in an index register, and the address of $X(0)$—that is, $x+5$—appears in the address field. In general, if the offset is m, the address of the word with index i is $x+i-m$, and the address field, when an index register is used, should contain $x-m$.

> The IBM 700 series are distinct from other computers in that the values of index registers are *subtracted* from the address field, rather than added to it. These machines use **backward arrays,** in which the addresses range from x to $x-n$ for indexing from 0 to n, or from $x-1$ to $x-n$ for indexing from 1 to n. For a backward array which is offset by m, the address field for variable indexing contains $x+m$; the address of the word with index i is $x-i+m$. The pseudo-operation BES n on these machines reserve n words and assigns the address of the word *following* these n words as the address of the array; thus arrays may be indexed from 1 to n without offset. Other arrays on these machines are ordinary or **forward arrays;** character arrays, for example, are normally forward arrays because of the way in which characters are read. For such arrays, another space-reserving pseudo-operation, BSS n , reserves n words and assigns the address of the first of these words as the address of the array.

3-2   Loops

A typical large computer contains between 2^{12} and 2^{18} instruction words; it executes instruction words at rates of from 100,000 to 1,000,000 per second. If the entire memory of a computer were filled with instruction words, each of which were executed only once, the program that they represented would be finished in less than one second. The great power and flexibility of computers lies in their ability to execute instructions and sequences of instructions repeatedly in a controlled manner. One way in which this is done is by means of subroutines, which are called repeatedly. Another, and more direct, way of executing a sequence of instructions a given number of times is by means of a **loop.**

In algebraic languages, loops, or **iterations,** are given by words such as *perform* or *do* or *for.* In FORTRAN, for example, we may write

```
        DO 17 I = 1, 100
17      C(I) = A(I) + B(I)
```

The result of this is the same as if we had written 100 statements as follows:

```
        C(1) = A(1) + B(1)
        C(2) = A(2) + B(2)
              .  .  .
              .  .  .
              .  .  .
        C(100) = A(100) + B(100)
```

(In ALGOL, the same loop would read FOR I := 1 STEP 1 UNTIL 100 DO C(I) := A(I) + B(I) .) The use of the loop saves space in coding, and it also saves space inside the computer, reducing the number of instructions required.

It is also possible to produce effectively the same result in an algebraic language in another way, without using an iteration statement. For example, we might write in FORTRAN:

```
        I = 1
17      C(I) = A(I) + B(I)
        I = I + 1
        IF (I-100) 17, 17, 18
18      (next statement)
```

The effect of this is as follows:
(1) I is set to 1.
(2) Since $I = 1$, $C(1) = A(1) + B(1)$ is performed.
(3) I is set to $1 + 1$, or 2.
(4) $I - 100$ is equal to -98. The IF statement specifies that if $I-100$ is less than zero, control passes to statement number 17; if $I-100$

is zero, to statement number 17; if I−100 is greater than zero, to state-ment number 18. In this case, control passes to statement number 17.

(5) Since I = 2, C(2) = A(2) + B(2) is performed.

(6) I is set to 2 + 1, or 3.

(7) I − 100 is equal to −97, so control passes to statement num-ber 17.

This process continues until I = 99, at which point:

(1) C(99) = A(99) + B(99) is performed.

(2) I is set to 99 + 1, or 100.

(3) I − 100 = 0, so control still passes to statement number 17.

(4) Since I = 100, C(100) = A(100) + B(100) is performed.

(5) I is set to 100 + 1, or 101.

(6) I − 100 = 1, which is greater than zero. Therefore, control passes to statement number 18, and the loop is finished.

This process gives the key to the operation of a loop. There are three steps which are taken at the end* of every loop. The index is *in-cremented,* in this case by 1; the index is *compared* with the maximum value; and control is *conditionally transferred,* depending upon whether the maximum value has been effectively reached. The iteration state-ment in an algebraic language performs these operations automatically. Any program in an algebraic language which uses iteration statements can, however, be rewritten without iteration statements, using the process described above.

In machine language, the statement $C(I) = A(I) + B(I)$ might appear as

```
LD    A,1
AD    B,1
ST    C,1
```

if index register 1 contains the value of I. The index incrementation, comparison, and conditional transfer are specified explicitly. We intro-duce a new operation in our machine language which does this:

Increment, compare, and transfer   ICT   X,I,M,A

This instruction increments index register X by the number I, compares the result with the number M, and transfers to A if the result is less than or equal to M. Such an instruction is called an **index transfer.** In practice, three separate instructions are often used here—one for incrementation, one

---

* A loop may also be written with these steps taken at the *beginning* of the loop. This is useful in case the number of times the loop is to be performed—i.e., the number of iterations—may be zero. In this case the entire loop will be **skipped;** a transfer will be made around it.

for comparison, and one for transfer. Many computers, however, have in-structions which perform two or all three of these functions simultane-ously. Using this new instruction, the given loop is performed as follows, assuming that the arrays are indexed from 1 to *n:*

```
A       RE    100
B       RE    100
C       RE    100
START   LXI   1,1
P1      LD    A-1,1
        FA    B-1,1
        ST    C-1,1
        ICT   1,1,100,P1
```

The operation of an index transfer is slightly different if the incre-ment is negative—that is, if it is a **decrement.** A decrement of n is the same as an increment of $-n$. Transfer is now made if the decremented index is *greater than* M. Hence we introduce another index transfer in-struction:

Decrement, compare, and transfer   DCT   X,I,M,A

which *decrements* the index register X by the number I, compares the result with M, and transfers to A if the result is greater than M. Some loops may easily be written using either increment or decrement index transfers. For example, suppose that we had written our loop in FOR-TRAN as follows:

```
        I = 100
17      C(I) = A(I) + B(I)
        I = I - 1
        IF (I) 18, 18, 17
18      (next statement)
```

This loop is equivalent to the loop as originally given; it corre-sponds to giving the same 100 statements as before, but in reverse order. The advantage of using a decrement instead of an increment is that the index may then be compared with zero, rather than with a maximum value, a more difficult process. Using our new loop statement, we can accomplish this process as follows:

```
A       RE    100
B       RE    100
C       RE    100
START   LXI   100,1
```

```
P1      LD      A-1,1
        FA      B-1,1
        ST      C-1,1
        DCT     1,1,0,P1
```

Incrementation by positive and negative numbers, or incrementing and decrementing, are sometimes called **forward** and **backward incrementation** respectively. Usually, backward incrementation involves a comparison with zero, as above. The increment or decrement is very often equal to 1, but it may be greater than 1, as when multiple arrays are processed.

In the IBM 700 series, forward incrementation is accomplished by two instructions: TXI, which transfers and increments (in this situation, the transfer is simply to the next instruction) and TXL, which compares and transfers. Backward incrementation may be performed using TXI and TXH (Transfer on Index High), but it is more common to use TIX, which does all three functions at once. The instructions TXI, TXH, TXL, and TIX all have 15-bit address fields and 15-bit **decrement fields.** In the case of TIX, the index is decreased by the amount given in the decrement field; the result is compared, not with zero, but with the decrement itself, which facilitates indexing of arrays from 1 to n instead of from 0 to $n-1$. (Why?) Note that backward incrementation on a backward array is the same as *forward* incrementation on a *forward* array, such as a character array; this is the justification for subtraction of index values in these machines.

Many instructions, such as BCT on the IBM 360, IJP on the CDC 1604, and JGD on the UNIVAC 1108, perform incrementation by -1, comparison with 0, and conditional transfer. A few computers perform our loop operation in one instruction in any case; an example is BXH on the IBM 360. This instruction uses three registers: one for the index, one for the increment, and one for the **comparand,** or value with which the index is to be compared. In the UNIVAC 1108, the index is kept in the right half of the index register, and the increment is kept in the left half; incrementation of an index may be specified following *any* instruction (except one with immediate addressing) using a special field of the instruction word.

When working with loops in machine language, or when working with loops without using an iteration statement in an algebraic language, extra care must be taken to ensure that the loop mechanism is correctly set up. An incorrectly programmed loop may cause the computer to go into an **endless loop,** in which it cycles over and over again through the same instructions without escape. This is one of the most common mistakes made by programmers, and is a particularly expensive one, because unless an endless loop is noticed by the operator of the computer, many minutes of valuable computer time may be wasted.*

* Many computers have a "time limit" feature: the programmer may specify, normally on a system control card, the maximum amount of time he wants his program to run. The computer will then proceed to the next job in sequence after this amount of time, even if it is in an endless loop.

3-3   Conditional Transfers and Skips

The index transfers described above are examples of *conditional transfers*—instructions which sometimes transfer and sometimes do not. Many other types of conditional transfers exist on various computers; among these are the following:

(1) *Register transfers,* which transfer if $A = 0$, $A \neq 0$, $A > 0$, $A < 0$, $A \geq 0$, or $A \leq 0$, where A denotes the contents of some register.

(2) *Condition code transfers,* which transfer if some condition has occurred: a register has overflowed; an attempt was made to divide by zero; a floating point operation has produced a number out of range; or an input-output device is busy.

(3) *Memory transfers,* which resemble register transfers, except that A now denotes the contents of some memory word. These require two address fields, one to denote the memory word and one to denote the transfer address.

Similar to the transfer instructions are the **skip instructions** or **test instructions.** A skip instruction, instead of transferring to an arbitrary address, will simply skip the next instruction. When we refer to a "skip instruction" we imply, of course, a conditional skip; instructions which *always* skip are very rare (although such instructions do exist on the PDP-6). A skip instruction does not need an address field for the transfer address, and may therefore use its address field for other purposes. Among the types of skip instructions are as follows:

(4) *Memory skips,* which skip if $A = 0$, $A \neq 0$, $A > 0$, $A < 0$, $A \geq 0$, or $A \leq 0$, where A denotes the contents of the addressed memory word.

(5) *Comparison skips,* which skip if $P = Q$, $P \neq Q$, $P > Q$, $P < Q$, $P \geq Q$, or $P \leq Q$, where the contents of a register and of the addressed memory word are denoted by P and Q respectively, or on some computers by Q and P respectively. This is a source of confusion and programming errors unless the direction in which the comparisons are made on a given computer is always kept in mind.

(6) *Input-output skips,* in which the address is coded to represent some input-output condition which may or may not have occurred.

A skip may also, of course, be of types (1) or (2) above, in which case the address field is not needed at all. Or a conditional transfer may be of the comparison type if there are two register fields to denote two registers which are being compared.

Skip or test instructions other than index transfers may be used in a loop in case the index is to be kept in memory, rather than in an index register. For example, the following loop (given in FORTRAN) calculates the factorial of 15:

```
        FACT = 1
        DO 27 I = 1, 15
27      FACT = FACT*I
```

(We ignore for the moment the fact that some versions of FORTRAN do not permit the programmer to use expressions such as FACT*I, where FACT is real—that is, floating point—and I is an integer.) In machine language, there is no reason to suppose that the index I will be kept in an index register, since it is never used as a subscript or as anything else but the index. In fact, it is probably better here to keep the variable I as a floating point number. We introduce two new instructions:

| Test equal to Y | TE | Y |
| Test unequal to Y | TU | Y |

These instructions skip the next instruction if the accumulator and the memory word Y are equal or unequal respectively. Using TE, we give machine language code for the above example:

```
I       RE    1
F16     CO    16.0
F1      CO    1.0
FACT    RE    1
P1      LD    F1
        ST    FACT
        ST    I
P2      LD    FACT
        FM    I
        ST    FACT
        LD    I
        FA    F1
        ST    I
        TE    F16
        TR    P2
```

We assume that floating point data words may be indicated by the data instruction CO, using a variable field in floating point format. Note that we wished to transfer to P2 if the accumulator was *unequal* to 16.0, and that for this purpose we used the test *equal*. This illustrates the fact that when a test instruction is followed by a transfer, the transfer is made if the test is *not* satisfied. Also, even though the final value of I is 15, the accumulator is compared with 16. The reason for this is that the index is incremented *before* the test; on the last iteration, the value of I is 15 within the loop and 16 after incrementation. This difficulty may be circumvented by using a test *greater* rather than a test equal. We introduce two more new instructions:

Test greater than Y	TG	Y
Test less than or equal to Y	TL	Y

Thus TG skips if the accumulator is greater than Y. (We repeat that this is an arbitrary convention; on some computers, "test greater" would mean: skip if the *memory word* Y is greater than the *register*.) Now we may alter the code given above by changing the floating point constant 16.0 to 15.0, and by changing the TE instruction to TG. The reader may verify that the algorithm still works.

Some computers have conditional instructions which neither transfer nor skip, but instead set the contents of certain **condition registers.** Such an instruction may then be followed by another which transfers if a given condition register has been set. On the IBM 1400 series and the Honeywell 200, there are four one-bit condition registers called "B=A," "B≠A," "B>A," and "B<A"; A and B refer to the two addresses given by the comparison instruction. In addition, there are other condition registers for such things as input-output conditions. On the IBM 360, there is a two-bit comparison register; a large group of instructions sets the condition register to any one of two, three, or four possible values.

3-4   Address Modification

On some computers it is necessary to reference an array without using index registers; there may, for example, be no index registers, or none available for the present computation. The programmer may then use **address modification,** a technique by which an address is calculated and stored. In the usual form of address modification, the address is stored directly into an address field somewhere within the instruction codes. This may be done by shifting and masking, but is usually done with a special instruction. We introduce such an instruction:

Store address	SA	Y

This instruction stores the accumulator into the address field of instruction word Y. The following code executes the loop example given earlier, without any index registers:

```
L1    CO   1
L100  CO   100
CNT   RE   1
A     RE   100
B     RE   100
C     RE   100
A1    CO   A
B1    CO   B
C1    CO   C
T1    RE   1
T2    RE   1
T3    RE   1
P0    LD   A1
      ST   T1
      SA   P1
      LD   B1
      ST   T2
      SA   P2
      LD   C1
      ST   T3
      SA   P3
      LD   L1
      ST   CNT
P1    LD   0
P2    FA   0
P3    ST   0
      LD   T1
      AD   L1
      ST   T1
      SA   P1
      LD   T2
      AD   L1
      ST   T2
      SA   P2
      LD   T3
      AD   L1
      ST   T3
      SA   P3
      LD   CNT
```

```
AD    L1
ST    CNT
TE    L100
TR    P1
```

The first nine instructions in this program, starting with P0, compute and store the address fields of P1, P2, and P3 for the first iteration. This is done because at the end of the loop these address fields have different values. Computing these values and storing them at this point allows this section of code to be executed more than once. In general, computing initial values of data, address fields, and registers is called **initialization.** If this section of code were to be executed only once, we could omit the initialization, and write

```
P1    LD    A
P2    FA    B
P3    ST    C
```

instead of the code actually given for P1, P2, and P3; this would ensure that the cells P1, P2, and P3 contain their initial values at the start of the entire program which contains this section of code.

Another way to modify addresses is to use indirect addressing. Here the words to be modified are no longer instruction words, but data words which contain the indirect addresses. As an example, we could have left out all the store-address instructions above, and written

```
P1    LD*    T1
P2    FA*    T2
P3    ST*    T3
```

instead of the code actually given.

Some computers have special instructions which increase the value of a memory word by one; among these are RAO on the CDC 1604, MIN on the SDS 930, and AOS on the GE 625 and the PDP-6. Using such instructions, sequences such as LD   T1 ; AD   L1 ; ST   T1   may be replaced by a single instruction.

The use of arithmetic instructions, usually addition, when dealing with addresses, assumes that an address may be treated as an integer. On the IBM 1400 series, this is not true; addresses are coded using a complex scheme by which 16,000 possible addresses are represented by three characters. Therefore, these machines have a special instruction, MA (Modify address), which adds a given integer to a given address field and leaves the result in the address field. Addition takes place in a manner dictated by the method of address coding.

Still another method of modifying addresses is to modify the entire instruction word, instead of just the address field. Here, however, a strange problem arises. If the op-code field is the left-most field of an instruction word, as is usually the case, some operation codes will produce *negative* instruction words. If the integer representation is signed magnitude, adding 1 to the entire instruction word will produce an address field which is one *less* than what it was before! This is not a problem, however, if the integer representation is one's complement or two's complement. (Why?)

If the computer does in fact have index registers, but these are all in use when an array must be referenced, the best technique usually is to **save and restore an index register.** A data word is set aside for the index register, which is stored before the array references are made and reloaded again after processing of the array is finished.

Address and instruction modification, if it is done at all, should be done with great care. It is wise to denote in some way that a given instruction is to be modified. Some programmers do not like to use an address field of zero, as we have done here for the instruction words P1, P2, and P3, because it may be confused with an actual address of zero. Instead, a special symbol is used, which is equal to zero, but which signifies to the programmer that this instruction word is modified. For some computers, particularly those with extensive memory protection schemes, address modification is actively discouraged.

3-5 Multiple-word Arrays

An **array of *n* double precision integers** is a sequence of $2n$ memory words having consecutive addresses. The first two words contain the first double precision integer, the third and fourth words contain the second double precision integer, and so on through the array. In a similar manner, an **array of *n* double precision floating point numbers** is a sequence of $2n$ memory words.

Reference to a double precision number in an array is complicated by the fact that the index register contains *twice* the actual index of a given double precision number. In some loops, this causes no problem. The following code implements the first example of this chapter, assuming now that the arrays A, B, and C are arrays of double precision integers indexed from 0 to 99:

```
A      RE   200
B      RE   200
C      RE   200
START  LXI  0,1
```

```
P1      LD   A+1,1
        AD   B+1,1
        TO   P2
        ST   C+1,1
        LDI  0
        TR   P3
P2      ST   C+1,1
        LDI  1
P3      AD   A,1
        AD   B,1
        ST   C,1
        ICT  1,2,199,P1
```

The ICT instruction at the end of the code increments index register 1 by 2, so that index register 1 successively assumes the values 0, 2, 4, etc. If the index register contains i, then the address A,1 refers to the word at location A+i, and the address A+1,1 refers to the word at location A+i+1; these are the upper and lower portions, respectively, of the corresponding double precision word. The body of the code follows the procedure of the last paragraph of §1-6, using a new conditional transfer instruction:

Transfer if overflow occurred   TO   Y

The loop in this example used the index only as an index, or subscript, and not as an operand. If the loop has the form

```
        DO 17 I = 1, 100
17      C(I) = I + A(I) + B(I)
```

in which I is used as an operand, then another complication occurs. The index used to reference the array is twice the number needed in the actual computation. One solution is to use two index registers, one of which is incremented by 2 and the other incremented by 1. Comparing, of course, needs to be done only on one of the index registers. Alternatively, we may use one index register and a memory cell which is incremented as in §3-4.

An array in which two words are used for each number or other data item is called a **double-word array.** Besides double precision, there are several other situations in which double-word arrays may occur. Two words, for example, may serve to denote a *complex number.* A complex integer or floating point number may be given by its real and imaginary parts, expressed as integers or floating point numbers; or it may be given in polar coordinates. A *two-dimensional vector* may be expressed as a pair of integers or floating point numbers. Sometimes, information which might have been expressed in the form of two single-word arrays is given by one double-word array. For example, in an assembly program, each symbol (represented by one word of character codes) has an address, which is an integer. The symbols and the addresses could be kept in separate arrays, but sometimes they are kept in one double-word array: first a symbol, then its address, then the next symbol, and so on. (We ignore for the moment the fact that in some assemblers two or more words of character codes are required for each symbol.) Such an array is sometimes called a **serial array;** the two single-word arrays to which it corresponds, taken together, are called a **parallel array.** Any double-word array may appear in memory as either a serial or a parallel array; for example, the upper portions of all the double precision numbers in an array may be kept in one single-word array, and the lower portions in another. In such an array, the upper portion of a number is kept in cell $x+i$, where i is the index, and the lower portion is kept in cell $x+i+n$, where n is the length of the array. This is a disadvantage of using parallel arrays; if the length of the array is changed, the program may have to be changed in several places. Parallel arrays are advantageous on computers in which several instructions assume the index increment (or decrement) to be 1, such as the CDC 1604 and 3600.

All that has been said about double-word arrays extends immediately to the case of **multiple-word arrays,** in which each number or other data item takes up more than two words. Triple precision integers or floating point numbers, or three-dimensional vectors, may, for example, be contained in **triple-word arrays.** Multiple-word arrays, like double-word arrays, may be either serial or parallel, and the index register used to index an n-tuple array must contain n times the actual index of the data item.

3-6   Multiple Arrays

A **double array** (or **two-dimensional array**) **of integers** is an array of integers in which each integer has two indices. If the first index ranges from 1 through m, and the second ranges from 1 through n, then m and n are the *dimensions* of the array, and there are $m \cdot n$ integers in the entire array. A **double array of floating point numbers** is an array in which each floating point number has two indices. Double arrays are used in most algebraic languages; the number with indices I and J in the double array called A is normally referred to as A(I, J) or A[I, J].

A double-word array may be treated as a double array in which one of the dimensions is 2. To specify an array X of 100 two-dimensional vectors, for example, we may give the dimensions as 2 and 100; the x component of the ith vector is then $X(1, I)$, and its y component is $X(2, I)$. Similarly, a multiple array in which each data item uses n words may be treated as a double array in which one of the dimensions is n. A matrix is represented as a double array; if the matrix is rectangular, its dimensions are unequal. Correlations in statistics are also represented by double arrays.

Double arrays may be contained in the computer in several ways. The most economical way to store an array with dimensions m and n is to treat it as a single array of dimension $m \cdot n$. If the indices range from 1 through m and from 1 through n respectively, then the elements of the array A may be stored in either of the following two orders:

$$A(1, 1), A(2, 1), \ldots, A(M, 1), A(1, 2), A(2, 2),$$
$$\ldots, A(M, 2), \ldots, A(1, N), A(2, N), \ldots, A(M, N)$$

called a **column representation** or a **column-wise** or **column array**; or

$$A(1, 1), A(1, 2), \ldots, A(1, N), A(2, 1), A(2, 2),$$
$$\ldots, A(2, N), \ldots, A(M, 1), A(M, 2), \ldots, A(M, N)$$

called a **row representation** or a **row array**. In either case, the length of a row is n and the length of a column is m; the number of rows is m, and the number of columns is n.

When an element of a row or column array is referenced, the index which appears in the index register must normally be computed and placed in the register. It is usually impossible simply to place the two indices in two index registers, because most computers do not have instructions in which two index registers are added to the address; such an instruction would have to contain two index register fields.

A few computers, such as the IBM 360, do indeed have instructions in which two index registers are added to the address; several other computers, such as the PDP-6 and the UNIVAC 1108, have instructions with two index register fields, which, however, are not used in this way. On the IBM 360, one index register is normally used as a base register; even when this is not the case, as for an array at the lower end of memory, one index register must still contain m times (n times) the actual index for a column (row) array. Also, these instructions do not improve the situation for arrays with more than two indices.

The computation of the actual index for element (i, j) involves the computation, for column arrays, of $(j - 1) \cdot m + (i - 1)$ if the indices start at 1, or of $j \cdot m + i$ if the indices start at 0. For row arrays, the corresponding computations are $(j - 1) + (i - 1) \cdot n$ and $j + i \cdot n$. In each case, the index is placed in an index register. In order to allow a single subroutine to calculate the index when the values of i and j (but not m or n) are known, the values of m and n are sometimes placed in a standard location relative to the array, such as just before the array.* If the subscript range is from m_1 to m_2 and n_1 to n_2, respectively, there may be four of these values; or there may be only the value m (for a column array), depending on the particular subroutine. Information such as this, which is associated with an array, is sometimes called a **dope vector.**

Incrementation of an index register is slightly easier. If the index of element (i, j) has been calculated, incrementing the index register by 1 will produce element $(i+1, j)$ for a column array, or element $(i, j+1)$, for a row array; incrementing the index register by m will produce element $(i, j+1)$ for a column array, and incrementing the index register by n will produce element $(i+1, j)$ for a row array.

The following code, written in FORTRAN, illustrates a computation which is often carried out with matrices. The double arrays A, B, and C all have equal dimensions n.

```
      DO 33 I = 1, N
      DO 33 J = 1, N
      SUM = 0
      DO 31 K = 1, N
   31 SUM = SUM + A(I, K)*B(K, J)
   33 C(I, J) = SUM
```

The matrix represented by the array C and calculated in this manner is called the product of the matrices represented by the arrays A and B. We shall now give a machine language program which accomplishes the same result. The arrays A, B, and C are taken to be indexed from 1 to n, so that, for example, the first element of A (that is, A(1, 1)) is actually at A+1. Notice that we do not calculate the indices each time, but increment them whenever possible. The number n is contained in the cell N. Also notice that in order to store the array C by columns, a different order of calculation from the one above is used.

```
      A      RE      1000
      B      RE      1000
      C      RE      1000
      N      RE      1
```

---

* This is especially helpful in a subroutine, one of whose parameters is the name of a multiple array whose dimensions are not known within the subroutine.

```
PB1     RE      1
PB2     RE      1
SUM     RE      1
START   LX      N,6
        LXI     1,2
        SX      PB2,2
        LXI     1,4
P1      LXI     0,1
        SX      PB1,1
        LX      PB2,2
        AX      N,2
        SX      PB2,2
        LX      N,5
        TR      P2A
P2      LX      PB2,2
P2A     LX      PB1,1
        AXI     1,1
        SX      PB1,1
        LX      N,3
        LDI     0
        ST      SUM
P3      LD      A,1
        FM      B,2
        FA      SUM
        ST      SUM
        AX      N,1
        AXI     1,2
        DCT     3,1,0,P3
        ST      C,4
        AXI     1,4
        DCT     5,1,0,P2
        DCT     6,1,0,P1
```

This code uses six index registers; on a machine with fewer than six index registers, some of the functions which we have performed in index registers would have to be performed using memory words. As usual we have made an arbitrary choice as to the lengths of the arrays A, B, and C. In some situations, the arrays will be exactly as long as needed; we have chosen to reserve a fixed number of words for each array, and the code which we give will therefore work for arrays of any dimension $N \le 31$ (since $31^2 < 1000 < 32^2$).

3-7 Arrays of Variable Length Data

So far we have not considered arrays which can, for example, contain both single precision and double precision integers. If it is necessary to have such arrays, it is always possible to consider a single precision integer as a double precision integer with zero in the upper portion. Sometimes, however, the data which is contained in an array is contained in a variable number of words per data item. For example, we may have an array of people's names, which range from 5 to 30 characters in length. Such an array is an **array of variable length data.**

If variable length data in an array are to be processed *sequentially*—that is, one by one, starting from the top or the bottom—then it is necessary only to be able to distinguish where one piece of variable length data stops and another begins. This may be done in a variety of ways. If each item consists of characters, a special character (such as the period) may be used to separate two character strings. This special character will never be used for any other purpose. Sometimes an unused character code, one that does not correspond to an actual character (sometimes called an *idle character*), is used for this purpose. On the IBM 1400 series, a word mark (one of the bits in the 8-bit word) is set to 1 to denote the start of a new data item. If the items do not consist of characters, the start of a new item may be denoted by some distinguishing characteristic of the first word of each item: having its sign bit negative, or its left half non-zero, or its index field non-zero. Or a field of the first word of each item may contain the length of the item in words. In each case, it is possible to process all the items in the array in sequence. The following loop causes the subroutine PRO to be called once for every item of an array of variable length data in which the index of the current data item is in index register 1. The length of the array is 1000, and the sign bit of the first word of each item is negative. It is assumed that the subroutine PRO saves and restores index register 1 if it uses this register. (For a description of the instruction PT, see Appendix A.)

```
TBL     RE    1000
START   LXI   0,1
P1      PT    TBL.1
        CA    PRO
        ICT   1,1,999,P1
```

In practice, the array itself may have variable length. The length of the array may be kept as a variable; or an item of a special format may be used to specify the end of the array. The following loop causes the subroutine PRO to be called once for each item under the condition that the right-most six bits of each item contains its length in words. The last word of the array contains the integer −1.

```
LM1    CO    −1
X1     RE    1
MASK   CO    63
TBL    RE    1000
START  LXI   0,1
P1     CA    PRO
       SX    X1,1
       LD    TBL,1
       AND   MASK
       AD    X1
       ST    X1
       LX    X1,1
       LD    LM1
       TE    TBL,1
       TR    P1
```

When the length of the array is kept as a variable, a problem arises. The loop instructions in our machine language, and in many computers, use immediate addressing in the comparison. In our instruction ICT, the index is compared with the *number* M, not with the number in the cell with address M. If the length of the array is the variable M, the latter type of comparison is indicated. The loop may, of course, be written without an instruction of this type, using separate increment, compare, and transfer instructions. If the given computer has no compare instructions using direct addressing involving index registers, the contents of the index register may be brought into an accumulator for comparison purposes. In computers with many registers, comparison is sometimes made with the contents of a register; this register may then be loaded, using either direct or immediate addressing, before the loop is started.

3-8 Pointers

When variable length data is to be *indexed*, rather than processed sequentially, the methods introduced above will not work. In this case we must know where each piece of variable length data starts. One way to do this is to have another array containing indices in the first array. To reference the nth variable length data item, we load the nth item in the index array and use this as an index. For example, suppose that five data items are contained in an array, containing 6, 3, 4, 7, and 2 words respectively; these all occupy sequential addresses, so that the first word of each item may be indexed by 1, 7, 10, 14, and 21 respectively. To reference the fourth item, we pick up the fourth word of a table containing the numbers 1, 7, 10, 14, and 21; this will be 14. The fourth item now has the index 14. Using this method, a separator between items is not necessary if the item length is known; this length may often be inferred from the form of the data.

Indices which are kept in this way are called **index pointers;** an array such as we have used above is a **pointer array.** Instead of using indices, we could have used the actual addresses of the first word of each variable length data item. To reference an item we would then pick up its address, put it in an index register, and reference it using this index register with an address of zero. Such addresses are called **address pointers.** Address pointers and index pointers are sometimes called **absolute pointers** and **relative pointers;** indices themselves are sometimes called **relative addresses,** in contrast to ordinary or **absolute addresses.** Pointers are used for many purposes other than handling variable length data; their most important use, in lists, will be discussed in the next chapter.

One widespread use of pointers is in representations of multiple arrays. A double array may be considered as an array of arrays; a matrix, for example, may be considered as an array of its columns. Such an array may then be treated as if it were an array of variable length data; that is, we have a pointer array giving the start of each column. This is called the **indexed representation** of a double array. It uses up more space than the standard row and column representations, but has the advantage that the calculation of an index no longer involves multiplication. In order to reference element (i, j) of such a double array, we pick up element i of the pointer array, consider this as the index of an array, and pick up element j of this array. This is particularly important on machines in which multiplication is slow. Either index or address pointers may be used in an indexed representation. Sometimes the indexed representation actually saves space, because columns of the double array can be duplicated; if two columns are the same, the second column need not appear at all, and the respective pointers can both point to the same column. An extreme example of this is a constant $m \times n$ array of zeros; here all we need is a single column of n zeros, and a pointer array of m pointers, each of which points to this column.

A triple array may be considered as an array of double arrays, and thus may be given by an array of pointers to double arrays—i.e., to their own pointer arrays. A constant triple array of $m \times n \times p$ zeros may be given by $m + n + p$ words, using the same ideas as are used above. In general, however, $(m+1) \cdot (n+1) \cdot p$ words will be used, as contrasted with $m \cdot n \cdot p$ in the row or column representation. Which representation is to be used in a given instance will depend on the application. Most algebraic languages, however, produce code in which a specific choice of representation for multiple arrays is made once and for all.

3-9   Sorted Arrays

An array is **sorted** if its elements are arranged in ascending order (or descending order) by addresses.

Two binary words are compared by comparing their bits from left to right until a bit position is found at which one of the words contains zero and the other contains one. The second of the two words will then be greater, unless the bit position is the sign bit; in signed-magnitude representation, the second of the two words will be greater only in absolute value. In signed-magnitude and one's complement representations, minus zero is less than plus zero. All this assumes, of course, that the binary words to be compared represent integers. For normalized floating point numbers, one word is less than the other if the corresponding real number is less than the other in the usual sense; this is ensured by the exponent bias, and may easily be verified. Thus a real array is sorted if its elements are arranged in integer ascending order. A sorted array of character codes is *alphabetized* in the usual sense if the following three conditions hold:

(1) The words of character codes are *left justified*. If the first character of each word is at the left, then two words which have the same first character will have their leading bits alike and will thus be compared on the basis of the remaining characters, as in alphabetization; i.e., one word will be less than the other if the corresponding character string precedes the other in dictionary order.

(2) The sign bit does not interfere. Unless special precautions are taken, a negative number will be less than a positive number, even though, when considered as character code words, the first character of the first word follows the first character of the second, since its highest order bit is a 1.

(3) The character codes for the blank character and the letters A through Z are arranged in ascending order. (The arrangement of all the characters of any computer in order of their character codes is called the **collating sequence** of the computer.)

The FIELDATA character code, used on the UNIVAC 1107 and 1108 and many other computers, specifies that all letters of the alphabet, and the blank, have 6-bit codes of which the first bit is zero; numbers and most of the special characters have codes of which the first bit is 1. Hence the sign bit does not interfere with comparison. The IBM 700 series has a comparison instruction which treats its 36-bit word as *unsigned;* therefore, left justified character strings will compare properly. The IBM 1400 series has a character-by-character compare instruction which works properly for character strings and unsigned integers, but not for signed integers (in the overpunch representation typical of this machine) unless all the signs are the same. To compare two signed integers, they must be subtracted, and the result tested for a negative sign. When 5-bit or 7-bit character codes are used with a 36-bit word, the 35 bits exclusive of the sign bit may be used if comparisons are to be made. The IBM 360 has separate compare instructions for full word, half word, decimal, and logical representations.

The following code inserts the word at W1 into the sorted array TBL of length N, in its proper order. As soon as the proper order is found, all succeeding entries in the table must be adjusted; that is, the contents of each word must be stored in the word with address one higher.

```
          DO 131 I = 1, N
          IF (W1 − TBL(I)) 131, 131, 135
131       CONTINUE
          I = N + 1
135       J = N + 1
137       IF (J − I) 141, 141, 139
139       TBL(J) = TBL(J − 1)
          J = J − 1
          GO TO 137
141       TBL(J) = W1
          N = N + 1
```

In this example, the entries at the end of the table are adjusted *forward;* they must be adjusted from back to front. If a word is to be *deleted* from a sorted array, all succeeding entries are adjusted *back.* Otherwise, there will be a "hole" in the table, a word which is not a bona fide entry; and although this will cause few difficulties if there is only one "hole," the table will be considerably harder to manage if there are several. The following code deletes TBL(I) from the sorted array TBL of length N:

```
          N = N − 1
          IF (N − I) 175, 173, 173
173       DO 174 J = I, N
174       TBL(J) = TBL(J+1)
175       (next statement)
```

PROBLEMS

1. A programmer wishes to transfer to D21 if cell N is zero. He writes

    TZ   N,D21

   The assembler, however, flags this as an error; indeed, such an instruction cannot exist on his computer because it would require two fields of address size (one for the address of N and the other for the address of D21). Describe how he may accomplish his objective by means of test instructions. Assume that the transfer instruction is TR and that there are two test instructions, ZT and NZT, which test for a memory word containing zero and non-zero respectively.

2. The following description of an instruction is given in the operations manual of a computer: "COG—Compare Greater. General form, COG   R,M . The contents of the memory cell M are compared with the contents of the register R. If they are greater than the contents of R, the next instruction is skipped; otherwise the next instruction is executed in sequence." A programmer writes COG   2,3 , followed by a transfer to Q9. Under what conditions will this sequence proceed to Q9?

3. Suppose that a certain loop is to be performed from $I = 1$ to N. If N happens to be zero, a difference of opinion exists as to whether the loop should be performed exactly once or not at all; some algebraic languages make one convention and some make the other. Suppose now that a machine language loop is being written, in which the loop count N may (but does not necessarily) assume the initial value zero. How does the choice discussed above affect the way in which such a loop is coded?

4. In many loops the process to be performed is slightly different the first time through the loop. A test may be made to see whether the index is equal to its initial value; if it is, the loop is performed in an altered manner. However, if a loop is coded in this way, this test will then be made each time the loop is executed, using up a considerable amount of time. A better method consists of starting the first iteration of the loop in the middle of the loop. For example, consider the following loop:

```
        DO 604 K = 1, N
        IF (K—1) 602, 603, 602
602     A(K) = A(K)*FACTOR
        B(K) = B(K)*FACTOR
        C(K) = C(K)*FACTOR
        D(K) = D(K)*FACTOR
        E(K) = E(K)*FACTOR
603     A(K) = A(K) — DELTA
        B(K) = B(K) — DELTA
```

$$C(K) = C(K) - DELTA$$
$$D(K) = D(K) - DELTA$$
$$604 \quad E(K) = E(K) - DELTA$$

Show how this loop may be rewritten so as to avoid the IF statement. Do not use a DO statement and do not increase the total number of lines of code by more than three.

5. Consider the following statement: "Address modification is incompatible with the newly emerging style of programming. This partially explains the popularity of machines with large numbers of index registers and, to a lesser extent, double indexing—both of which reduce the necessity for address modification." Assuming the truth of the first statement, which is debatable, can the second be justified, and if so, how? (Hint: What technique or techniques may be used as a substitute for address modification if a large number of index registers are present, or if instruction words contain two index register fields? Describe in detail.)

6. (a) A forward array C contains 50 double precision numbers. The two words of C(0) have octal addresses 30274 and 30275. What are the octal addresses of the two words of C (29)?

(b) A backward array D contains 30 complex numbers. The real part of D(1) is at octal address 23772 and its imaginary part is at octal address 23771. What is the octal address of the imaginary part of D(20)?

(c) A forward array E contains 75 real three-dimensional vectors. The x, y, and z components of E(1) are contained at hexadecimal locations 1396, 1397, and 1398 respectively. What is contained at hexadecimal location 1400?

(d) A forward array P contains 20 complex three-dimensional vectors. The real and imaginary parts of the x component of P(1) are contained at octal locations 131225 and 131226 respectively. The y and z components of P(1) follow; the real part of the x component of P(2) is thus contained at octal location 131233. Where is the imaginary part of the y component of P(9)?

(e) A forward array Q contains 6 complex, triple precision, three-dimensional vectors. Each component of each vector uses 6 consecutive locations, consisting of 3 consecutive locations for the real part followed by 3 consecutive locations for the imaginary part. The x, y, and z components of each vector are in sequential order. The vectors range from Q(0) to Q(5) and use octal locations 7000 through 7153. Where is the real part of the z component of Q(4)?

7. Each of the following programs has one or more errors. Some of the errors are programming errors which may be corrected by changing a statement; in other cases, the ideas underlying the program may be faulty. In each case, analyze and correct the error or errors.

(a) The sum of the squares of the integers from 1 to 100 is to be found and the result placed in NSSQ:

```
        NSSQ = 0
   1    I = 1
        NSSQ = NSSQ + I*I
        I = I + 1
        IF (I - 100) 1, 1, 2
        (next statement)
```

(b) Two complex vectors of dimension N are kept in the arrays G and H, where

DIMENSION G(100), H(100)

and $N \leq 50$. That is, G(1) and G(2) are the real and imaginary parts, respectively, of the first component of the vector G; G(3) and G(4) are the real and imaginary parts, respectively, of the second component of G, etc.; and similarly for H. It is desired to set Z equal to the product of the Kth component of G and the Jth component of H (as complex numbers), where $K = 5*L$ and $J = N - K$, and where the complex number Z is expressed as $X + Yi$:

```
    K = 5*L
    J = N - K
C FOR THE PRODUCT OF TWO COMPLEX NUMBERS A + BI AND C + DI,
C THE PRODUCT IS E + FI, WHERE E = AC - BD AND F = AD + BC.
C FIRST CALCULATE AC - BD
    X = G(K)*H(J) - G(K+1)*H(J+1)
C NOW CALCULATE AD + BC
    Y = G(K)*H(J+1) + G(K+1)*H(J)
```

(c) The arrays V and W, each of dimension 25, are being compared to see if they contain equal entries. If they do, transfer is made to statement 135; otherwise, transfer is made to statement 136:

```
        I = 1
   134  IF (V(I) - W(I)) 136, 133, 136
   133  I = I + 1
        IF (I - 25) 134, 135, 135
   135  (continue if arrays are equal)
        ...
   136  (continue if arrays are unequal)
```

(d) The scalar product of two three-dimensional real vectors R and S is to be found and placed in PROD. The vectors R and S are kept in double precision and are of DIMENSION 6; thus R(1) and R(2), R(3) and R(4), and R(5) and R(6) respectively designate the first, second, and third components of the vector R, and similarly for S. The result PROD is a double precision quantity and is therefore of DIMENSION 2. This program calls subroutines DPAD(X, Y, Z) and DPMUL(X, Y, Z) for adding or multiplying, respectively, two double precision numbers X and Y, each of dimension 2, and placing the result in the double precision number Z of dimension 2:

```
        DIMENSION CP(2), PROD(2), R(6), S(6)
        I = 1
        PROD(1) = 0
        PROD(2) = 0
3       CALL DPMUL(R(I), S(I), CP)
        CALL DPAD(CP, PROD, PROD)
        I = I + 1
        IF (I − 3) 3, 3, 4
4       (next statement)
```

(e) An integer array M has dimension 10. If any element of this array is less than the following element, it is to be decreased by one. If any element is now greater than the following element by more than 5, it is to be set to zero:

```
        I = 1
7       IF (M(I) − M(I+1)) 8, 9, 9
8       M(I) = M(I) − 1
9       I = I + 1
        IF (I − 10) 7, 10, 10
10      IF (M(I) − M(I+1) − 5) 12, 12, 11
11      M(I) = 0
12      I = I + 1
        IF (I − 10) 10, 13, 13
13      (next statement)
```

(f) An integer array L has dimension 10. The elements of this array are to be altered as follows: If $L(I)$ is greater than $L(I-1)$, then $L(I)$ is to be decreased by 1, for each I, $2 \leq I \leq 10$. The average of all the elements of L (as a real number) is then to be calculated and stored in X:

```
        I = 1
23      IF (L(I) − L(I+1)) 24, 25, 25
24      L(I+1) = L(I+1) − 1
25      I = I + 1
        IF (I − 10) 23, 26, 26
26      W=L(1)+L(2)+L(3)+L(4)+L(5)+L(6)+L(7)+L(8)+L(9)+L(10)
        X=W/10.0
```

(g) A real array E has dimension 50. For each element x of E, the quantities $x^3 + 5x^2 - 14x + 7$ and $x^2 - 20x + 5$ are to be calculated. If both these quantities are negative, the given element is to be set to zero:

```
        I = 1
71      X = E(I)
        Y = X*X*X + 5.0*X*X − 14.0*X + 7.0
        IF (Y) 72, 78, 78
72      Y = X*X − 20.0*X + 5.0
        IF (Y) 73, 78, 78
```

```
73    I = I + 1
      E(I) = 0.0
      GO TO 79
78    I = I + 1
79    IF (I − 50) 71, 71, 80
80    (next statement)
```

8. (a) A forward double integer array L with dimensions 15 and 20 is given in a column representation. What number results from subtracting the address of the cell containing L(2, 7) from the address of the cell containing L(5, 8)?

(b) A backward double floating point array P with dimensions 10 and 50 is given in a column representation. What is contained in the cell whose address is 100 (decimal) greater than the address of the cell containing A(6, 20)?

(c) A forward double floating point array R with dimensions 8 and 60 is given in a row representation. What number results from subtracting the address of the cell containing R(5, 1) from the address of the cell containing R(7, 3)?

(d) A forward triple integer array M with dimensions 8, 16, and 40 is given in a column representation. The cell containing M(1, 1, 1) has octal address 25344. What is the octal address of the cell containing M(3, 12, 10)?

(e) A forward double array of complex numbers, Z, with dimensions 71 and 11, is given in a column representation. The first cell of this array has octal address 3617. What is the octal address of the last word of the array?

9. (a) Verify the statement implied in the text that the binary representation of a normalized floating point (real) number is greater, as a binary integer, than the binary representation of any smaller normalized floating point number. What happens if the numbers are allowed to be unnormalized?

(b) Suppose that an array of *right* justified, zero filled character code words is sorted according to the representations of these words as binary integers. If this array is printed out, will it be in any apparent order? Assume that, in the collating sequence, the blank comes before A.

(c) Arrange the following left justified, blank-filled character code words in the order in which they would appear when sorted, assuming that, in the collating sequence, the blank character comes between R and S:

J
JPRIME
JA
JULY
JAM
JAZZ
JAMB

Chapter 4

LISTS

4-1   Items and Lists of Items

The data in a computer may be grouped *physically* into bits or digits, character codes, words, half words, double words, or pages (which are collections of words whose addresses have the same leading bits). The data in a computer may also be grouped *logically* into integers, real (floating point) numbers, complex numbers, three-dimensional vectors, instruction words, double precision numbers, and in many other ways. Logical grouping of data is dependent on the program which uses the data; some programs use more types of data than others. Each type of data uses a certain number of words, which may be variable, and which may be a non-integral multiple of one word. When these are grouped into arrays, we have called them "data items." We now reserve the word **item** as a technical term, meaning a logical "piece of data" in its most general sense, which is stored in a data word or in several data words with consecutive addresses. Like the word "set" in mathematics, the word "item" has no precise definition. An item may consist of one or more numbers in any format or in several different formats; it may consist of a collection of data of various types, such as a character string, a number, a one-bit flag, etc. A word, or a part of a word, used as storage for part of an item is called a **field,** and the arrangement of an item into words and/or fields is called the **format** of the item. The **length** of an item may be expressed in bits, characters, or words, or, on a decimal computer, in digits. If the length of all items of a certain type is the same, they are called **fixed length items;** otherwise, they are called **variable length items.** The **address** of an item is the address of its first word (or, less frequently, of its last word).

A **list** (or **chain**) is an ordered collection of items, each of which contains a pointer to the next item. The pointer, as we have noted, may consist of either the address of the next item or an index of this item in some array which contains all elements of this list. The items do *not* necessarily have to have consecutive addresses; this distinguishes a list from an array.

The following algorithm adds the integers in a list and leaves their sum in the accumulator. The list is assumed to be of two-word items; the second word is the address of the next item on the list, or zero if this is the last item on the list, whereas the first word is the integer.

1. Load index register 1 with the address of the first item.

2. Set an accumulator to zero.

3. AD   0,1 . This adds the integer in an item to the accumulator.

4. Load index register 1 with the address of the next item, which is contained in the cell whose address is one greater than the current contents of index register 1.

5. If index register 1 does not contain zero, go to step 3.

> Implementation of this algorithm depends strongly on the computer involved. If there is more than one accumulator, many instructions will have two register fields, one for the accumulator number and one for the index register number, and hence there is likely to be a single instruction which implements our step 4. If there is only one accumulator, it may happen that no instruction has two register fields. An index register may be loaded from a memory word, but not from a memory word whose address is *indexed,* as is necessary in this case. The indexed memory word may be brought to the accumulator first and taken from there to the index register; or the index register may be stored in the address field of the instruction which loads the index register.

Logically, a list of integers is similar in some ways to an array of integers, and the same is true for lists of floating point numbers or other fixed length items. As we have seen, such a list may be processed from the first item to the last, although it may not be indexed; finding the nth item in a list takes n steps instead of one. Also, an extra address field is needed in each item when it is to be contained in a list rather than an array. Although lists have several advantages over arrays, these may not apply in certain simple situations. In practice, lists, in some form, and arrays are used with approximately equal frequency.

4-2   Insertion and Deletion

When a program uses several arrays stored one after the other in memory, these arrays must have fixed (maximum) sizes. To increase the maximum size of an array, it would be necessary to adjust all arrays which follow it, and then to change all references to those arrays, i.e., all address fields whatsoever which contain locations within these arrays. When a program uses several lists, however, the size of each list can be increased and decreased very easily. In fact, when data is stored on lists rather than on arrays, it is not necessary to have a fixed maximum size at all, or to keep space on lists for any more items than are actually on the list.

Suppose that we have a large array of cells in which list items are stored. The current length of this array may be kept as a variable. Now, when it is necessary to add a new element to a list, this variable may be increased, and a new list item linked on to the list by setting a pointer within it to the start of the list. We note that adding an element to an array normally means adding it to the end of the array, whereas adding an element to a list may be and often is accomplished by adding it to the *beginning* of the list, called the **head** of the list.

We illustrate this procedure for the two-word items described above. The large array is denoted by LS; it is 4000 words long, which allows space for 2000 possible items. The cell LSL is an index pointer to the first word of the last item in the array LS; it is one less than the current length of LS. The array LH contains the heads of 75 lists; each word in LH contains a pointer to the first word of a list. Suppose that a new item is to be added to the nth list, where n is contained in index register 1. We may now proceed as follows:

1. Load index 2 with the element in LH,1 .

2. Load index 3 with LSL.

3. Increase index 3 by 2 (the length of an item); check whether the maximum length (4000) has been exceeded; store index 3 in LSL.

4. Store index 2 in LS+1,3 ; that is, set the second word of the new item to point to the item which was formerly the head of this list.

5. Store index 3 in LH,1 (to denote the new head of the list).

This example assumes that pointers are indices in the array LS. We may also use address pointers; in this case the current length of the array, as given above, is replaced by the address of the current end of the array.

We may also insert a new item in the *middle* of a list. Suppose that index 2 already contains a pointer to an element on a list, and we wish to insert an item between this element and the next one. In this case, we may take the following steps:

1. Load index 3 with LSL.

2. Increase index 3 by 2 and check whether the maximum length has been exceeded; store index 3 in LSL.

3. Load the accumulator with the element in LS+1,2 (the next item of the list).

4. Store the accumulator in LS+1,3 (that is, let the new item in the list point to its successor).

5. Store index 3 in LS+1,2 (that is, let the item to which index 2 points, point to the new item).

The same procedure could be used to insert an item at the *end* of a list. The last element of a list must contain a special pointer which denotes this fact. Usually, a zero pointer will suffice, because the cell with location 0 is not available for list space. If indices rather than addresses are being used as pointers, the array can be indexed starting at 1, making the zero pointer again available as an end flag.

Items may also be deleted from a list. Suppose that we wish to delete the item which *follows* the item pointed to by index 2. Then we may do the following:

1. Load index 3 with the element in LS+1,2 (the item to be deleted).

2. Load the accumulator with the element in LS+1,3 (the item after the one to be deleted).

3. Store the accumulator in LS+1,2 .

Note that we cannot delete the item to which a given index register points unless we know the preceding item in the list. It is not possible, using the kind of list which we have been considering, to deduce which item precedes a given item without searching the entire list from the beginning.

An array, such as the array LS, which is used to contain all items (of a given format) that may occur in lists is called **list space** or **free storage.** A single array may be used as list space, or several arrays may be used. In our example, only part of the list space, lying below the index LSL, is actually in use at any time; the remainder of LS is the **available space** for later insertions.

4-3 The List of Available Space

The procedures of the preceding section have one important drawback when both insertions and deletions are continuously being made. The variable which indicates the current size of list space is increased on insertion and is not decreased on deletion. When this variable reaches its maximum value, there may be space left by items which have been deleted, and which can be used for new items; but the deleted items are presumably scattered through list space, and we do not know where they are. If all this available space were on a list, we could proceed by taking items from this list, one at a time, as they are needed for insertions.

The use of a **list of available space** is a device due to Allen Newell, which now normally is used whenever insertions and deletions are continuously made. It assumes that all the space which is currently available is always on a single list. If a program starts with all lists empty, then *all* list space must be considered to be available, and it is placed on a single list by a simple loop; this is called initializing the list of available space. When we wish to insert an item on a list, we delete one item from the head of the list of available space and then insert it. When we wish to delete an item from a list, we delete it and then insert it at the head of the list of available space. This procedure assures us that there will always be available space, as long as all the possible items in list space have not been used.

The following code illustrates the use of a list of available space. It is part of a computer system for control of a factory which manufactures parts. A three-word item describing each part is kept in memory at all times. There are 60 working areas within the factory. With each working area, there is associated a list of all parts which are currently at that working area. When a part moves from one working area to another, an item must be taken off one list and put on another. When a part is finished and leaves the last working area, an item must be deleted; similarly, when a part enters the factory, an item must be inserted on the list corresponding to the first working area.

The list space, LS, is an array with dimension 12000; it is assumed that no more than 4000 parts will be in the shop at any one time. LASH is the head of the list of available space. The working area list heads are given in the array LWA; each word in this array points to the head of a list for a given working area. The code is written in FORTRAN IV; all pointers are indices within the array LS. The format of the items is such that the first word of each item contains the address of the next item; a zero pointer is used to denote the end of a list.

(1) To insert a new item on the list whose head is at LWA(I):

```
M = LS(LASH)
LS(LASH) = LWA(I)
LWA(I) = LASH
LASH = M
```

(2) To delete the first item of the list whose head is at LWA(I):

```
M = LS(LWA(I))
LS(LWA(I)) = LASH
```

```
LASH = LWA(I)
LWA(I) = M
```

(3) To delete the first item of the list whose head is at LWA(I) and insert it as the first item of the list whose head is at LWA(J) (this operation does not affect the list of available space):

```
M = LS(LWA(I))
LS(LWA(I)) = LWA(J)
LWA(J) = LWA(I)
LWA(I) = M
```

(4) To delete a list item whose index is LP, immediately preceded on its list by an item of index LC:

```
LS(LC) = LS(LP)
LS(LP) = LASH
LASH = LP
```

(5) To move a list item whose index is LP, immediately preceded on its list by an item of index LC, to the head of the list whose current head is at LWA(I):

```
LS(LC) = LS(LP)
LS(LP) = LWA(I)
LWA(I) = LP
```

(6) To initialize the list of available space:

```
    DO 3 I = 1,11995,3
3   LS(I) = I+3
    LS(11998) = 0
    LASH = 1
```

This last operation should be especially noted. When the program is started and there are no lists, *all* the space in the list may be considered to be available. Therefore, all the items in the array LS must be collected onto a list of available space. The fact that the last item on the list of available space has a zero pointer affects the error checking operations that can be made; for example, each time an item is inserted, we can check the list of available space to make sure it is not exhausted.

If deletions are not to be made, so that the method of the preceding chapter can be used, it is advisable to use it, because it is faster and also because list items may be of differing lengths. This method, in which the current length of list space plus one is always an index pointer to the next available word of list space, may be termed the use of an **array of available space.**

4-4   List Structures

An array of variable length items may be stored as a list of variable length items in which each item is itself treated as a list. An item of length n is treated as a collection of n two-word items, each containing a pointer to the next. Insertions and deletions may now be made on these lists, producing a list of items of changeable length. This is a special case of the concept of a **list of lists.** A list which is contained on another list is called a **sublist** of that list. As usual, a list is "contained" on another list if the second list contains a pointer to the first. A list which has no sublists may be called a **simple list.**

The sublists of a list may have sublists, and so on ad infinitum; the object which we obtain in this way is called a **list structure.** The concept of list structure may be defined recursively; a list structure of integers, for example, is defined to be a list which may contain integers and/or other list structures of integers. A list structure of items of length greater than one may be treated as a list of pointers, each of which points to such an item; pointers to items and pointers to sublists have the same length, and thus the list items can all have the same length, namely the number of words necessary to store two pointers.

The use of **S-expressions** to denote list structures is a device due to John McCarthy, which provides a way to visualize any list structure. In the S-expression notation, any item on a list which is not a pointer to a sublist is assumed to have a name of some kind. A simple list is then denoted by the names of its items in order, separated by blanks (or commas) and enclosed in parentheses. Thus

$$(A \ B \ C \ D \ E \ X \ Y \ Z)$$

is an S-expression denoting a simple list of eight items. A list which is not simple is denoted in the same way, except that whenever a sublist occurs, the S-expression which represents the sublist appears in the main S-expression. Thus

$$(A \ (B \ C) \ D \ (E \ (F \ G)))$$

is an S-expression denoting a list of four items. The first is called A; the next is a list containing B and C; the next is called D; the next is a list of two items, of which the first is called E and the second is a list containing F and G.

The following S-expression represents the numbers from 1 to 100 in a way which exhibits their prime factors. Each prime number is contained on the list; each number that is not prime is represented by a list of its prime factors.

(1 2 3 (2 2) 5 (2 3) 7 (2 2 2) (3 3) (2 5) 11 (2 2 3) 13 (2 7)
(3 5) (2 2 2 2) 17 (2 3 3) 19 (2 2 5) (3 7) (2 11) 23 (2 2 2 3)
(5 5) (2 13) (3 3 3) (2 2 7) 29 (2 3 5) 31 (2 2 2 2 2) (3 11)
(2 17) (5 7) (2 2 3 3) 37 (2 19) (3 13) (2 2 2 5) 41 (2 3 7) 43
(2 2 11) (3 3 5) (2 23) 47 (2 2 2 2 3) (7 7) (2 5 5) (3 17)
(2 2 13) 53 (2 3 3 3) (5 11) (2 2 2 7) (3 19) (2 29) 59 (2 2
3 5) 61 (2 31) (3 3 7) (2 2 2 2 2 2) (5 13) (2 3 11) 67 (2 2
17) (3 23) (2 5 7) 71 (2 2 2 3 3) 73 (2 37) (3 5 5) (2 2 19)
(7 11) (2 3 13) 79 (2 2 2 2 5) (3 3 3 3) (2 41) 83 (2 2 3 7)
(5 17) (2 43) (3 29) (2 2 2 11) 89 (2 3 3 5) (7 13) (2 2 23)
(3 31) (2 47) (5 19) (2 2 2 2 2 3) 97 (2 7 7) (3 3 11) (2 2
5 5))

> The IBM 700 series has two fields of the (type A) instruction word, the *address* field and the *decrement* field, in which pointers may be kept; instructions also exist on these machines for index registers to be loaded from and stored into an arbitrary address or decrement field. The CDC 1604 and 3600 have a similar feature with the address fields of each of the two instructions contained in a word. The UNIVAC 1108, the PDP-6, the IBM 360, and many other computers contain half-words, where pointers may be stored efficiently. On other computers, such as the CDC 6600 and the SDS 930, list processing is slightly more unwieldy. On the Honeywell 800, four address fields are available per word.

4-5 Threaded Lists

When an instruction word on the IBM 700 series is divided into address and decrement fields, each of which may contain a pointer, there are two three-bit fields left over (the prefix and tag fields). In list processing languages, and in list processing in general, on machines of the 700 series, use is very often made of these extra fields. In the IPL-V language, for example, they are known as the P and Q fields, and may take any value from 0 through 7. Other computers do not have these fields, but it is usually possible to include at least two one-bit flags along with each pair of pointers. One of these may now be used to designate the start of a sublist; if this flag is present, one of the pointers indicates the next word of the main list, whereas the other indicates the start of the sublist. The other one-bit flag may be used to designate the end of a list. We have denoted the end of a list by a special pointer, as a zero pointer; if the end of a list is denoted by a one-bit flag, a pointer becomes free for other use.

The **threaded list** is a concept developed by Alan Perlis which uses **this** pointer to advantage in the following way. Each word which ends a list contains a flag denoting this fact and a pointer to the *head* of the list. Thus each list is **circular;** procedure from one element of the list to the next repetitively results in an endless process of cycling through the list. Each list, however, has a definite start and end.

Circular lists have many other uses in specialized forms of array processing. The usual situation is one in which every fourth element of an array, for example, is to be treated differently from the others. Or perhaps there are four separate formulas, one to be used for elements 1, 5, 9, 13, ..., the next to be used for elements 2, 6, 10, 14, ..., and so on. In these cases, it may save time and space to collect the aspects of the formulas which are different into items on a circular list. The following process is an example of this; the formulas are

```
C(I) = A(I) + A(I)² + A(I)³ + A(I)⁴ + B(I)
C(I) = A(I) + 2*A(I)² + 3*A(I)³ + 4*A(I)⁴ + B(I)
C(I) = A(I) + 3*A(I)² + 6*A(I)³ + 10*A(I)⁴ + B(I)
C(I) = A(I) + 4*A(I)² + 10*A(I)³ + 15*A(I)⁴ + B(I)
```

We construct a circular list with index pointers by constructing an array as follows:

```
CL(1) = 5.    CL(2) = 1    CL(3) = 1     CL(4) = 1
CL(5) = 9     CL(6) = 2    CL(7) = 3     CL(8) = 4
CL(9) = 13    CL(10) = 3   CL(11) = 6    CL(12) = 10
CL(13) = 1    CL(14) = 4   CL(15) = 10   CL(16) = 15
```

This is a circular list of four-word items; the first word in each item points to the next item. We may now write

$$C(I) = A(I) + CL(J+1)*A(I)^2 + CL(J+2)*A(I)^3$$
$$+ CL(J+3)*A(I)^4 + B(I)$$

where J has been set initially to 1; when I is increased by 1, we perform

$$J = CL(J)$$

to advance the circular list. This may also be done in machine language; if J is kept in index register JX, CL(J+1) may be loaded in one instruction by performing LD   CL+1,JX .

The threaded list provides a very fast method of cycling through all the elements of a list structure in order. In general, although a list structure is nonlinear in form, its elements may be linearly ordered in a natural way; this is, in fact, the order of the elements in the corresponding S-expression. The first element of a sublist immediately follows the preceding element or sublist of the main list; the last element of a sublist is immediately followed by the next element or sublist of the main list. Since the end of each sublist points to the head of the sublist, we may proceed immediately to the next element on the main list; this is called **threading** through the list. As we shall see in Chapter 7, there are ways to thread through a list structure which is not explicitly threaded, using recursion, which involve only a very slight increase in time and space over this method.

4-6   Two-way Lists

The lists that we have discussed are one-way lists, that is, they are capable of being processed only in one direction. If a pointer to a list element is contained in an index register, we may find the element which follows it, but not the element which precedes it, unless we have saved it at some other point; therefore we cannot start at the end of the list and process it back to the head. A **two-way list** is a list which may be processed in both directions. Two-way lists, also called **symmetric lists,** have been most extensively investigated by Joseph Weizenbaum, who programmed the language SLIP (Symmetric List Processor) to handle such lists.

An item in a two-way list contains *two* pointers, one to the following element and one to the preceding element. Two-way lists therefore take up more space than one-way lists. There are exceptions to this statement, mainly on machines on which a one-way list wastes a certain amount of space which a two-way list does not; for example, a one-way list of integers on the IBM 700 series requires two-word items, but so does a two-way list because both pointers can be kept in the same word. In general, however, two-way lists should be used only when their other advantages are sufficient to offset the extra space requirements.

The end of a two-way list may be signified by zero in the pointer to the next element; the *beginning* of a two-way list will then also be signified by zero in the pointer to the *preceding* element. Pointers in two-way lists may be either addresses or indices as usual. Any element in a two-way list may be deleted from that list if only its location is known, which is not the case with one-way lists. Since both the preceding element and the following element are known, we need only to store a **forward pointer** (or a **right pointer**) to the following element in the preceding element, and a **backward pointer** (or **left pointer**) to the preceding element in the following element. The deleted element may then be placed on the list of available space, if there is one.

4-7   Common Sublists

When a list occurs more than once as a sublist in a list structure, it is sometimes possible to save space by keeping the list in only one place in memory. Each time the list occurs as a sublist, there will be a pointer to it. For example, the list whose S-expression is

$$(A \ (B \ C \ D) \ E \ (A \ (F \ (B \ C \ D) \ G \ H)))$$

has the **common sublist** (B C D); even though the list has 12 items, only 9 items are necessary to store the list within the computer.

Devices, such as the common sublist, by which items on a list may have more than one role are known as **internal linkage.** The processing of lists with internal linkage involves various special problems, which may in any case be solved by eliminating the internal linkage, but which are usually solved by modifying its form. In the case of common sublists, the most important problem of this type arises when a list structure is to be deleted. (In this and the following section, when we speak of *deleting* a list, we are mainly concerned with returning space to the list of available space.)

When we delete a list, do we delete all its sublists? If there are no common sublists, the answer is certainly yes. But if there are common sublists, as we have considered them above, the answer cannot be determined. Any sublist might also be a sublist of another list which has not yet been deleted. This problem is called the **responsibility problem;** it originally arose in the form: "Which routine in a list processing system should have the responsibility of deleting sublists?" It is often solved by modifying the form of the common sublist mechanism, usually by the use of reference lists or reference counts.

A **reference list** for a common sublist is a list of all locations containing pointers to the common sublist. When reference lists are used, it is always possible to determine whether a sublist is common or not. When a list is being deleted and a sublist is encountered, the reference list for that sublist should contain the location on the original list which points to the sublist. If it contains *no other* items, the sublist may be deleted. In any event, the relevant item on the reference list should be deleted from it.

When common sublists are the only form of internal linkage, **reference counts** may be used instead of reference lists. The reference count mechanism depends on the fact that the only information in the reference list which is actually used in the deletion process is the *number* of references to a given common sublist. Therefore, the responsibility problem may be solved in this case by associating with each sublist a field containing an integer called its reference count. This is the number of references to this list. When a new list is formed which contains this list as a common sublist, the reference count is increased; when the sublists of a list are being deleted, the reference count is decreased, and any sublist with a reference count of zero is deleted.

Both one-way and two-way list structures may use common sublists; the reference list and reference count mechanism are the same in each case.

4-8 Linked Lists

There is a much more extensive method of saving space in list processing than the use of common sublists. It works only for one-way lists, not for two-way lists, and creates a host of problems. In certain cases, however, these problems may be solved quite elegantly.

Suppose that two lists have the same last few elements. For example, consider the lists whose S-expressions are

(A B C D E W X Y Z) and (F G H W X Y Z)

The technique is to store the final portion of each list, (W X Y Z) in this case, only once in memory; the preceding elements then contain identical pointers. Lists such as these are said to be **linked.** In a linked list, the element at which the link occurs will have more than one preceding element; this is the reason that linking does not work with two-way lists. When linked lists are used extensively, the amount of core that is saved may be quite considerable.

The first serious problem that arises with linked lists is that, if it is possible to link the end of one list onto the middle of another, it is theoretically possible to link the end of a list onto the middle of itself, producing a circular list. True circular lists do not have S-expressions, and programs which process ordinary lists may not be able to process circular lists. If a program has mistakes in it, a circular list may be formed by accident, if a link is made in the wrong place. These problems may be solved by checking out a program under the assumption that it makes no links, and adding the link mechanism to it after checkout.

Deletion, as before, causes problems. When two lists are linked it is not even possible, in general, to delete every *element* of a list, because a link might have been made to the last few elements of the list. To remedy this situation we may introduce **link reference lists** or **link reference counts,** which are quite similar to ordinary reference lists and reference counts; with each element to which a link is made, there is associated either a list of all references to that link, or an integer giving the number of links to that point. When a new link is made, an element is added to the reference list, or the reference count is increased; when a list containing a link is deleted, an element is deleted from the reference list, or the reference count is decreased. In either case, the proper decision may be made about whether to delete the cell at which the link occurred, i.e., to return the space which it uses to the list of available space.

The use of link reference lists or link reference counts suffices as long as there are no circular lists. If there are circular lists, in the most general sense, neither counts nor lists will prevent available space from being lost in cycles. When a list links to itself, there are now two references in the link reference list, or the link reference count is 2. When the elements of this list are deleted one by one, a single element is removed from the link reference list, or the link reference count is reduced to 1. Therefore, the cycle is not deleted; as far as the program is concerned, there is another list which needs this link at this point. Actually, there may be such another list, if another link to the cycle exists at a different point of the cycle.

When one-way lists are processed using common sublists and linked lists, the list of available space may be handled using a completely different technique, developed by Daniel Edwards and known as **garbage collection.** Under the special conditions under which it is operative, garbage collection is quite elegant. It removes the need for reference counts or lists of any description; it even removes the need for deletion in the sense in which we have used it. Lists may still be removed from consideration, but the space which they use is not returned to the available space list (this is sometimes called **abandoning** a list, rather than deleting it). Instead, the list space is allowed to fill up; when it is full, a new list of available space is created by a process of elimination. An item is defined to be available if it is not unavailable; the unavailable items are those which are currently on some list. During garbage collection, all lists which are currently operative are cycled through, and each element on each list receives a special one-bit flag. Then the entire list space is processed as an array, and all items which do *not* have this flag are collected to form a new list of available space. At the same time, all flags are turned off. The time taken by garbage collection is supposedly comparable to the time taken by deletions and manipulating reference lists or reference counts, although thoroughness demands that this be determined experimentally in any given situation.

4-9 Dynamic Data

In some large-scale programming systems it is necessary to move data around in memory during the course of a computation. An excellent example of this is a program which continuously forms and deletes *arrays,* rather than lists, using an array of available space. Let us assume that all arrays are contained within an **array space** AS, of large dimension, which is somewhat analogous to a list space. At any time the variable ASL (array space length) indicates how much of the array space has been used. All arrays currently in use are between AS(1) and AS(ASL). If a new array of length N is to be formed, it will use the cells AS(ASL+1) through

AS(ASL+N), and the variable ASL is increased by N. This process continues until ASL cannot be increased further without becoming larger than the dimension of the array space AS. At this point, certain arrays have been deleted, and we are left with a problem analogous to that of handling lists with an array of available space: the entire array space has by no means been used, and yet there is no general way of finding space for a new array. In special cases, of course, there are ways of finding such space. If all the arrays contained in the array space have the same length, they may be treated as items in a list space. Similarly, if there are only a small number of distinct array lengths, several list spaces, each containing items of a different length, may be used. Even when the length of a general array is arbitrary, it may be possible to find space for certain small arrays even when the array space is effectively full. A list may be kept of deleted arrays, arranged by sizes; if the size of the largest deleted array is greater than or equal to the size of the new array, space may be found. Adjacent deleted arrays may be combined into larger deleted areas to aid this process. In general, however, it will not be possible to find space in this way for an arbitrary array whose size is less than the total number of words currently taken up by deleted arrays.

When the array space is full, it is possible to move the currently undeleted arrays back in such a way that they occupy sequential addresses from $AS(1)$ to some value $AS(n)$, where n is taken as the new value of ASL. Two pointers K1 and K2 are initialized to 1; at each stage in the loop, $AS(K1)$ is set equal to $AS(K2)$, K1 and K2 are each increased by 1, and if K2 points to a deleted area, it is further increased until it points to an undeleted area. The process terminates when K2 is equal to the size of the array space. This process is called **collapsing** or **compactifying** and the arrays which are moved in the process are called **dynamic arrays.**

Suppose that A is a dynamic array, and J is a pointer to A. If A is moved, as by a compactifying process, J must be changed if it is to be used after A is moved. Of course, J may be a variable which was used before compactifying and is not to be used again; in such a case, we say that J is not **currently active.** All currently active pointers must be changed when compactifying is done, and this normally means that the compactifying program itself will change, or update, all these pointers. This requirement places a strict discipline on programs which use dynamic data, because it means that *the locations of all currently active pointers must be known at all times.* If the arrays were not dynamic, this would not be a necessary condition; in fact, its observance would waste considerable time. A pointer is treated just like any other variable, and even a register, whose contents are saved through a subroutine (such as a compactifying process) is quite likely to contain a pointer.

One way to keep track of the currently active pointers is to require all pointers to be in a special array, or space, reserved for pointers. A search is then made through this array when compactifying takes place. If the program which uses an array space also uses a list space, a list may be kept of the locations of the currently active pointers; or a separate list may be kept for each dynamic array. Or the convention may be made that there is exactly one pointer to each dynamic array; all reference to the array must be made through this pointer. In any case, the discipline mentioned above must be faithfully observed. For instance, if J5 is a currently active pointer, then it is unwise to set J6 = J5 + 2, say, since this operation makes J6 a currently active pointer itself. It should be noted as such, unless it is quite certain that no operations which could cause compactifying to occur—such as creation of new arrays—will take place until J6 is no longer needed.

Compactifying may be combined with garbage collection. In general, the program must be able to determine which arrays have been deleted. This may be done by keeping a list of deleted arrays; but it may also be done by the compactifying program, which makes a search of all currently active pointers and marks those elements of the array space which are currently in use. Any element of the array space not so marked may now be considered to be in a deleted array. Thus multiple references to the same array may be made and deleted in arbitrary order, much like references to a common sublist. The extra search takes a certain amount of time in each compactification; but in a complex situation this time may be exceeded by the amount of time it would take to delete each array, keep track of a reference count, and place the array on a list of deleted arrays.

PROBLEMS

1. In most machine languages, *literals* are allowed. A literal is an expression in the variable field which directs the assembler to simulate immediate addressing in a situation in which instructions which use immediate addressing are nonexistent or inappropriate. In our machine language, we will denote literals by a preceding equal sign. Thus the instruction

$$\text{LD} \quad =4$$

accomplishes the same task as

$$\text{LDI} \quad 4$$

(See also Chapter 1, problem 2.) In order to do this, the assembler places a constant word containing the number 4 in a special location, and a pointer to this location in the address field of the LD instruction. A second literal with the same constant reference, such as

$$\text{AD} \quad =4$$

causes the assembler to generate an identical pointer.

(a) Suppose that a machine language has both direct and immediate addressing instructions, such as LD and LDI in the above example, where the immediate addressing instruction takes the contents of the address field and places it in the accumulator. Under what conditions, assuming that both instructions have the same execution time, would the direct addressing instruction be used with a literal, rather than the immediate addressing instruction?
(b) What would be the effect of using a literal with an *indirect* addressing instruction?
(c) In one assembly language, an octal literal is denoted by $=\emptyset$; thus $=\emptyset 77$ is the same as $=63$. In another assembly language, symbolic literals may be used; thus if TBL is a symbol which has the octal value 30772 in an assembly, then $=$TBL is an allowable literal, producing in the address field a pointer to a word containing the octal number 30772. What difficulty would arise if it were attempted to include both these conventions in the same machine language?

2. The array L of dimension 10 is a list of five integers expressed in two-word items. The second word of each item is the integer and the first word is an index pointer to the next item on the list, or zero for the last item on the list. The values of $L(1)$ through $L(10)$ are as follows:

$$L(1) = 5$$
$$L(2) = 6$$
$$L(3) = 9$$
$$L(4) = 5$$
$$L(5) = 0$$
$$L(6) = 3$$
$$L(7) = 1$$
$$L(8) = 8$$
$$L(9) = 7$$
$$L(10) = 0$$

(a) Which two-word item on this list is the last item?
(b) What are the five integers on this list, in order?
(c) Which two-word item on this list is the first item?

3. Which of the following are S-expressions? State why the others are not S-expressions.
(a) (2 5 (3 6) 4 (3 7))
(b) (2 8 (3 (((2 5) 6 (3 9)) 1 3)) 6 4))
(c) (4 (8 (3 7)) 2 ((9 1) 8 (7 6 (3 5 9))))
(d) ((6 2 5) 3 8 9) 2 1 5) 4 (((7 2 3) 1)

4. Consider the S-expression
(5 (6 7 (1 2 4 (3 6))) 8 (1 ((5 4) 7)))

(a) How many elements are on the main list? (Remember that elements consist of *numbers* and *sublists*. An element of a sublist is not an element of the main list.)
(b) How many elements are on the sublist beginning with 6?

(c) How many lists are there?

(d) What is the maximum sublist depth?

(e) What is the total number of pointers that would be needed to represent this S-expression in a computer?

5. In each case below, find the S-expression that has been represented in the given computer in the given way. Zero pointers denote the ends of lists, and the content of each item is either a number or a pointer to a sublist. All numbers are less than 100; all pointers are greater than 100.

(a) The IBM 7094 has 36-bit words and 15-bit address fields. A list of one-word items is constructed on this machine in which the right half of each word is the content of the corresponding item, and the left half contains the right justified pointer to the next item or zero. An S-expression starting at address 16604 is given as follows in octal:

ADDRESS	CONTENTS
16604	016607000002
16605	016610000004
16606	016612000007
16607	016613000003
16610	000000016611
16611	016615016614
16612	016616000005
16613	016605016606
16614	016617000006
16615	000000000002
16616	000000000010
16617	000000000001

(b) The CDC 6600 has 60-bit words and 18-bit address fields. A list of one-word items is constructed on this machine in which the right-hand 18 bits of each word is the pointer and the rest of the word is the content of the corresponding item. An S-expression starting at address 033227 is given as follows in octal:

ADDRESS	CONTENTS
033227	000000000033231033234
033230	000000000000004000000
033231	000000000033235033233
033232	000000000000011000000
033233	000000000000002000000
033234	000000000000001033240
033235	000000000000003033230
033236	000000000033237000000
033237	000000000000003033232
033240	000000000000005033236

(c) The SDS 930 has 24-bit words. A list of two-word items is constructed on this machine in which the first word of each item is the content of the item and the second word is the pointer to the next item or zero. An S-expression starting at address 00502 is given as follows in octal:

ADDRESS	CONTENTS
00502	00000002
00503	00000514
00504	00000510
00505	00000516
00506	00000504
00507	00000000
00510	00000010
00511	00000522
00512	00000520
00513	00000000
00514	00000004
00515	00000506
00516	00000007
00517	00000512
00520	00000003
00521	00000524
00522	00000011
00523	00000000
00524	00000004
00525	00000000

6. Suppose that a list is to be built up by adding new elements onto the *end* of the list, instead of onto the beginning. What extra information must be kept in this case? How many extra instructions are needed each time an element is added to the list?

7. A *matrix*, i.e., a square array such as

$$\begin{pmatrix} 3 & 4 & 6 & 7 \\ 2 & 1 & 5 & 6 \\ 7 & 0 & 3 & 5 \\ 8 & 3 & 6 & 4 \end{pmatrix}$$

may be represented as an S-expression, such as

$$((3\ 4\ 6\ 7)(2\ 1\ 5\ 6)(7\ 0\ 3\ 5)(8\ 3\ 6\ 4))$$

and represented in a computer as a list structure. Some matrices, however, can be represented more compactly (i.e., using fewer locations in memory) by using a linked structure. A certain 4 by 4 matrix has been represented in the UNIVAC 1107 computer, which has 36-bit words and 16-bit address fields. The linked structure consists of one-word items, of which the right half is the content of the item and the left half contains the right justified pointer to the next item or zero; other conventions are as in problem 5 above. The structure starts at location 053321, and is given as follows in octal:

ADDRESS	CONTENTS
053321	053322053330
053322	053323053327
053323	053324053326
053324	000000053325
053325	053326000000
053326	053327000000
053327	053330000000
053330	053331000001
053331	053331000000

(Note: Ignore the fact that the sublists do not terminate; any program which references this structure will presumably not look for any elements of any sublist beyond the fourth, since it is known that this represents a 4 by 4 matrix.)

(a) Write this matrix as a 4 by 4 square array.

(b) Suppose that this matrix were represented as an S-expression in the memory of this computer without using linked lists. How many additional cells would be required?

(c) Suppose that this matrix were represented in this computer as a double array in column notation. How many additional cells would be required?

8. Five applications of list processing are described below. In each case tell whether, in programming such a system, one would use an array of available space, a list of available space with garbage collection, or a list of available space with items returned to it by deletion. Briefly state the reason for your choice.

(a) In an assembler, a symbol table is built up in the first pass. This is a table of "elements" which may be either simple items or lists of items. None of these elements is ever removed from the symbol table. In the second pass of the assembler, these lists are used, but no new lists are added.

(b) A matrix processing system uses a list of lists to determine a matrix. It includes a subroutine which deletes a given matrix. In order to save space, a matrix all of whose rows are the same may consist, within the system, of a list of identical pointers to a single row. Also, if two rows are the same except for the first few elements, one of them may link into the middle of the other. (See also problem 7 above.)

(c) A system which simulates a factory contains, for each work station, a list of parts at that work station. A part can be, at any given time, at only one work station. Elementary operations include moving a part from one work station to another, adding new parts as they enter, and deleting finished parts as they leave. The total number of parts in the factory at any given time is variable, but can never be more than 2000. Each part is completely described by a five-word item.

(d) A program to play the game of bridge contains for each player a set of four lists, one for each suit. As the program proceeds, cards are removed from these lists one at a time and "played" to each trick in turn.

(e) A generalized list processing system contains the following operations on lists: create a new list; put a given list on another list as a sublist; create a link from the end of a given list to an arbitrary item.

9. A certain computer has 24-bit words and 15-bit address fields, and contains a list space of one-word items, each of which contains a non-negative integer and a pointer.

(a) If absolute pointers are used, what is the largest integer that can be contained on lists in this list space?

(b) What is the largest integer if relative pointers are used and the list space is 1,024 (decimal) words long?

(c) Suppose that integers from 1 to 9,999 must be contained on these lists. Assuming relative pointers are used, what is the maximum allowable size of the list space?

(d) Suppose that the form of the list space is modified so that each one-word item contains a pointer to the next item and a pointer to the content of the item (which is presumably not contained in the list space). Assuming relative pointers are used, what is the maximum possible size of the list space?

Chapter 5

SEARCHING AND SORTING

5-1   Timing

A process which looks for a particular element of an array or of a list is called a **search process** or a **search algorithm.** By a "particular element" we mean one which satisfies some condition such as being equal to a given word, greater than a given word, or equal as a list structure. If the elements of an array or list are ordered, such that each item is greater than the preceding, then it is said to be **sorted** (in ascending order). A **sort algorithm** arranges the elements of an unsorted array or list so that they are sorted.

There is a large variety of search and sort algorithms. No single search algorithm is best for all searching problems, and the same is true for sorting. When a program is being written, the programmer should know how to compare the various algorithms which may be used as to their efficiency in the use of space and time. *Space* refers to the amount of memory used by a given method. This is usually relatively easy to determine; if a standard subroutine is used for searching, the number of cells which it uses should accompany its description, and similarly the lengths of any arrays which it may use can be found easily. *Time,* that is, the amount of time the computer takes to perform a given process, is much harder to determine accurately; however, in many cases, various methods of performing a process differ in timing by large factors, so that the timing advantage of one method over another is quite evident.

Each operation, or instruction, takes a certain amount of time to execute. These times are contained in the operations manual of the computer. They are usually expressed in microseconds (1 microsecond = 10^{-6} seconds), although in very fast computers they may be in nanoseconds (1 nanosecond = 10^{-9} seconds). These times are useful in comparing one computer with another in regard to speed—for example, if the installation of a new computer is being considered. In the comparison of one method of programming with another on a single machine, however, all that matters is the *relative* speed, i.e., the ratio of the time taken by one instruction with the time taken by another.

A **synchronous** computer is one in which a clock cycle has been set up to regulate the timing of all instructions. We say that a synchronous computer has a "one-microsecond cycle time," a "three-microsecond cycle time," or the like. On a synchronous computer, each instruction takes an integral number of cycles; if the circuitry corresponding to a given instruction is such that it finishes operation before a cycle is finished, the remainder of that cycle is not used. Timing on a synchronous computer is often referred to in cycles rather than microseconds, when only relative speed is important; we speak of "two-cycle instructions" or "eight-cycle instructions." A large class of instructions on a synchronous computer will, in fact, take one or two cycles; exceptions include the multiplication and division operations, operations on large amounts of data such as a block transfer operation, the input-output instructions, and sometimes others.

In an **asynchronous** computer, the end of each instruction initiates the next. Hence no time is wasted at the end of cycles. On many asynchronous computers a much greater variation in the timing of a single instruction is allowed than on synchronous computers, with the result that a range of times may be given for each instruction, instead of a single time. This makes the timing of a given subroutine more difficult to determine empirically. On an asynchronous computer, timing will be expressed in microseconds, using decimal fractions if necessary; an instruction may, for example, be listed as taking from 2.8 to 3.2 microseconds.

Many computers, both synchronous and asynchronous, have a **real time clock,** a device which allows the computer to determine its own timing. In a typical real time clock operation, a register or a special memory cell is incremented by one during each cycle. The cycle of a real time clock on a synchronous computer is usually much larger than the computer's cycle time, and may be as great as 16 milliseconds (1 millisecond $= 10^{-3}$ seconds), or 1/60 of a second. By determining the time value before and after a computation and subtracting, the computer can determine how much time it took, to the nearest clock cycle. The term *"real time"* arose initially in contrast with simulation programs in which the time is kept as a variable stored in memory, to be incremented, or stepped, under program control. It is also used to describe processes in which the computer is controlling a device and must receive input signals and transmit output signals within a certain maximum time in order to control the device effectively. Examples of such *real time processes* are satellite control, ship control, and factory control (often called *process control*). An airline reservation system or a national defense air raid warning system is also spoken of as operating "in real time."

5-2   Linear Search

The word "search," used without any qualifier, usually refers to a linear search. In a linear search the program simply considers one element of the array or list after another, until it finds the condition it is looking for. The following routine, written in FORTRAN, searches an array KV of N integers for one that is equal to M:

```
        DO 128 I = 1, N
        IF (KV(I) − M) 128, 129, 128
128     CONTINUE
        (continuation if no integer in the array KV is equal to M)
        . . .
129     (continuation if the integer KV(I) is equal to M)
```

If there is no integer equal to M in the array, we may wish to **insert** M in the array. Searching and insertion are, in fact, very often done together. In this case the program above would continue:

$$N = N + 1$$
$$KV(N) = M$$

If the maximum size, or dimension, of the array KV is KVMAX, we might also continue:

```
128     N = N + 1
        IF (N − KVMAX) 129, 129, 199
129     KV(N) = M
        (continuation if the array has not become too large)
        . . .
199     (continuation if the array has become too large)
```

Less frequent is the situation in which more than one element of an array is equal to some variable. In many situations this will never happen; for example, if an element is added to the array only after an unsuccessful search. Even when there are duplicate elements in an array, the above type of search is sometimes used; in this case, only the first match will be found.

When an array is *sorted,* an unsuccessful linear search takes less time than if the array is unsorted. The following routine searches the array KV as above, with the additional assumption that its items are in ascending order:

```
      DO 128 I = 1, N
      IF (KV(I) — M) 128, 129, 1281
128   CONTINUE
1281  (continuation if no integer in the array KV is equal to M)
      . . .
129   (continuation if the integer KV(I) is equal to M)
```

When $KV(I) - M$ is greater than zero, or when $KV(I)$ is greater than M, we do not have to search any farther. Since the elements of the array are in ascending order, no further element of $KV(I)$ can be equal to M.

The linear search of a list is exactly analogous to the linear search of an array. Passage from one element of the list to the next is made in the usual way, and the end of a list is sensed by a pointer which is zero, or equal to a special constant. A list which is added to by searching and insertion should be kept sorted if possible; as we have seen, we may insert an element into a sorted list in such a way that the list is still sorted, whereas this is not possible with a sorted array without adjustment. If insertion is required, we remove an element from the list of available space, test for no more available space, and add the element to the given list in a manner analogous to the insertion procedure for arrays described above.

> Some computers have linear **search instructions,** which are faster in their operation than linear searches. As we have seen above, there can be two possible outcomes of a search; either a match is found, or it is not. A search instruction is thus basically a test; if a match is found, the instruction skips, otherwise it does not skip. In the typical form of search instruction, the search count is placed in an index register; this index register is then referenced in the index register field, the address field containing the address of the start of the array. If the search succeeds, the index of the match is left in the index register. The UNIVAC 1108 has a special **count register** which contains the search count, allowing both the index and an arbitrary increment to be kept in the index register; if the search succeeds, the index of the match, *plus the increment,* is left in the index register. Most of these instructions search arrays, although the CDC 3600 has an instruction which searches a list.

5-3   Binary Search

Binary search is a technique for searching a sorted array, which is much faster than linear search. In a binary search, comparison is made with the element at the center of the array; whichever way the comparison goes, the element being searched for is now known to lie in some array which is one half as long as the original array. Comparison is now made with the element at the center of this array, and the process continues. If there are 2^n elements in the array, n tests are necessary; there is an additional equality test necessary at the end unless it is already known that the element is somewhere in the array. In general, if there are x elements in the array, the maximum number of tests required is $a+1$, where a is the smallest integer which is greater than or equal to $\log_2 x$.

Binary search cannot be applied to unsorted arrays, or to simple lists, sorted or unsorted; its great speed, however, makes it ideal for sorted arrays. The following code, written in FORTRAN IV, searches the array A of length N for the floating point number X. The elements of A are assumed to be in ascending order. As usual, the operator .GT. means "greater than"; the operator .EQ. means "equals."

```
         I = N - N/2
         INDEX = I
         GO TO 11
10       I = I + INDEX
11       IF (INDEX .EQ. 1) GO TO 14
12       INDEX = INDEX - INDEX/2
         IF (X .GT. A(I)) GO TO 10
         I = I - INDEX
         GO TO 11
14       IF (X .EQ. A(I)) GO TO 16
         I = I + 1
         IF (X .EQ. A(I)) GO TO 16
         (continue if no element of A is equal to X)
         . . .
16       (continue if A(I) = X)
```

We note the statement $I = N - N/2$, instead of simply $I = N/2$. Division of integers by the computer is almost always done without rounding; the quotient of 17 by 2, for example, is 8. In this case we want to round the quotient upward; therefore, we produce $17 - 8 = 9$ (in this case). The same may be said of the later instruction $INDEX = INDEX - INDEX/2$. Another way to produce the same result as $I = N - N/2$ is to write $I = (N+1)/2$.

As an example, we trace this routine for $X = 60.0$ and a table A of dimension 8, i.e., DIMENSION A(8) and $N = 8$, such that $A(1) = 10.0$, $A(2) = 20.0$, etc., with $A(8) = 80.0$:

1. I is set equal to 4.

2. INDEX is set equal to 4.

3. Control goes to statement 11.

4. INDEX is not equal to 1, so control does not go to statement 14.

5. INDEX is set equal to 2.

6. X is greater than A(4), since 60.0 is greater than 40.0; therefore control passes to statement 10.

7. I is set equal to $4 + 2 = 6$.

8. INDEX is not equal to 1, so control does not go to statement 14.

9. INDEX is set equal to 1.

10. X is not greater than A(6), since 60.0 is not greater than 60.0; therefore control does not pass to statement 10.

11. I is set equal to $6 - 1 = 5$.

12. Control passes to statement 11.

13. INDEX is equal to 1, so control goes to statement 14.

14. X is not equal to A(I), since 50.0 is not equal to 60.0.

15. I is set equal to $5 + 1 = 6$.

16. X is equal to $A(I) = 60.0$; therefore control passes to statement 16.

There is another type of binary search in which each comparison is a three-way test—that is, a test whether X is greater than, equal to, or less than A(I). In this type of search, if there are x elements in the array, the total number of tests required may be anywhere from 1 to $a+1$, where a is the greatest integer in $\log_2 x$. The following code, written in FORTRAN II, searches the array A of length N for the floating point number X; the elements of A are assumed to be in ascending order.

```
         I = N - N/2
         INDEX = I - I/2
         GO TO 121
   10    I = I + INDEX
   11    IF (INDEX - 1) 12, 14, 12
   12    INDEX = INDEX - INDEX/2
   121   IF (X - A(I)) 13, 16, 10
   13    I = I - INDEX
         GO TO 11
   14    IF (X - A(I)) 15, 16, 15
   15    (continue if no element of A is equal to X)
         ...
   16    (continue if A(I) = X)
```

In order to determine the efficiency of this method, we determine the average number of tests required. There will be one element for which a single test is required, two for which two tests are required, four for which three tests are required, and in general 2^i for which $i+1$ tests are required, where i ranges from 0 through $a-1$. For the remainder of the elements, $a+1$ tests are required; there may be anywhere from 1 to $2a$ of these. If these last elements are excluded, the total number of elements is $\sum_{i=0}^{a-1} 2^i = 2^a - 1$, and the average number of tests is

$$\frac{1}{2^a-1} \sum_{i=0}^{a-1} (i+1) \cdot 2^i = a - 1 + \frac{a}{2^a-1}$$

as may be determined by induction. Hence the average number of tests exceeds $a - 1$, and the inclusion in this average of any additional elements which require $a + 1$ tests does not alter this fact. Hence, on the average, the first method will never require greater than two tests more than the second method.

Which of the two methods is more efficient depends on the computer and on the size of the array. On most computers, a three-way test is implemented by performing two tests—one for "greater than" and one for "equals." If the first test succeeds, the second test is unnecessary, and thus the three-way test takes half again as much time, on the average, as a two-way test. Therefore, if the size of the array is large enough, the first test is more efficient. The IBM 700 series has a three-way test instruction, CAS (Compare accumulator with storage), and no two-way tests of this type; therefore, on these computers, the second type of test is more efficient.

There are a few special situations where a linear search will actually be faster than a binary search. One important situation is that in which some of the elements in a table are searched for much more frequently than others; another is that in which the tables are small, so that the greater length of each step in a binary search outweighs the difference in the number of steps.

5-4   Searching and Insertion in Binary Trees

A **binary tree** is a collection of items arranged as in the figure on p. 101. Pointers are, as usual, represented by arrows; an arrow from one item to another represents an address field in the first item carrying the address or the index of the second item. The **address** of the binary tree is taken to be the address of its **root item** (the item at the bottom of the figure). The root item contains two pointers. Either or both of these pointers may be zero; if they are both zero, the tree contains exactly one item. As with the termination of a list, we may replace the word "zero" in the above sentence by any constant fixed number denoting the end of a branch of the tree. A pointer which is not zero will point to an item with the same

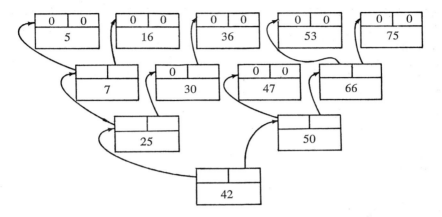

format as the root item, and which is itself the root of a binary tree. In fact, this is the most concise way to define a binary tree:

A binary tree consists of a root item containing two pointers, each of which is either zero or else points to the root item of a binary tree with the same root item format.

From this definition it is clear that a binary tree can have any length; it does not need to contain exactly as many items as the binary tree in the figure. What makes the tree "binary" is that each item contains two pointers. The definition is recursive; it defines a binary tree in terms of other binary trees. The two binary trees to which the root item of a binary tree points may be called the *left branch* and the *right branch* of the binary tree.

A binary tree is **sorted** if *every* item in its left branch precedes the root item and if the root item precedes *every* item in its right branch. The word "precedes" may have different meanings here, depending upon the format of the items. The binary tree of integers in the figure is sorted in the sense that any integer precedes any larger integer.

As we have seen, searching an unsorted array of length n requires n steps, whereas insertion may be done in one step; searching a sorted array of length n may be done in approximately $2 + \log_2 n$ steps using a binary search, but insertion requires $n/2$ steps on the average (for adjustment); searching a sorted list requires $n/2$ steps on the average, whereas insertion may be done in one step. The binary tree allows both searching and insertion to be performed very rapidly. In fact, searching a binary tree of length n requires a number of steps ranging between $1 + \log_2 n$ and n, depending on how well the tree is balanced; insertion may be done in one step after searching.

A binary tree is (perfectly) **balanced** if its left and right branches contain the same number of elements and if these branches are themselves balanced. In this sense, only trees of $2^n - 1$ elements may be perfectly balanced. For a general tree containing n elements, we require only that the left and right branches contain numbers of elements which differ by at most one. A still weaker definition of balance, which usually suffices for searching purposes, depends on the concept of the **height** of a binary tree, which is the length, in items, of the longest connected path from the root to the top of the tree. A tree of height n is then said to be balanced if it contains between 2^{n-1} and $2^n - 1$ elements.

5-5 Hash Code and Hash Tables

The **hash table** or **scatter storage table** is the fastest known method of searching and insertion. It allows either searching or insertion *in one step,* almost always, unless the table is over half full. In a hash table, the position of any item in the table is determined by its **hash code,** which is a number easily obtained from the item.

The simplest hash code is the **division hash code.** If the array has length n, and the largest integer that may be contained in a computer word is k, the division hash code of a word is found by dividing it as an integer by n. This produces a quotient and a remainder; the remainder is an integer between 0 and $n - 1$, and may be used as the table index.

As presented so far, this method fails if any two elements of the array have the same index. In the actual application of hash tables, the entire table is first set to some initial value which will never occur as meaningful data (usually zero, but sometimes -1 or -0). For insertion, the hash code of a word is found, and the word at the corresponding index tested to see whether it is equal to the initial value. If so, the number is inserted at that point; otherwise, the table is linearly searched in a forward direction from that point until a word is found which is equal to the initial value. When such a word is found, the insertion is made at that point. If the end of the table is reached during the linear search, it is continued from the beginning of the table. For searching the hash table, the hash code of a word is found, and the corresponding index compared with the word and then with the initial value. If it is equal to neither of these, the next word in the table is similarly compared. If the initial value is ultimately found by this procedure, the word is not in the table.

The division hash code has the disadvantage that sometimes it does not produce indices which are equally distributed. Ideally, the hash code of a given word in a hash table should be a random number in the range 0 to $n-1$, where n is the length of the table. The entries in the hash table will usually themselves be quite far from random, and the choice of a good hash code in a given situation may be a matter of trial and error.

One method of increasing randomness in a hash code is to multiply the item beforehand by a large number, preferably one whose bits are in a "random-looking" order, and then use some of the bits of the result as the hash code. This means that the length of the hash table must be a power of 2.

Hash tables have a few disadvantages which appear in special situations. Of all the search methods presented thus far, the hash code method is the only one which requires a table of fixed size specified in advance. In some computers it is more expensive, either directly or indirectly, to use a large amount of the available memory than a small amount. In particular, this will usually be true in a multiprocessing or time-sharing situation. In this case, a linear array becomes attractive, since only a small amount of the array needs to be specified at the start, and the memory cost of a particular computer run is only the cost of the memory that was actually used. Lists and trees also have this property; an array whose items are to appear on lists or on trees may be treated as an "expanding" array, just as if it were a linear array. A hash table, however, must be specified in advance, and the entire table is always potentially in use.

Hash tables are also not easily amenable to processing in other ways than searching and insertion. We have seen that the use of a list rather than an array for any purpose implies that the elements can no longer be indexed; reference to the nth item on a list takes n steps, whereas reference to any item of an array takes only one step as soon as its index is known. A list, however, can still be processed from one end to the other. With hash tables, this is no longer possible without cycling through the entire table, a very inefficient process if the number of entries currently in the table is much less than the size of the table. If the entries in a hash table must be processed, one method is to keep a separate array of pointers to the elements currently in the hash table. This array need never be searched, since it will be evident from the standard hash table search whether a given word is or is not in the hash table. Whenever an element is inserted in the hash table, a pointer to it is inserted in the pointer array.

5-6   The Hash Table of Lists

It is quite often true that a combination of representation methods for data has better characteristics than any simple method. The *hash table of lists,* or *hybrid hash table,* is one of the most popular of the so-called "hybrid" or combination methods. A smaller hash table is used than in the standard hash table method; each entry in this table is taken as the head of a list. When an element is inserted in the table, it is inserted on the list corresponding to its hash code. When a search is made, the hash code of the item to be searched for is calculated, and the corresponding list is searched linearly. If the item is not found, it may be added to the table by adding it at the head of this list. Unlike the standard hash table, the hash code of an item always applies to that item; no item, for example, is ever placed on the list whose head is at the following position in the table. Thus the hash table of lists does not become unwieldy as its size grows, and, in particular, its size does not have to be specified in advance, as in the case of the standard hash table; the size of the original table is usually negligible compared to its potential size, i.e., the sum of the lengths of all the lists.

As an example of the use of hash tables of lists, we consider the case of a macro assembler. (For a general discussion of macros, see §6-2.) Suppose that a macro called GC is given as

```
GC    MACRO    (dummy symbols A, B, C, N, R)
      LX       R,N
P1    LD       A
      FA       B
      ST       C
      DCT      N,1,0,P1
      END      (of macro)
```

The symbol P1 is defined for use inside the macro only. It cannot be referred to by assembly source code lines which do not involve GC. If the macro GC is used more than once, P1 is not, effectively, a duplicately defined symbol, since each reference to P1 (in the DCT instruction) refers to a specific instance of P1. But now suppose that some assembly source code line actually defines a symbol called P1. Then, when the DCT instruction is assembled, the assembler has two symbols called P1 in its symbol table, and it must be able to select the value corresponding to the occurrence of P1 *within* the macro, rather than outside it. We could, of course, define such symbol duplication to be an assembly error, but this would make general-purpose macros very difficult to write. If one programmer uses a macro written by another, he may very easily choose a symbol for use in his assembly which is also contained in the macro.

This problem is solved by using a hash table of lists for the symbol table. Each symbol which is defined outside a macro is inserted in the hash table along with its value. Now suppose that a symbol is already in the symbol table and an identical symbol is defined within a macro. This symbol is then placed on the same list as the original symbol, since the hash codes of two identical symbols are obviously the same. The symbol defined within the macro is inserted after the symbol defined outside the macro. Since new items are inserted at the *head* of a list, the symbol defined within the macro will precede the other symbol on the list. Now suppose that this symbol is referenced later, as in the DCT instruction in our example. A search routine will be called to find the value of this symbol. This routine will return the value of the symbol defined within the macro, since this is the first matching symbol on the list which it encounters. The result is that, within the macro, all references to a symbol defined within that macro are made properly, regardless of the existence of another symbol with the same name defined outside the macro. When the end-macro statement is encountered, all symbols defined within the macro are deleted from the symbol table. Therefore, further references to such symbols will not refer to definitions made within a macro.

5-7 Sorting by Searching

We now consider the process of sorting an array or a list in memory. Such a process is called an **internal sort,** in contrast with processes which act on an amount of data too large to be contained in memory, such as one or more tapes; these will be discussed in the next chapter.

The simplest sort algorithms arise from linear search algorithms, which are modified to search for the largest elements of an array or list in one complete scan of the table. A linear search for the largest element of an array or list of length n requires n steps; at each step, if the current item is larger than the current largest item, it becomes the new current largest item. To sort a list, we search for the largest element, place it on a new list, and delete it. Then we search again for the largest element, place it at the head of the new list, and delete it from the old list; this process continues until the old list is empty, at which point the new list is sorted (in ascending order). If the list is to be sorted in descending order, we need only to search for the smallest element each time instead of the largest. To sort an array (in ascending order), we search for the *smallest* element, make it the first element of the new array, and then mark it as having been found already; this may consist of simply storing a very large number in it. Now we search for the smallest element again, place it next in the new array, and mark it; this process continues until the new array has the same number of elements as the old array.

The following program, written in our machine language, sorts a list of two-word items with address pointers. The first word of each item contains a pointer, or zero for the end of a list; the second word contains a floating point number. In this routine the head of the list is at LH;

the head of the new (sorted) list is at NLH; the number currently being compared is at X; the start address of the program is P2; and T1, T2, and T3 are temporary symbols.

```
     X    RE    1
     T1   RE    1
     T2   RE    1
     T3   RE    1
     LH   RE    1
     NLH  RE    1
     P2   LDI   0
          ST    NLH
          LD    LH
          TZ    P8
          ST    T3
          LX    LH,2
          LD    1,2
          ST    X
          LD    0,2
          ST    T2
          TZ    P7
          LX    T2,1
     P3   LD    1,1
          TG    X
          TR    P5
     P4   LD    0,1
          TZ    P6
          SX    T1,1
          LX    T1,2
          ST    T1
          LX    T1,1
          TR    P3
     P5   ST    X
          SX    T2,1
          SX    T3,2
          TR    P4
     P6   LX    T2,2
          LX    T3,1
          LD    0,2
          ST    0,1
     P7   LD    NLH
          ST    0,2
```

```
        SX    NLH,2
        ZT    T2
        TR    P2
   P8   LD    NLH
        ST    LH
```

Sorting programs may also be based on other types of searching. A hash table may be adapted for sorting if the hash code corresponds to the sorting method—that is, if one item is greater than another if and only if the hash code of the first item is greater than the hash code of the second. Use of such a hash code is dependent on a relatively equal distribution of the items to be sorted over their possible values. The best case for this method occurs where each item contains an integer from 1 to n, each of these integers occurs in exactly one item, and the items are to be sorted in order of these integers; then the integer itself can be used as the "hash code" and the table sorted in n steps. A hash table of lists may also be used in this way, but each of the lists must now be sorted by some other method. An ordinary binary search, of course, assumes that the array or list is already sorted; a binary tree, however, may be adapted for sorting by inserting each element in it and then extracting all the elements of the tree in order.

5-8   Interchange Sort

An **interchange sort** is a sort process in which elements of a table which are out of order are interchanged until they are in order, i.e., until no more interchanges need be performed. An interchange sort of an array has one important advantage over a sort by linear searching: it requires no extra space. In the sort by linear searching, the original array and the new sorted array must be distinct; if there are n items in the array, space is required for $2n$ items. In an interchange sort, the array to be sorted is rearranged until it is sorted; no extra space is required.

Interchanging two elements of an array involves a special technique, which, although very simple, depends on the computer and the language involved. If $A(I)$ and $A(J)$ are to be interchanged, we cannot, for example, say (in FORTRAN)

$$A(I) = A(J)$$
$$A(J) = A(I)$$

to interchange $A(I)$ and $A(J)$. (Why?) The following sequence will work:

$$X = A(I)$$
$$A(I) = A(J)$$
$$A(J) = X$$

but it is translated into six instructions, which is much too many for such a simple operation. Nevertheless, in FORTRAN and ALGOL, one cannot do any better.

An interchange operation in machine language normally takes four instructions. If there are two full-size registers, we merely load them both, and then store them both in the opposite order. Some machines have **exchange instructions,** which exchange the contents of an accumulator with a memory word; this allows us to exchange two memory words in three instructions using one register, by loading the first, exchanging the accumulator with the second, and storing the first. Some algebraic languages, such as JOVIAL, have exchange statements, which allow us to exchange two variables directly; these are compiled into one of the sequences mentioned above.

There are various types of interchange sort. One is almost exactly like the sort by linear search, except that in the search for the smallest element, instead of keeping a current smallest element, elements which are found to be smaller than the first are interchanged with the first (in the first stage). Thus the first stage ends with the smallest element first. Now the first element is ignored, and the array from indices 2 through n is examined in the second stage, placing its smallest element first, that is, second in the original array. This procedure is repeated $n-1$ times to sort the entire array.

Another interchange sort takes advantage of the fact that a table of length n can be tested to see whether it is sorted in n steps. The sort tests the first element against the second, the second element against the third, and so on. If it finds no two elements out of order, the file is sorted. If it finds two elements out of order, it interchanges them and records the fact. After it has tested all elements, it cycles back to test the table in its new order, if and only if an interchange has been made on the current pass over the table. This method has the advantage that if the table is already sorted, or close to being sorted, only n steps are required (or only slightly more than n).

Still another type of interchange sort is known as the **bubble sort.** It shares the advantage of the previous sort, and has the added advantage that it is slightly faster on the average. A bubble sort of an array of length n consists of n stages. At stage i, the first i elements of the array are assumed to be in order. Item $i+1$ is now compared with item i. If it is smaller than item i, it is interchanged with item i, and then compared with item $i-1$. This process continues until item i has reached its proper place in the table, at which point the first $i+1$ elements of the array are in order.

In any interchange sort, an interchange of any two items takes at least $4x$ operations on most computers, where x is the number of words per item. If x is large, the procedure can be speeded up by means of **address tables.** In this procedure, a table of pointers to each item is constructed, and then, instead of sorting the original items, we sort the address table. Two words in the address table are compared by comparing the items to which they point. The address table may be either an array or a list, depending on how much space is available. At the end of the sort, the order of the original items may be found by scanning the address table. Address tables may be used with any sorting method, not only with interchange sorts; whether they are economical depends on the amount of space and time available.

5-9   Classification and Selection

Sorting by classification or selection is much faster than the methods of the last two sections. A classification sort takes $n \log_2 n$ steps, where n is the number of items; a selection sort takes nk steps, where n is the number of items and k is the number of bits in the word being compared.

In a **classification sort,** the table to be sorted is considered as a table of n items consisting of j groups of m items each, where each group of m items is sorted and $jm = n$. At the start of the sort, $m = 1$, so that each group consists of one item and the table may be in any order; at the end of the sort, $j = 1$, so that there is one group of $m = n$ sorted items, i.e., the entire table is sorted. At each stage, the table is processed to produce a new table in which the value of m is multiplied by two and the value of j is divided by two. Each stage takes n steps, and at the end of k stages, the value of m is multiplied by 2^k and the value of j is divided by 2^k; if $2^k = n$, then $k = \log_2 n$, the total number of stages.

Each stage proceeds as follows. Two pointers are initialized, one to point to the start of the table, and one to point to the start of the second half of the table. The items to which the pointers point are now compared, and the smaller item becomes the first item of the new table. The pointer corresponding to this item is advanced; thus the first groups of the two halves of the table are **merged** to form the first group of the new table. This procedure is now repeated with the second groups of the two halves of the table, etc.; if the total number of groups is an odd number $2k+1$, the "second half" of the table actually contains the last k (or $k+1$) groups.

For a classification sort of an array, two arrays are used; at each stage, either the first array is processed to form the second, or vice versa. For a classification sort of a list, the old list may be deleted after each stage; the middle of the new list must be marked when it is passed, so that it can be used to initialize the second pointer in the following stage.

The **selection sort** or **radix sort** is an adaptation for the computer of a sorting method which is common on mechanical sorters, or **tab sorters.** A standard card has 80 columns, each one of which may contain a code for any character. In sorting cards mechanically, only one column at a time is considered. A moving pointer on the sorter may be set to refer to any of the 80 columns. When cards contain numeric data only, i.e., only one punch in the given column and in one of the rows 0 through 9, the sorter directs all cards containing a given punch into a particular hopper. By collecting the cards in the proper order, the operator can sort the cards numerically by the given single column. Suppose, however, that a certain deck of cards contains a numeric field which is more than one column in length, i.e., a number which is more than one digit long. In this case, the cards may still be placed in ascending order on this particular field by sorting several times in order, once on each digit, with the *lowest order (right-most) digit taken first*. When a deck which is already in ascending order of the lowest order $k - 1$ digits of the number is sorted on the kth digit, the result will be in ascending order of the lowest order k digits.

On a decimal computer, this process carries over without much change. The table to be sorted is arranged first by its lowest order digit. This may be done by setting up ten lists, one for each digit, and placing each element at the head of its list. The process is then repeated for the next higher order digit, starting with the list corresponding to the digit 9, then 8, 7, etc. (because the *last* items of any list are always inserted first). The process is then repeated again, for a total number of times equal to the number of digits.

On a binary computer, the process is considerably easier. In the first place, bits are used instead of digits; there need to be only two lists, and in fact, if there is enough space, two *arrays* will suffice. These two arrays, of course, are processed into two other arrays, so it is necessary to have a total of four arrays, which are processed back and forth. The items with zero in a given bit position will be placed in the first array in order, and the items with one in this position will be placed in the second. Selection sorting on a binary computer does not work for *signed* integers in a signed-magnitude format; these should be converted to one's or two's complement before sorting and then reconverted afterward. Even in one's complement or two's complement, the sign bit must be treated separately; items with 1 in the sign bit are less than, rather than greater than, items with 0 in the sign bit.

PROBLEMS

1. Three computers are all assumed to use our textbook machine language, but the timings of the instructions are different on each computer. A table is given below of the timings for several instructions, in microseconds:

	COMPUTER I	COMPUTER II	COMPUTER III
LD	3.6	3.4	3.2
ST	7.2	5.2	3.2
AD	4.0	3.4	3.2
SU	4.0	3.4	3.2
MU	27.4	8.7	5.4
DI	42.5	12.3	8.1
RSL	10.0	6.1	5.8
LSL	10.0	6.1	5.8
FA	12.0	9.8	6.1
FS	12.0	9.8	6.1
FM	31.3	13.8	11.4
FD	31.3	16.2	11.2

State what would be the fastest way, on *each* of the three given computers, to compute the following:

(a) $z = x^2 - y^2$ (floating point).
(b) $a = b/6$ (floating point).
(c) $a = 9d$ (floating point).
(d) $n = 8m$ (fixed point).
(e) $n = 10m$ (fixed point).

2. Suppose that the elementary operations of a certain computer are subject to the following execution times:

Load—2 cycles
Store—2 cycles
Add—3 cycles
Subtract—3 cycles
Multiply—7 cycles
Divide—11 cycles
Load an index register—3 cycles

In each of the following, which of the two given operations would be faster:

(a) Calculating $k + k + 5$ or $2k + 5$?
(b) Calculating $n^2 + 2n + 4$ as $(n*n) + (2*n) + 4$, or as $(n + 2)*n + 4$?
(c) Calculating the area of a polygon with vertices (x_1, y_1), (x_2, y_2), ..., (x_n, y_n) according to the formula

$$x_1y_2 + x_2y_3 + \cdots + x_{n-1}y_n + x_ny_1 - y_1x_2 - y_2x_3 - \cdots - y_{n-1}x_n - y_nx_1$$

or according to the equivalent formula

$(x_1-x_2)(y_1+y_2)+(x_2-x_3)(y_2+y_3)+\cdots+(x_{n-1}-x_n)(y_{n-1}+y_n)+(x_n-x_1)(y_n+y_1)$?

(d) Calculating the binomial coefficient

$$\frac{n!}{k!(n-k)!}$$

as it stands (by multiplication of the two terms in the denominator) or by taking the numerator, $n!$, and then dividing first by $k!$ and then by $(n-k)!$?
(e) Loading A(I, J, K), where the indices I, J, and K have just been calculated, if multiple arrays are stored using a column representation, or using an indexed representation?

3. The ages of 100 people are in an array of dimension 100. Another array of dimension 100 is to be filled with the "age code" of each of these people, as follows:

Under 21—Code 1
21 to 64—Code 2
65 and over—Code 3

In order to do this, the following algorithm is used:

1. Set index register 1 to 100.
2. Load an age.
3. Subtract 21.
4. Skip if positive.
5. Transfer to step 13.
6. Subtract 44.
7. Skip if positive.
8. Transfer to step 11.
9. Load the code 3.
10. Transfer to step 14.
11. Load the code 2.
12. Transfer to step 14.
13. Load the code 1.
14. Store as the age code.
15. Subtract 1 from the index.
16. Skip if non-zero.
17. Transfer to step 2.
18. Transfer to next algorithm.

Suppose that this algorithm is performed on a computer in which each of the steps above is performed in one instruction, and these instructions have the following timing:

Load—2 cycles
Store—2 cycles
Add or subtract—3 cycles
Add or subtract, immediate addressing—3 cycles
Transfer—4 cycles
Set or increment index register—2 cycles
Skip instructions—3 cycles

Suppose further that, for the ages currently in the array, the age codes are calculated as follows:

15 people with age code 1
60 people with age code 2
25 people with age code 3

How much time, in cycles, does the entire algorithm take?

4. An array **A** of dimension N is to be linearly searched for an element A(K) which is between 101 and 200, inclusive, and is not equal to 128. If such an element is found, its value is to be stored in I; otherwise, I is to be set equal to zero. The following flowchart is set up for this algorithm; it has three errors in it. Correct the errors and state what would happen if the algorithm were run without the corrections.

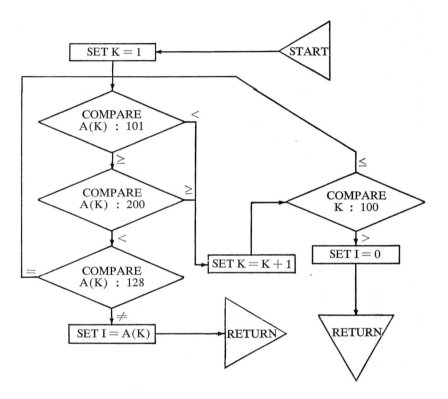

5. The CDC 1604 has a linear search instruction called EQS (Equality Search). This instruction compares the indexed word in memory with the contents of the accumulator. If they are equal, the next instruction is skipped, and the index register contains an index pointer to the found word. If they are not equal, the index register is tested. If it is zero, the next instruction in sequence is taken, and the EQS instruction has failed. If the index register is not zero, it is decreased by one and the comparison process continues.

(a) Can this instruction be used to search lists?

(b) Can this instruction be used to search arrays of items containing more than one word?

(c) The CDC 1604 also has another instruction called MEQ (Masked Equality Search) which is the same as EQS except that both quantities to be compared are masked by the contents of the Q register before comparison. Can this instruction be used to search a program for an instruction word with a given operation code?

(d) Can the instruction MEQ be used to search an array of quantities which are less than full word size, such as an array of characters? What difficulty is encountered in finding the *first* matching item in this way, if more than one item in the array is a matching item?

6. Searching and insertion operations are to be carried out on a one-way list which is kept sorted. Searching therefore takes an average of $n/2$ steps, where n is the length of the list, whereas insertion may be performed by changing two pointers. The following improvement in this scheme is proposed: "Suppose that instead of one cell LH pointing to the head of the list, we have a cell LH pointing to the head and a cell LM pointing to the *middle* of the list. Now, when we search the list, the first thing we do is compare the element to be searched with the middle element. Thus we can determine whether the element to be searched is in the top half or the bottom half of the list. In either event, we have only half the list to search. Thus search time will be improved by a factor of almost 2, without affecting insertion time."

(a) Though the general scheme outlined above will work, there is one false statement made. What is it?

(b) Suppose that deletion operations were to be carried out on the above list, in addition to searching and insertion. What difficulty would arise?

7. Three methods of producing a 12-bit hash code to be used in a 4096-word hash table are being considered. One consists of simply using the left-hand 12 bits of the given word. Another involves taking the exclusive OR of the left-hand 12 bits and the right-hand 12 bits. A third method consists of performing a floating point multiplication by the constant 10.66 and taking the right-hand 12 bits of the result. In each of the following cases, state which method or methods mentioned above would produce completely unusable hash codes (such as the same hash code for all data) and explain why. Assume that the sign and exponent of floating point numbers together take up 12 bits.

(a) The data to be placed in the table consists of a collection of more or less random two-character symbols (P5, Q7, V3, etc.), right justified and zero filled. (Assume 6 bits per character, 48 bits per word.)

(b) Same as above, but left justified and blank filled.

(c) The data to be placed in the table consist of a collection of symbols all of which begin with GEN, such as GEN1, GEN5A, GENB, GEN82, etc. These symbols are left justified.

(d) The data to be placed in the table consists of floating point representations of positive integers between 5000 and 7000.

8. Sorting of a very small number of items is sometimes performed without looping. Thus the following algorithm sorts three items:

1. Compare the first with the second. If the first is greater, interchange the first and second items.
2. Compare the second with the third. If the second is greater, interchange the second and third items and again compare the first with the second. If the first is greater, interchange the first and second items.

Thus, to sort three items, a maximum of three interchanges is necessary. Derive a formula for the maximum number of interchanges required to sort n items in this way.

9. If an array of items to be put in some order is already known to be in a closely related order, sorting time may sometimes be reduced. How may n items be quickly placed in ascending order:

(a) If they are already in descending order?

(b) If they are currently in order of their magnitudes as integers? (Assume that the items are to be placed in a second array in ascending order.)

(c) If they are almost in order, but each item is out of place by no more than two positions?

Chapter 6

FILE PROCESSING

6-1 Types of Memory

A **file** is a sequence of items. The word "sequence" implies that the items are kept "sequentially," but the meaning of this word depends on where the items are. If the items are in memory, "sequentially" means having consecutive addresses; in this case, a file is simply an array. Such a file is called a **memory file** or a **core file;** the memory of a computer, as we have been using the word, may also be called **core memory** or **core.** This involves a slight play on the word "core"; the memory of a computer is its center, or core, in contrast to the information contained on the tape units or elsewhere, but core memory actually derives its name from the fact that each bit is physically represented by a toroidal piece of iron oxide, or ferrite, known as a **ferrite core,** which may be magnetized in one of two directions. Some computers use thin films or plated wires instead of ferrite cores, but the main memory may still be called core unless more than one type of main memory is used.

If a file is kept on **tape,** its items are kept one by one along the tape. A computer tape, like a sound recording tape, is simply a tape of iron oxide with a backing; tapes may have several tracks, or, less frequently, may be capable of recording on either side. Tiny areas of iron oxide receive one of two possible values of magnetization, which determine bit values. These areas may be of various sizes and occur on the tape packed closely together, to a greater or lesser degree; the **packing density** of a tape is usually expressed in bits per inch of tape.

Some computers also have devices for storage of data in which any piece of data may be referenced in a relatively short time (from 1/60 of a second to about one second) and in which data in sequence may be transferred into and out of core at a high rate of speed as soon as access has been made to the start of the data. These devices include drums, disks, magnetic card devices, magnetic tape loop devices, and various others. A drum or a disk is simply a rotating cylinder or disk which is coated with ferrite; disk devices usually contain several disks rotating at once. These devices have finite memory size, and unlike most tapes, they have the property that their locations may be *addressed,* in much the same way that core is addressed.

Transferring data from a tape, drum, or disk into core is known as **reading;** transferring data from core to a tape, drum, or disk is known as **writing.** A file is read or written by means of a **head,** which is somewhat like the recording head of a sound recording tape. A computer tape has two heads, one for reading and one for writing. Drums and disks have many heads; on most disk units, the heads are contained on "arms" which move back and forth over the surface of the disk, whereas on most drum units the heads are fixed, and consequently there must be more of them. Drums are more expensive per bit, on the whole, than disks, but they are also much faster, since the continuous rotating motion is faster than the discontinuous arm motion.

Files which are on tape may be read or written only from one end to the other. In order to operate on a number which is contained somewhere on a tape, the computer must read or pass over the entire tape up to that point; files in core, however, may be processed in any order, while files on drum or disk may be broken up into subfiles which can be accessed randomly, although it would take a large amount of time to access one word at a time from randomly selected addresses on a drum or disk. Tapes and similar media such as paper tapes and cards are said to be **accessed sequentially,** and the devices connected to a computer, such as tape units, which contain data that may be processed in sequence only are collectively called its **sequential access storage.** All other storage is called **random access storage,** although this term is most often used to refer to drums, disks, and the like, which are more properly called **intermediate access storage.** Core memory and other parts of the computer containing data that may be processed immediately—such as thin film or plated wire—are said to be **accessed directly,** and the main memory of a computer, together with its registers, is called collectively its **direct access storage.** (This term is also used in some quarters as synonymous with random access storage.)

Direct access storage is most closely analogous to "remembering" data, as performed by a person carrying out a calculation. The analogy between a person and a computer expressed in the terms "memory," "reading," and "writing," is carried, in programmers' slang, to a conclusion which is ridiculed by some and hailed by others as the key to advances in programming. A computer is said to *know* an integer if it contains this integer somewhere in direct access storage. A computer is said to *know a concept* if it contains a code in memory which expresses this concept within the context of the program. For example, a computer processing cards, each of which contains data about a certain person, would know that a person is married if the code on the card indicating that he is married had been stored somewhere in memory. When the next card is read, the code indicating whether the next person is married may be stored in the same cell. In this case the computer *forgets* whether the first person is married. On the other hand, the computer may wish to *remember* the marital status of all the people whose cards it is processing, by storing the codes in different words of memory. The main memory, of course, is finite; a computer, like a human being, is capable of remembering only a finite amount of information. If a program has a mistake in it, so that codes are stored in the wrong places, the marital status code for a person may be interrogated by the program and control transferred in error to a section of the program which is applicable only to cards denoting married persons. In this case the computer *thinks* that a person is married when in fact he is not. More specifically, the computer program, or even the particular subroutine currently operative, would be referred to as thinking. A program may *decide* whether a person is married even if this fact is not directly known; for example, a program may check the age code and store the marital status code for unmarried if the age code is less than 16. Or it may call a subroutine which tries in various ways (by checking the number of exemptions, etc.) to determine whether the person is married; when the subroutine returns control to the main program, the marital status code will be left in a register for the main program to store in the proper location in memory. In this case we may say that the main program *asks* the subroutine, or the subroutine *tells* the main program, whether the person is married. The semitechnical terms "know," "remember," "forget," "think," "decide," "ask," and "tell" refer to computer processes which can, if desired, be described mathematically.

6-2   Elementary File Processes

File processing is a general term connoting any computation process on a file (usually, one which is not a core file). Any process which takes place on an array from one end to the other may take place on such a file. Information is transferred from an input file into the computer, processed, and new information transferred from the computer to an output file. We say that the computer **reads** the input file, and **writes** the output file. Any file process may read one or more input files and may write one or more output files.

The simplest file processes are those which **copy** information from one file to another. Among these are the following:

(1) **Tape copy.** One input tape and one output tape are used. An amount of information, called a **record,** is read from one tape and written on the other. The process is repeated until the end of the input tape is reached. Alternatively, several output tapes may be used, and the information written on all of them.

(2) **Card-to-tape copy.** One card reader and one output tape are used. Each card is read and then written on tape; or several cards may be read and a single tape record written all at once. This process is repeated until there are no more cards, or an end card, in the card reader. Card-to-tape copy may be used on a small computer to prepare tape for input to a large computer.

(3) **Tape-to-printer copy.** One input tape and one printer are used. Each tape record is read and printed on one or more lines. This process is used to obtain a listing of the contents of a tape.

(4) **Card-to-printer copy.** One card reader and one printer are used. Each card is read and printed on one line. This process is used to obtain a listing of a deck of cards.

(5) **Tape-to-card copy.** One input tape and one card punch are used. Each tape record is read and punched on one or more cards. Tape-to-card copy is used to prepare, on a small computer, object decks produced by an assembler or a compiler on a large computer.

Every copy process uses a loop; the input is read, the output is written, and the program recycles to read more input. The input information does not need to be contained in core all at once. This is, in fact, characteristic of all file processes.

Another file process is the **compare.** In a tape compare, two tapes which are presumably identical are read and checked for discrepancies. If any are found, these are printed and/or written on an error file. A slightly more involved tape process is **merging,** or the production of one sorted tape from two or more sorted tapes. All the input tapes are presumed to be sorted in the same way—that is, the same comparison is made between their items. The first item of each tape is now read. Of the items now in core, the smallest is written on the output tape, and another item is read from the tape which contained this item. If there are no more items on this tape, the item corresponding to it is set greater than any possible value; the process then repeats until there are no more items on any input tape.

Extraction of items from one tape onto another is a more general tape process. The extraction may be on any basis, and some tests performed to determine if an item is to be extracted are quite complicated. At its simplest, extraction consists of reading a tape, finding all items having a certain value in a certain field, and writing these on a new tape. The loop consists of reading, testing, and either writing or not writing, depending on the results of the test. This process is very commonly performed for anthropologists, political scientists, demographers, and other such specialists who are performing series of statistical tests on census data, survey data, and the like.

Still other common tape processes are **blocking** and **unblocking,** which refer to changing the size of records. Blocking and unblocking may apply also to card-to-tape, tape-to-card, and tape-to-printer copy operations. A record on tape may include the information on more than one card; but only one card can be read at a time. Therefore, several cards may be read and one tape record written, and the process repeated; the tape record is then sometimes called a **block,** to distinguish it from the images of card "records," or cards, which it contains; the program has *blocked* the records (arranged them in a block). The reverse procedure, reading a tape and printing or punching the original records one by one, is then called unblocking.

A program may contain, as subroutines, one or more file processes. If it contains more than one, it may produce files which are not part of the final output. These are called **intermediate files,** or more informally, **scratch files** (by analogy with "scratch paper"); if they are tape files, the tapes are called **scratch tapes.** Arrays in core which are used only for intermediate results are likewise sometimes called **scratch arrays** or **scratch memory.**

The elementary file *operations* that take place within an elementary file process are reading and writing. The main loop in such a process will contain one or more of these operations. There are, however, other elementary file operations which take place outside the main loop, either before it or after it. There may, in addition, be other associated processes which must take place before a file can be used or after use of a file is complete. It is customary for the read and write operations on a file to be performed by subroutines; thus one subroutine will read data into an array and perform all associated operations (such as unblocking). If this is done, the processes that are carried out before and after reading or writing are also grouped into subroutines, known as *opening* and *closing* routines.

A file is said to be **open** at any point in a program after the opening subroutine has been performed and before the closing subroutine has been performed. Reading and writing cannot take place, by convention, until the given file is open; the file process is not complete until the file is closed. The opening and closing processes are different for reading and for writing; thus we speak of subroutines which **open to read, open to write, close read,** or **close write.** Thus a close write subroutine, for example, will write an end-of-file mark on a tape, and may rewind the tape. An opening subroutine for a tape file will make sure that the tape is ready to read or ready to write.

One important process which is often performed by opening routines is that of writing and checking labels. If a large number of tapes are handled every day by the operators of a computer, it is very important that computer time not be wasted, or information lost, because the operator put the wrong tape on the machine. A **label** on a tape is a special record which is written by the computer when a file is opened to write; this record serves as identification for this file. When the file is opened to read, this record is read, and the program performing the file process may now check whether the tape which was mounted is the right tape. A label record usually contains not only the name of the file as it is conventionally referred to, but also the date on which the file was written (although this may be a simple "week code" from 1 to 52). If the file takes up more than one reel of tape, a tape reel sequence number is also included and checked when the file is opened to read.

Blocking and unblocking also affect the opening and closing of files. When several logical records are contained in a block, a pointer to the current logical record must be kept; as records are read or written, this pointer is advanced. When the file is opened, either to read or to write, the pointer is set to point to the first logical record in the block. Even more important is the action taken by the close write routine when a file is blocked. When a blocked file is being written, logical records are accumulated into a block, which is written only when it is full. At the end of the process, this block will, in general, not be full; but the records which it contains must still be written on the file. This process is performed in the closing routine.

Some file processes use a special variable which is zero whenever the given file is closed. This prevents reading and writing operations from being performed in error on a closed file. Opening operations on open files and closing operations on closed files may also be treated as errors, but more often they are ignored. Such a way of operation is useful if, for example, the program must be stopped because of error conditions. Unless the program keeps its own record of which files are open, so that it can close all open files before exiting, it is easiest to close *all* files, regardless of whether or not they are open.

6-3   File Searching

A linear search may be carried out very easily on a tape file. The time taken to search an entire tape is approximately, and quite often exactly, the time taken to read the tape, since tape reading and other computer instructions often take place simultaneously.

When a sorted tape is being searched, several search operations may be combined into one. This is accomplished by a **comparison merge.** The items to be searched are first sorted in the same order in which the tape is sorted. This sorted file of items, whether in core or not, is then read together with the original sorted file. The first item of each file is read and the two items compared. If they are identical, a match has been found; if the item from the file of items to be searched is greater than the other, then a new item is read from the original sorted file, and if it is not greater, then no match exists for this item and a new item is read from the file of items to be searched. Insertion of items which do not appear may also be done at the same time, by writing all distinct items on an output tape.

This procedure saves so much search time that it is often used even when its use distorts the logic of its program. For example, let us consider an assembly program on a computer that is very small, so that the table of symbols has to be kept as a file outside of core. Each time a line is read, this table must be searched for any symbols that appear on that line. This amounts to one complete search per line. The process can be greatly speeded up by reading several lines at once and collecting all the symbols that have to be searched. All the searches are now made at once, and the items which match are also brought into core. The assembly process is now performed on these lines using information in core, and a new set of lines is brought in.

A variant of this procedure may be used on arrays, i.e., files in core, when several linear searches are to be made at once. An array in core which is sorted can, of course, be searched with a binary search; but if several searches are to take place at once, the comparison merge in core may be faster than a succession of binary searches.

Other search methods do not work well on tape files. If a file is small enough that it may be brought completely into core, it may there be subjected to a binary search or hash table search. It is possible to conceive of the words on a tape being numbered sequentially, and these numbers being treated as addresses. A binary search of a tape could conceivably then be carried out by positioning the tape each time a comparison is made to the word with which the comparison is to be made. It is not hard to see that such a process would be *slower* than a linear search of the tape. This fanciful example illustrates a general principle: tape files are *sequential* files, and the fastest tape processes are sequential processes.

To change an item in a tape file, it is necessary to make a complete new tape file. This is true even when the length of the item is not increased. The difficulty is technical, not theoretical—such an operation cannot be implemented on present-day tape units, with very few exceptions. To *insert* a new item in a tape file, of course, requires a complete new file to be written for a different reason: there is not enough physical space on the old tape to hold a new item. Changing items and inserting items, like searching, are best performed in groups. That is, the insertion program, instead of inserting each item when it is given, collects these items until there are a certain number of them and inserts them all at once. If a search must be made before the items are inserted, however, it must not only search the file itself but also must check all the items in the current group. Therefore, this current group must be a table that is accessible to the search program and the insert program. Such a table is called a **dribble table.** It collects small amounts or "dribbles" of entries into a larger group, which is inserted all at once.

The dribble table technique may also be used on arrays in core. Even if an array is sorted and hence can be binary-searched, insertion still takes $n/2$ steps on the average, where n is the length of the array. Instead of inserting every element, we can build up a dribble table as an array, and insert all the elements in this array when it reaches a certain size. A similar method may also be used with binary trees, where both searching and insertion are fast, but balancing the tree takes a relatively long time—in this case, we balance the tree only at every nth insertion, where n is suitably chosen.

6-4   Information Retrieval

The problem of arranging a file searching program so that the required searching is performed with maximum efficiency is called the **information retrieval problem.** This phrase is actually a misnomer, because it implies that there is a single problem with a single, although as yet unknown, solution. Actually, information retrieval problems have various solutions, depending on the problem, which may itself change with time.

The variable quantities in an information retrieval problem are as follows:

(1) *Space.* The amount of memory in a given system, including available space on tape units, disk drives, and elsewhere, may be limited. In this case some solutions to a given information retrieval problem, which

would require larger amounts of space, may not be possible. Or they may save so much money that it pays to acquire the extra memory.

(2) *Time.* Depending on how the problem is attacked, a single search may take place in a greater or lesser amount of time, or a run comprising many searches may take place in a greater or lesser average time per search.

(3) *Cost.* When an information retrieval problem is posed within the context of a single computer system, cost depends only on space and time; but information retrieval problems are frequently considered when a new system is being contemplated, and different possible systems are being compared. A system using disks may be faster than a system using tapes, but questions then arise as to whether the extra cost of a disk system will pay for itself.

(4) *Retrieval rate,* i.e., the number of items per minute (or per hour, or per second) that the system is expected to retrieve. If time is not important, large retrieval rates may be achieved very easily. If it is stipulated that any item must be retrieved within the time it takes to make one complete pass over the file—say, from a few minutes to an hour—then items to be found on the next pass may be collected and sorted during the present pass, and the program simply goes through the file continuously, making one pass after another.

(5) *Extent of organization* among the items to be retrieved. This covers such questions as: How much cross reference is there among items? To what extent is it necessary to find an item, obtain a cross reference, find the cross-referenced item, and so on? If cross references occur in a random fashion, this process becomes very time-consuming if tape files are used, and random access storage must be considered.

The successful solution of information retrieval problems often involves duplication of information—keeping current information in more than one place to facilitate processing. For example, suppose that a large file, which is to be updated daily, is processed by linearly extracting certain information from it and printing it; in commercial programming, this is called a **report.** A file is assumed to be sorted in some way for the purposes of the report, and it is kept sorted in this way; updating the file consists of sorting the new items and the references to items to be deleted, and processing this new file with the current file. Now suppose that the file must be sorted in a different way for the purposes of a second report. If we sort the file for this purpose, we will sort it daily, since it is updated daily. Alternatively, we may keep a dribble table of new items which accumulate over a period of a week, and sort the file weekly. However, we can avoid any sorting at all by keeping two files—one consisting of the items sorted in one order, and the other consisting of the same items sorted in the other order. Both files are now updated daily, or at longer intervals if a dribble table is kept. This process may save a great amount of time when tape files, rather than drum or disk files, are used, since in this case sorting is a time-consuming operation.

Another type of decision commonly found in information retrieval is the frequency with which various data-rearranging operations take place. An example is the length of time a dribble table is kept; it may be found that computer time is saved if the dribble table is accumulated for a month, rather than a week. Or it may be that the number of new items accumulated each week varies over so wide a range that it is more feasible to merge the dribble table when its size reaches a certain maximum, rather than at fixed time intervals.

Theoretical considerations are of only a limited value in information retrieval. There are a few guidelines of a general nature: tape sorting of large files should be avoided whenever possible; searching of tape files should be rearranged whenever possible so that more than one search is performed at the same time. Choices between one particular system and another, however, are highly dependent on the particular data at hand.

6-5   File Sorting

Sorting of large files has been the subject of much theoretical work, mainly because of the large amounts of machine time involved in a sort. There is no one best method of sorting a file of a given length. Much depends on the relative cost of various types of memory such as tape, drum, and disk; a file may be partially sorted already, making short cuts possible. A sort using intermediate access storage is faster than a tape sort by a factor which may exceed 100, and hence intermediate access storage should be used whenever possible. However, many computers on which sorting is performed do not have such storage; also, many sort algorithms on drum or disk are modifications of tape sort algorithms.

On most computers it is not necessary to write a complete sort program each time a new type of sort is required. Generalized sort programs, which are really sorting-oriented languages, are available. Such a program has statements describing the files to be sorted and the way in which they are to be sorted, together with the form of the output file. Alternatively, a generalized sort program may be called as a subroutine, and the file descriptions supplied to this subroutine in the form of tables.

With every method of sorting a file, there is associated a test algorithm to determine which of two items is greater. In a generalized sort program, there is sometimes a facility for the user of the sort program to insert his own subroutine, which is called each time it is necessary to determine the order of items. In practice, however, most sorts are based on comparisons between certain fields of words in each item, which are contained in standard relative locations in the items. These fields are called **sort keys.** If there is more than one sort key, a definite order is specified for the keys. To decide which of two items is greater, the first key of one item is compared with the first key of the other. If these two keys are the same, the second key of the first item is compared with the second key of the second item, and so on through the keys. If two items have *all* their sort keys identical, the sort program may make an arbitrary decision as to which item is to be taken first; or it may indicate an error.

As an example of the use of sort keys, consider the following words of twelve octal digits:

```
466372631145    461307701243    735541001263    046637126330
364511001024    210374662511    343552661700    124351467355
253660012736    213650561350    213554726325    304526631265
617660245764    731264500342    630113255553    041377477240
```

Suppose that these words were divided into fields, which are to be considered as sort keys, as follows:

Field 1	Digits 1–3
Field 2	Digit 4
Field 3	Digits 5–6
Field 4	Digits 7–10
Field 5	Digits 11–12

Then the following table gives the result of sorting these fields in three different ways; the "A" or "D" after each field number stands for "ascending" or "descending."

Field 4 (A)	Field 3 (D); Field 1 (A)	Field 2 (A); Field 3 (A); Field 5 (D)
364511001024	041377477240	630113255553
735541001263	210374662511	731264500342
253660012736	466372631145	461307701243
046637126330	731264500342	124351467355
617660245764	253660012736	466372631145
630113255553	617660245764	210374662511
124351467355	213554726325	041377477240

041377477240	343552661700	364511001024
731264500342	124351467355	304526631265
213650561350	213650561350	735541001263
466372631145	735541001263	343552661700
304526631265	046637126330	213554726325
343552661700	304526631265	046637126330
210374662511	630113255553	213650561350
461307701243	364511001024	617660245764
213554726325	461307701243	253660012736

Sorting by searching is not economical for files which are too large to be kept in core. This is true even when the searches are grouped. For example, suppose that a file contains n items, of which c items can fit in core at one time. The first c items are read, sorted, and output; the next c items are read, sorted, and merged with the output to provide a new output file; and the process continues until the input file is exhausted. The number of merges in such a process would be n/c. In contrast, the sort processes that we shall study usually require k merges, where $m^k = n/c$, for some number of intermediate files m.

One core sorting process which generalizes easily to file sorting is the selection sort. A two-file selection sort is performed as follows. The key is treated as a binary integer; all the items which have a zero at the right-most position of this integer are written on one intermediate file, and all other items are written on another intermediate file. These two files are now treated as one file, and selection is made on the second bit from the right. That is, the first file is read, and its items written on two other intermediate files; when the first file is finished, the second file is read and its items are written. Then the process is repeated on the third bit from the right, and so on until the file is sorted. The process requires a total of four intermediate files; at alternate stages, files 1 and 2 are input and files 3 and 4 are output, and vice versa.

Another variation of the selection sort is the four-file selection sort, requiring a total of eight intermediate files. In this type of sort, the bits in the key are considered two at a time. Items are written to one of four intermediate files, depending on whether the two bits currently being considered are 00, 01, 10, or 11, respectively. In general, a selection sort may consider n bits of the key at a time, requiring a total of 2^{n+1} intermediate files. When drum or disk storage is used, various drum or disk addresses may be considered as the start addresses of intermediate files; the use of 32 or even 64 intermediate files in such a process is not uncommon.

6-6 File Classification

The classification sort as performed in core generalizes fairly easily to a file sort. As a file sort, it is sometimes called a **sort-merge,** because the phases of the sort, when considered as file operations, are file merge operations. The standard classification sort-merge consists of one sort phase, several merge phases, and a final merge phase which is different from the others. We shall describe this sorting method from scratch, without reference to the previous chapter.

In the sort phase, the input file is read until its items fill core memory. These items are then sorted (or they may be sorted as they are read in) by any core sorting method, and output. Now the input file is read again and the process repeated. The output file is now partially sorted; it consists of n groups of items, each of which is sorted. This file is now processed to produce a sorted file in a total of k merge phases, where $2m$ tapes are available and $m^k \geq n$. If the sort is performed on drum or disk, the variable m represents the number of drum or disk files that can comfortably be read or written in one pass.

The merge phases proceed as follows. The output from the initial sort phase is written on m tapes, one after the other. These m tapes are now read all at once for the first merge phase. One item is read from each tape, and the loop consists of writing the smallest of these items on the output file and reading another item from the tape from which this smallest item was taken. For the final merge phase, the output file is a single file; for any other merge phase, the output consists of m files, written one after the other just as in the sort phase, and this provides input to the next merge phase.

The sorting process in the merge phases is complicated by the fact that the tapes are only partially sorted. If the groups on each of m tapes are of length $l,$ these are to be merged into a single group on the output tape of length ml. Therefore, when a group on any tape is finished, that tape should not be read again until one entire output tape group is produced. This may be done by filling the space normally used by the key of an item from this tape with the largest possible number, or by otherwise declaring it "ineligible." The actual key which has just been read, however, must be saved. When all tapes become ineligible, all these keys are read back into position, all tapes become eligible, and the process repeats. Since the groups on the output tapes are m times as long as the groups on the input tapes, there are $1/m$ as many groups on the output tape. If this process is repeated k times, there will be $1/m^k$ as many groups on the final output file, that is, one group; the file will be completely sorted.

In a variation of this procedure, an item is declared ineligible if its key is smaller than the current key. If the items in one group are all smaller than the items in the next group, the two groups are considered as one. This facilitates the sorting of a tape which is already partially sorted. The number of groups is counted at each merge phase, and when this number is less than m, the final merge phase is started.

A variation of both the classification and selection sorts involves division of each merge phase into two phases. In the first, the output is written on one tape, and in the second, this tape is distributed back onto m tapes. Thus only $m+1$ tapes are needed, instead of $2m$. If only tapes are available, and the number of available intermediate tapes is not a power of 2, this method may actually be superior, because it allows a larger number of bits to be treated at once (for selection sort) or a larger increase in group size (for classification sort), even allowing for the doubling of the number of passes.

Still another variation is known as the **cascade sort.** This is essentially a cross between the preceding two methods. Only $m+1$ tapes are used, but at the same time there are m input tapes and m output tapes. This is accomplished by using almost all the tapes both as input tapes and as output tapes on each pass. There is at the beginning of each pass an unequal distribution of items on the tapes, so that some tapes have fewer items than others. Therefore, as m tapes are merged onto one tape, one of the m tapes will be exhausted very quickly. The remaining $m-1$ tapes are now merged onto this tape until one of the $m-1$ tapes is exhausted. This tape is now used as an output tape for the remaining $m-2$ tapes, and so on. The relative members of items on each tape must be calculated precisely for maximum efficiency.

6-7   Two-way Tape Processing

Some tape units may be processed in two directions; we speak of **reading forward** and **reading backward.** Many tape units which can be read both forward and backward can be written only forward. In any event, writing backward on a non-addressable tape is troublesome; the spacing between bits as they are recorded on the tape is not exact, and writing backward the same amount of information which has been read forward does not necessarily position the tape where it was before reading. Most two-way tape processes consist of alternately writing forward and reading backward.

Most of the UNIVAC tape units (or UNISERVO units) can read backward; so can the tape units for the PDP series and the Honeywell tape units. Most of the IBM tape units cannot read backwards; neither can the CDC tape units. Intermediate-access storage units cannot read backwards because they continuously revolve in one direction. However, if a file consists of a list of tracks, the tracks may be read from last track to first. Reading backward in this sense should not be confused with reading in such a way that the information which is read enters core in reverse order; this is also possible on some computers. A more general facility is the so-called **scatter-read** and **gather-write,** in which data from a single record on an input device may be read into several arrays in different locations, and data from several arrays in different locations may be written at once on a device.

The ability to read backward adds to the capabilities of a tape unit in a way that is slightly analogous to using two-way lists instead of one-way lists. Processing may now be carried out in both directions, but it is still sequential; it proceeds from one end to the other. Some file processes are profoundly altered by the possibility of reading backwards. An example of this occurs in algebraic compilers. If the source code (i.e., the statements in the algebraic language) can be read by the compiler and a file written and subsequently read backwards, many of the problems in compiling have simpler solutions. For example, when the file is read backwards, the terminating statement of a loop is read before its first statement. Since the increment, compare, and transfer instructions of a loop often occur at the end of the loop, they will be generated first.

The time taken by a sort is also decreased when backward reading is allowed, usually by a factor of 2. In such a sort, *all* reading is generally done backward, except for the very first stage, and all writing is done forward. This makes it necessary to reverse the comparisons on every other stage, since alternate stages will be in ascending and descending order. However, except for this change, most of the sort algorithms remain the same, with the additional feature that no time is lost by rewinding tapes. In the classification sort, for example, ascending strings are read backward by one stage and merged. Since ascending strings are being read backward, the input tapes must originally have been in descending order. The output tapes, however, are written forward in ascending order. When these are read backward and merged in the next stage, they will enter core in descending order. The result of merging several strings in descending order produces a single string in descending order, and therefore each group on the output file will be in descending order; it is necessary only to output the largest element instead of the smallest. On the following merge phase, the items will again be read and merged in ascending order.

6-8   Drum and Disk File Processing

An intermediate-access storage device such as a drum or a disk differs from a tape unit in that files may be accessed at any point, not just at the beginning. Access to any word in a file usually takes less than half a second and may take an average of 1/60 second or less. This implies that optimal drum and disk processing is very different from optimal tape processing. In tape processing, there is usually a severe limitation on the number of available tapes, and therefore logically different types of information are often written on the same tape. With intermediate-access storage this is usually unnecessary; in practice, however, quite a few tape-oriented systems are converted to drum or disk with no redesign, so that the resulting system uses drum or disk in an inefficient way.

The best use of a device depends greatly on its timing characteristics; this topic is treated in more detail in Chapter 10. Also, on some intermediate-access devices, there is a minimum amount of information which can be written at one time. On a disk unit, for example, this may be called a **track** or a **sector;** if one track consists of 460 words, then no fewer than 460 words may ever be written at one time. This fact, which is a consequence of the design of the device, places a restriction on the organization of data in the device. It is not feasible, for example, to implement a hash table insertion and search on such an intermediate-access file; insertion in such a file would involve writing one word at a time, each word in a different portion of the memory of the device.

The most commonly used search method on drum and disk is one that uses **directories.** A directory, in this sense, is a record containing the drum or disk addresses of various records in the file, together with the first and last items of each such record. Let us assume that the file is sorted; each of its records will then be sorted, and will, in fact, contain only those elements that lie between its first and its last items in the given order. These two items correspond to the two words printed in boldface at the top left and the top right of each page of a dictionary; the directory here would correspond to a list of all pages with the two words which appear on each page associated with it. To search for any item, the directory is read into core, and the record on which it should be is found by a search (which may be binary) of the first and last items. Then this record is read, and the item is searched for on the record. The entire procedure resembles a binary search; it is actually possible to include only the first word of each record, since the first word of the following record may be used in the comparison instead of the last word of the first record.

A directory search may be carried out on more than two levels.

There may, in fact, be several directories, each covering a subsection of the file. A master directory now contains the drum or disk addresses of each of these directories, together with the first item indicated in each. Thus a search consists of reading the master directory, searching it, reading the directory which it indicates, searching that, and finally reading a record of items and searching it. If a large amount of searching is being done at once, the highest level directory may stay in core at all times.

Selection sorting and classification sorting apply to intermediate-access storage as well as tape. Sections of the given device are treated as "intermediate tapes," and there can be as many of these as there is room in core for buffers for them (i.e., arrays which contain as much information as will be written at once). It is not uncommon in drum or disk sorting to find 32-way or even 64-way merges. Drums and disks cannot be read backward, but this causes no problems. Two-way tape processing is faster than one-way tape processing because rewinding is eliminated; but with intermediate-access storage devices, there are no "rewind" operations anyway—each file is simply restarted at the beginning.

6-9 Tournament Sort

The **tournament sort algorithm** is not, strictly speaking, a complete sorting algorithm, but rather a method of speeding up processing in merge phases. It can be applied to any sort involving a merge, and is especially useful when large numbers of files are being merged.

We recall that in a merge algorithm the item which is output at any time is the smallest of m items in core, one for each of m input tapes. Since these items cannot be assumed to be sorted, it takes m steps to find this smallest item. However, the following search is taken over the same items, with one exception; we might intuitively guess that it should be possible to use some of the information obtained in a search to speed up the next search. The tournament algorithm in fact finds the smallest element, under these special conditions, in e steps, where $2^e = m$. Thus only five steps are required for a 32-way merge, or six steps for a 64-way merge. Drum and disk sorting is thus speeded up by a factor of five or more.

The tournament sort gets its name from the fact that the m items are arranged as players in an elimination tournament. Each item "plays" in the first round; only the winners in each round "play" in the next round. The winner of any "game" is the item that is smaller. Since the tournament sort is normally carried out on a number of items which is a power of two, there are no "byes" to worry about; in a selection sort, in fact, the number of intermediate files is always a power of two. If this number is 2^r, then r is the number of rounds.

At the start of the merge, one item from each file is read into core. A set of address tables is now set up, one table for each round of the tournament. A single address represents the winner; an address table of length 2 is set up for the "semi-finals," an address table of length 4 for the "quarter-finals," and so on. These tables are filled with the addresses of the "winners" or smallest items, taking the first round first and continuing through the "finals." The winner of the last round is, of course, the smallest item of all, and this is the item which is output.

A new item is now read from the file which contained the smallest item, and there are now two possibilities. Either this new item is now the smallest, or the new smallest item was already in the table. But in the latter case, the new smallest item *must have been directly beaten by the previous smallest item* in the previous tournament; and there are only r choices for such an item, where r is the number of rounds.

All tournaments after the first are actually carried out in the following manner. The one new item in the table is compared with the same item with which it was compared in the last tournament, on the first round. The address table for this round is modified in this position; the other positions in this address table are left alone, since all the other first-round decisions are the same as they were in the last tournament. The new address may, in fact, be the same as the old, but in any event the smallest of these two items is now compared with the same item with which it was compared on the second round in the last tournament. Thus one comparison is made per round, and a new smallest item is found; this item is then output, and the process continues.

PROBLEMS

1. In each of the core sorting situations described below, state which of the following sorting methods you would use, and why this method is appropriate: bubble sort; classification sort; selection sort. Also state whether address tables should be used, and if so, why.

(a) The five most common causes of automobile accidents in each of the 50 states of the U.S.A., over a ten-year period, are to be printed out. For a total of 500 times, the numbers of accidents due to any of nine different causes, including "miscellaneous and unknown," are input from cards; these nine numbers are sorted and the first five printed.

(b) There are 250 professors at a university. A nine-word item describing each professor is in core. These items are to be sorted and printed out in order of age, from the oldest to the youngest. 100 registers are available for temporary storage.

(c) A study is being made as to whether there is any correlation between the first letters of a person's first name, middle name, and last name in various countries. To do this, 5,000 names are taken randomly from a list of voters or a telephone book. They are already alphabetized in the usual way by the last names; they are now to be alphabetized by their first two initials. Each name in core consists of the first two initials followed by a surname; the entire collection of names takes up 11,000 words in core. Another 21,000 words are available for temporary storage.

(d) For the common stock of each of 3,000 corporations, a three-word item is in core describing its dividend and growth behavior as well as giving its price as of April 15. These three-word items take up the beginning of a 19,000-word array of available storage for sorting. They are to be sorted by the April 15 price.

(e) In a large tournament, there are 180 teams of four players each. Each player is described by a single word containing his player number and his handicap, which is a small integer. For each team, the total handicap is to be computed and the teams sorted by total handicaps. Each word in the computer is capable of containing two pointers, two handicaps, or one pointer and one handicap. The players have already been arranged in core by teams, so that there are 180 four-word items, each describing one team. At the end of the sort, these items are to occupy the same space they do now. 200 words are available for temporary storage.

2. A new disk unit is attached to a computer which has not previously used drums or disks. Five jobs commonly run on this computer are described below. In each case, state whether, and why, these jobs may be run faster if reprogrammed to use disk files rather than tape files. Assume that disk and tapes have the same basic speed (transfer rate).

(a) The payroll file, consisting of an item for each employee with his salary and deductions, is kept as a tape file and processed monthly to produce pay checks for everyone. (Assume that salaries and deductions are constant.)

(b) The library program file contains commonly used (object) programs. Each time a program is to be run, it is read into core from this file and executed.

(c) A program which translates from Russian into English uses a file of Russian words with their English equivalents. Each time a Russian sentence is read, the English equivalent or equivalents of each Russian word in the sentence are read from this file.

(d) The so-called "history" file, containing, for each job run on the computer, the running time, job name, and job number, is kept on tape. Each time a job finishes, an item is written on this file. The file is later printed for reference purposes (in the order in which it was written).

(e) A file describing each book in the physics library is kept on tape. The items, one for each book, are sorted according to their library call numbers. Once each month, a card file for new books and another card file for lost and discarded books are run against this file so that it may be brought up to date. These card files are likewise in call number order.

3. A tape is organized into 25 files, each of which contains 40 records. The following subroutines are given; in each case, N is the number of the tape unit on which the tape is mounted:

TRD(A, M, N)   Reads one record into array A of length M
TPFR(N)   Positions tape forward by one record
TPBR(N)   Positions tape backward by one record
TPFF(N)   Positions tape forward by one file
TPBF(N)   Positions tape backward by one file

Each of these operations ends with the tape positioned at the beginning of some record. In each case, assume that the tape unit is initially positioned at the beginning (or "load point"). Which record is read into the array A?

(a) TPFR(N)
    TPFF(N)
    TRD(A, M, N)

(b) TPFF(N)
    TPFR(N)
    TRD(A, M, N)

(c) TPFF(N)
    TPFF(N)
    TPFR(N)
    TPBF(N)
    TPBF(N)
    TPFR(N)
    TPFR(N)
    TRD(A, M, N)

(d) TPFF(N)
    TPBR(N)
    TPBR(N)
    TRD(A, M, N)

4. What is done by the program represented by the flowchart on p. 136?

5. The following two-word items are given in octal, where each word of each item uses 8 octal digits:

23635401-31003572	34027103-34332401
35402234-77462134	02533471-07345055
53462367-62137035	35276111-35247113
13645534-46210356	66232314-35620000
74663120-00354442	24355352-10235714
53452237-34664120	36255131-13460762
37213003-35445562	33377210-21374472

Sort these items in each of the following ways:

(a) By the first word of the item.
(b) By the second word of the item.

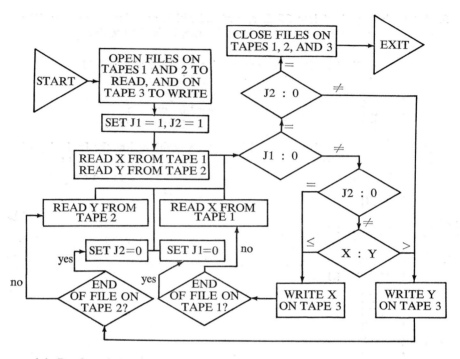

(c) By the left half of the first word of the item.

(d) By the sixth and seventh octal digits of the second word of the item.

6. The following five-word items are given in decimal, where each integer given in an item takes up an entire word:

1,4,2,5,3	2,7,6,1,3
6,3,3,7,4	5,3,0,15,8
2,1,5,3,3	1,4,3,8,3
4,6,2,10,1	7,4,3,12,3
2,4,3,11,3	1,4,2,6,3

Sort these items using each of the following sequences of keys:

(a) First word (ascending); fourth word (ascending).

(b) Third word (ascending); fifth word (descending); fourth word (descending).

(c) Fourth word (descending).

(d) Fifth word (ascending); second word (ascending); first word (descending); third word (descending); fourth word (ascending).

7. A list in the PDP-6 computer, which has 36-bit words and 18-bit address fields, is made up of one-word items, of which the right half is the pointer to the next item in the list and the left half is a pointer to the content of the item. This list is sorted by item content, taken as a positive integer, and ap-

pears in memory starting at location 535617 (octal); it is given as follows in octal. Fill in the X's with appropriate values for a table sorted in ascending order:

ADDRESS	CONTENTS
535617	XXXXXX535625
535620	XXXXXX535626
535621	XXXXXX535624
535622	XXXXXX535623
535623	XXXXXX000000
535624	XXXXXX535620
535625	XXXXXX535621
535626	XXXXXX535622
535627	000000000010
535630	000000000220
535631	000000000217
535632	000000100000
535633	000000000436
535634	000100000000
535635	000000000003
535636	000000000077

8. In each situation described below, a program has been written initially for tape units which cannot read backward. State whether any improvement in speed would result if tapes could be read backward, and if so, why.

(a) A tape contains exactly one file, of fixed length records, giving the purchases made by a certain department during March. Purchases for stationery are to be added up. If the total is so high that pilferage is suspected, a warning notice is to be printed and mailed to the head of purchasing for that department. This warning notice contains dates, amounts, and purchase order numbers for all March stationery purchases (in any order).

(b) Same, except that the purchase order numbers are to be printed in ascending order by date; the tape is itself in ascending order by date.

(c) Same, except that the tape contains several files, one for each department in the company. Assume that rewinding and backspacing are faster than any form of forward tape positioning.

9. A program reads a tape from one end to the other, processing each record on the tape in order. It then rewinds the tape and re-reads it, processing each record a second time. The rewind operation takes time, and it is therefore desired to rewrite the program so as to avoid the rewind. How can this be done, assuming that the total number of records on the tape is known in advance or is contained on the first record? (Hint for users of the IBM 7094: This type of reprogramming was done in the FAP assembler; the total number of records is supplied to the assembler via the COUNT pseudo-operation.)

Chapter 7

SUBROUTINES

7-1 Calling Sequences

The purpose of a subroutine is to perform some task* which is a part of the larger task performed by the routine which calls it. Most subroutines, however, do not do exactly the same task each time they are called. For example, a sine subroutine may take the number in an accumulator, find its sine, and place the sine in the accumulator. The operation of the sine routine depends on what number it finds in the accumulator. In logic, when we write sin (x), the variable x is called an *argument* or a *parameter*. In constructing subroutines, a number or item which is in a register or in some other place where a subroutine may reference it, and which may be changed each time the subroutine is called, is referred to as a **parameter.** In this case, there is one parameter, which the routine takes from the accumulator; the **value** of the function, i.e., the number which is sin (x), is often, as in this case, left in a register by the subroutine. We say that the subroutine SIN(X) is **entered** with x in the accumulator, and that it **exits with** or **leaves** sin (x) in the accumulator.

When there is more than one parameter, we must find some way of letting the subroutine have access to the parameters. If there is more than one accumulator, the subroutine may be entered with the parameters in several accumulators. This method fails when there are more parameters to a subroutine than there are registers in the computer. Another method, which is popular on certain small machines, is to set aside certain special locations in memory, into which the parameters are placed before the subroutine is called. There are as many of these locations as there are parameters of the subroutine, and they may be stored in the same general

---

* We use the word "task" here in the nontechnical sense. In multiprogramming (see Chapter 10), a *task* refers to one of several subprograms performed at the same time.

area of memory in which the subroutine is stored. This method may be used for all subroutines except those which have a variable number of parameters which increases without limit. On most smaller machines and on some larger machines, however, the subroutine and the main program must be part of the same assembly for this process to work, because reference cannot be made in this way, in one assembly, to symbols in another assembly. These considerations make this method unwieldy for standard subroutines (sometimes called **library subroutines**) which may be used by anyone programming under a given programming system; such routines normally are assembled separately, only their object decks being associated with the calling program.

The most common method of handling subroutine parameters is the **calling sequence.** Under this method, the instruction which calls the subroutine is immediately followed by a collection of data words. These may contain the parameters, but more commonly they will contain the *addresses* of parameters. The next instruction in the program follows the data words. In a variation of this procedure, the first "data word" is actually a transfer around the following data words to the next instruction in the program.

Reference to the parameters by the subroutine depends on how the subroutine is called. If the calling instruction leaves the return address in an index register, the parameters may be referenced in terms of this index register. For example, if the return address is in index register 1, then LD   1,1   will load the first parameter or the address of the first parameter; if parameter addresses are used, then LD*   1,1   (using indirect addressing) will load the first parameter. On some computers, the return address (the address referred to by (0,1) in this case) will be the calling instruction plus one, rather than the calling instruction itself; this improvement modifies the form of the references, so that the first parameter—actually the "zero-th parameter"—is now loaded by LD   0,1 or LD*   0,1 . Return from the subroutine is performed by a transfer to the word following the last data word. Thus in this case we may say TR   3,1 , if the parameters are numbered 0, 1, and 2.

If the calling instruction leaves the return address in memory, immediately preceding the code for the subroutine, an index register may be loaded with the return address, and reference made as above. In this case return is made by transferring, sometimes indirectly, to the first word of the program. Since this resumes the calling program at the address immediately following the call, this word should contain a transfer around the parameters; this is the variation mentioned above.

Conflicts may arise between the use of index registers by a subroutine and by the routine which calls it. A routine which uses index registers and calls a subroutine usually expects that the index registers are not changed by the subroutine. This does not mean that the subroutine cannot use index registers; but, if it does, it must **save** whatever index registers it uses when it is entered, and **restore** them before it exits. An index register is saved by storing it in a cell reserved for that purpose, and is restored by being loaded from that cell. Saving and restoring are especially important when return addresses are kept in index registers. If a subroutine calls another subroutine, and the same index register is used for the return address in both cases, the first subroutine must save that index register before calling the second subroutine and using the index register in the process. Failure to observe this precaution produces an endless loop.

7-2   Macro-instructions

Some subroutines are so small that they are best not treated as subroutines at all. Instead of calling a subroutine from several places, the code for the subroutine is repeated at each of these places. A section of code which occurs in this way is called an **open subroutine;** an ordinary subroutine is called a **closed subroutine.** The decision as to whether to treat a given task as a closed or open subroutine depends on many factors. In general, the more times a subroutine is called, the more space is saved if it is closed; the more parameters a subroutine has, the more time, and usually space, is saved if it is open; the more instructions a subroutine has, the more space is used if these are repeated. In doubtful cases, subroutines are usually best regarded as closed and later changed to open form if a more thorough analysis warrants it.

A closed subroutine can be easily changed; if a closed subroutine is changed, the effect of the change is felt at every place the subroutine is called. If the code for a subroutine is repeated explicitly, it must be changed at every place it appears if the task it performs is altered—a grave disadvantage for the open subroutine, since mistakes in this process are easy to make and hard to find. In order that an open subroutine may remain in easily modifiable form, it may be cast into the form of a **macro-instruction.** This is a single "instruction" with a mnemonic or operation code, selected by the programmer, that is equivalent in the assembly process to the set of instructions required by the open subroutine.

Macro-instructions, or **macros,** have a wide variety of uses. Some assemblers do not allow macro-instructions, because the facility for handling macro-instructions adds a great deal of code to an assembler, and therefore increases its cost; assemblers which do allow macro-instructions are sometimes called **macro assemblers.** A macro-instruction is defined by giving its name in the label field of a special pseudo-operation code (usually MACRO). This is followed by a number of assembly lines terminated by a line which ends the macro and which has another special pseudo-operation code (usually END or ENDM). The name of the macro may now be used as a pseudo-operation code, and it is equivalent to the set of assembly lines given in the definition of the macro. These may be operations, pseudo-operations, or other macros.

> The assemblers for the IBM 700 series, in their advanced versions, have another kind of macro-defining pseudo-operation, known as MOP; a macro in the MOP format is used by giving its name, not as a pseudo-operation, but as the first symbol in the variable field. The assemblers for the UNIVAC III and UNIVAC 1107 have a type of macro in which the operation codes in the macro definition must not generate any code, that is, must not be ultimately equivalent to any actual operations. Such a macro can now be called by including it with parameters in a variable field expression. Such a macro is said to be in *function format*, as contrasted with the ordinary, or *procedure format;* the corresponding pseudo-operations which define a macro are PROC and FUNC.

A macro-instruction, like a subroutine, may have parameters. When the macro is defined, the definition process must include a description of how the parameters are to be handled. Sometimes the programmer is allowed to specify dummy parameters in the variable field of the MACRO pseudo-operation; these dummy parameters may then occur anywhere in the macro definition. Sometimes the dummy parameters have standard names, and sometimes they have names which derive from the name of the macro; if the macro is called Z, the first parameter may be $Z(1)$ (or $Z(1, 1)$).

Macro-instructions may be used for open subroutines; the subroutine is defined as a macro, which is then used at each point at which the subroutine is needed. If the subroutine is to be changed, the macro can easily be changed, and the routine reassembled. A macro can even be changed so that its definition consists of a single instruction which calls a closed subroutine. When several programmers are working on a single program, one programmer can define tasks and design macro formats, while another can construct the actual macro definitions.

Whether open or closed subroutines are used, it is important for almost all large programs that they be kept **modular:** each task should correspond to a distinct subroutine. If the same task is performed more than once, it should be represented by the same subroutine each time it is performed. Most good programs will undergo a continuous process of modification and expansion, often by programmers other than those who worked on it originally. Modular programs are the easiest to modify, because extensions to a program are normally expressed in terms of changes to specific tasks.

7-3   Relocation

When a program has several subroutines, each subroutine occupies a certain portion of memory. If the program and all its subroutines are assembled at once, producing an object deck, the assembler determines which portion of memory each subroutine occupies. However, if the program and the subroutines are assembled separately, producing several object decks, the reserving or **allocation** of space in memory for each subroutine is still to be determined. Of course, a subroutine can be assembled in such a way that it starts at a fixed address determined by the programmer; but then it would have to be reassembled if it were used in any other context. What is needed is an object deck capable of representing a program whose starting address can be *arbitrarily determined* by the context in which it is used. Such an object deck is called a **relocatable object deck,** and the assembler which produces it is called a **relocatable assembler.**

A relocatable assembler assumes that the starting address of every program is taken to be a fixed integer (usually zero). The object deck contains instruction words which assume this; a transfer to the location which exceeds that of the start of the program by 24, for instance, is taken as a transfer to cell 24. When all assemblies have been made, the relocatable object decks are processed by a program called a **relocatable loader** (or **allocator**) which reads them and places the routines which they represent in core at distinct addresses.

The relocatable loader works as follows. Suppose that several routines have been loaded, and the last of these has the final address $n-1$. The start address of the current routine is taken to be $n;$ this is the **relocation base.** The relocation base is now added to the address fields of certain instructions; these instructions are said to be **relocated.**

Not all instructions are relocated by the loader. An instruction with immediate addressing which loads an index register with a count, for example, is not relocated; the address field stays as it is. An instruction whose address refers to a special fixed location in core, such as an addressable register, is also not relocated. Neither is a subroutine return or parameter retrieval which uses a small number as its address modified by an index register, nor is a list advancing operation which does the same. All instructions whose addresses refer to symbols within the assembly, including most transfers and operations on data, saving and restoring of index registers, and the like, are relocated; some instructions with immediate addressing are even relocated, as when an index register is loaded with the address of a fixed item.

In order to determine which instructions are to be relocated, an object deck may contain **relocation bits,** which are one-bit flags. In the simplest form of relocation, one bit is used for each instruction word; if the bit is zero, the address is not relocated, but if it is one, the address is relocated. The determination of the relocation bits is done by the assembler, which determines whether the address is relocatable. A symbol is relocatable, but a number is not; a symbol plus a number is relocatable, and further rules may be quite complex. An alternative is to use special cards, called **relocation cards,** to contain this type of information.

An assembler, or an object deck, which is not relocatable is called **absolute.** Some programs use absolute assembly, even on machines for which a relocatable assembler is available, because they use the entire memory of the computer, or because they depend on certain properties of their addresses—the fact that certain addresses have the highest order bit equal to 1, for example. In general, such programming is to be discouraged. Sometimes a relocatable loader, besides loading routines into core, will produce an absolute deck as a by-product, representing the entire "complex" of programs; this absolute deck may be loaded at a later time, a procedure which saves computer time by avoiding the relocatable loading process.

When several routines are loaded together, one routine may have an address field referring to an address in another routine. This will happen, for example, when one routine calls another. If this is the *only* type of cross reference between routines, it may be handled by the relocatable loader using a device known as a **transfer vector,** which is a set of words for each routine, one for each **global symbol** or **external reference,** or symbol in another program which is referenced in this program. Transfer is now made to the appropriate location in the transfer vector instead of directly to the routine involved; the loader fills the transfer vectors with transfers to the appropriate routines as soon as it has determined the starting addresses of all routines. Thus each subroutine call is made by two transfers, the first a subroutine calling instruction, and the second an ordinary transfer.

If there are other types of cross reference involved—if, for example, one routine loads data from another routine—a more complex type of loader, known as a **linking loader** or **linking allocator,** is necessary. Such a program loads routines and inserts references in a given routine to actual addresses within other routines, using the relocation bases of these routines which it has calculated. The relocation bits must now include information about external reference, and, in general, there will be more than one relocation bit per instruction. Other relocation schemes use more than one relocation base, or relocation of fields other than the address field.

7-4 Flags

A **flag** is a variable that is usually restricted to having small integer values which are codes for certain statements that can be made about data. Examples of such statements are that an input tape has reached the end, that an employee has reached his maximum FICA deduction, that an error has been made on an input card, and that an item has not been found in a table. More commonly, the statement represented by a flag will be much more complex; the truth of the statement may always be represented by 1, and its falsity by 0, no matter how complex it is. Flags which assume only two values may be called **logical flags.** A logical flag may be kept in a single bit; other flags may be kept in two, three, or more bits, although sometimes a flag will be kept in an entire word for the sake of simplicity.

If a program has a small number of flags, it is often expedient to keep them permanently in a register. This may simply be one of the accumulators, if there are several, or it may be a special register for flags, as the sense indicator register on the IBM 700 series. It is now possible to test a flag, set a flag to 0 or 1, or set several flags simultaneously to 0 or 1, in fewer instructions than we would need if the flags were in memory.

When two closed or open subroutines are almost alike, space may be saved by combining them into one subroutine and using a flag to distinguish cases. When the subroutine is entered, the flag is set to either 0 or 1. If the subroutines are open, the flag is tested at the end; a transfer is made to the location following the proper subroutine, depending on whether the flag is 0 or 1.

Flags are often used in conjunction with tests. It may happen in a program that the result of a test determines an action which cannot be performed at the time the test is made. In this case, a flag is set to 0 or 1 at the time the test is made, and tested later. The following algorithm is an example of this. It converts a signed integer to a string of characters. The right-most character position is specified, but the left-most is not; the integer is to be converted in such a way that there are no leading zeros. If there is a minus sign, it then appears immediately to the left of the left-most digit. Because the division logic in many computers makes calculation of remainders unwieldy for negative numbers, this algorithm works with positive numbers only. That is, each number is tested at the beginning; if it is negative, its absolute value is converted, and a minus sign is placed at the left of the number. However, we cannot place the "minus" character in its proper position at the time that we test if it is negative, because we do not know yet what character position the minus sign will occupy. Nor can we test the number at the point where the minus sign is stored, because by now is it positive, whether it was positive or negative to begin with. We could, of course, keep both the integer and its magnitude; but this is too much information. Instead, we simply keep a flag which is 0 if the number was positive and 1 if the number was negative.

The algorithm is given as a series of steps as follows:

1. Load the quotient register with X.

2. Load some other register (call it register C; this may be an accumulator, an index register, etc.) with 0.

3. If the quotient register is positive, go to step 6.

4. Load the quotient register with −X.

5. Load register C with 1 (or any non-zero quantity).

6. Store register C in the cell FLAG.

7. Divide the contents of the quotient register by 10. We assume that this leaves the quotient again in the quotient register and the remainder in a register R.

8. Store the register R in the next character to the left, and advance the character pointer one character to the left.

9. If the quotient register does not contain zero, return to step 7.

10. Load the accumulator with the character code for a minus sign.

11. If FLAG does not contain zero, store the accumulator in the next character to the left.

We note the usual algorithm for converting integers to character strings. Dividing an integer by 10 repeatedly will produce its digits from right to left as remainders, and the last digit is sensed by the fact that the quotient is zero. This works in any number system, and is discussed further in Chapter 11. Note also that the digits are assumed to have their own character codes, i.e., the character code for a "3" is 3, and so on; if this is not true, then character conversion may be appended to step 7.

7-5 Co-routines

The concept of **co-routines** is an extension of the concept of a subroutine. Every subroutine has a return address, which is saved while the subroutine is being performed, and which may be different each time the subroutine is called. When the subroutine is not being performed, no return address needs to be saved. Thus a subroutine is subordinate to its main program; the main program calls the subroutine and then takes up where it left off. In contrast, the relation between two co-routines is symmetrical. Each co-routine has a return address, and one of the two return addresses must be saved at all times. When control passes from one co-routine to another, the co-routine which is being entered takes up where it last left off, and the address at which the other co-routine transferred control, plus one, is saved as the return address to that co-routine. The instruction or macro which transfers control between co-routines is called a **bilateral linkage.**

> Bilateral linkage is relatively fast on most machines, but must be set up carefully. On machines which have an index linkage, bilateral linkage may be performed in one instruction if the index linkage is itself indexable. Linkage is made to location zero modified by an index register, and the return address is stored in the same index register. Such instructions include BAL on the IBM 360, LMJ on the UNIVAC 1108, and JSP on the PDP-6. If the index linkage is not indexable, bilateral linkage may be performed in two instructions, by storing the index register in the address field of the following instruction, which is a linkage using the same index register. On the IBM 700 series, the complement of the index must be stored (and this is not possible on the 704, 709, or 7090). On machines with a memory linkage, the best expedient is for one co-routine to return jump to location B1 and the other co-routine to location B2; location B1+1 contains a subroutine return to B2 and location B2+1 contains a subroutine return to B1.

The return address to a pair of co-routines must be *initialized*. The usual procedure is to pick one of the two routines in which to start, and initialize the return address of the other co-routine to be its starting address. If the return addresses are kept in memory, the initialization may be implicit—that is, one return address may already be in place when the routine is loaded, just like any other data word.

We illustrate these concepts by considering bilateral linkage between routines with no other transfer instructions than the linkages. If the sections of code between successive linkages in one co-routine are referred to as A1, A2, A3, etc., and in the other co-routine by B1, B2, B3, etc., then the order of execution of all these sections is as follows: A1, B1, A2, B2, A3, B3, etc. Thus one of the uses of co-routines is in a situation where several routines are "almost alike" but have small differences here and there. It is clear that simply by changing one instruction (the initialization of the return address) we could execute A1, C1, A2, C2, A3, C3, etc., or A1, D1, A2, D2, A3, D3, etc., substituting a different co-routine each time. Hence those parts of the code which are the same can be collected and separated by bilateral linkages to form the program A, whereas programs B, C, D, and so on, embody the differences between the various routines.

A powerful use of co-routines is in the **composition of file processes.** If one file process reads a file A and writes a file B, and a second file process reads file B and writes a file C, and if both processes can be kept in memory at once, then they may be composed; that is, a single routine may be written which has the effect of performing the two routines, one after the other, and which reads file A and writes file C; file B is rendered superfluous. The composition is performed by replacing the output and input operations involving file B by bilateral linkages. At every point in the first program at which a record is output to file B, the second program takes over; it assumes that it has just read a record from file B, but this record has actually been supplied by the first program through the bilateral linkage. This method may be extended to the composition of n file processes, each of which uses a file written by the previous one. Provided that all n programs can be kept in core at once, the initial input file may be read and the final output file written in one pass.

7-6 Recursive Routines

A **recursive function** is, roughly speaking, a function that can be computed. Precise definitions of recursive functions involve the ability to express the function in terms of simpler ones. Thus

$$f(x) = g(x^2 + x + 3)/h(5 + g(x))$$

is a recursive function if $g(x)$ and $h(x)$ are recursive functions. Using an algebraic language, $f(x)$ may in fact be computed, either directly or by a series of statements such as

```
A = X*X + X + 3
B = 5 + G(X)
F = G(A)/H(B)
```

where G and H are function subroutines which compute $g(x)$ and $h(x)$ respectively.

It is also permissible to define a recursive function $f(n)$ in terms of $f(n-1)$, or other values $f(m)$ for $m < n$; this is sometimes called "definition by induction." Thus the factorial function $n!$ or "n factorial" for positive integers n is defined recursively by

$$0! = 1$$
$$n! = n \cdot (n-1)!$$

From this we can deduce the usual explanation that "the factorial of n is the product of all the integers from 1 to n inclusive," and can write a routine to calculate the factorial of n:

```
        NFACT = 1
        DO 5 I = 1, N
   5    NFACT = NFACT*I
```

Suppose, however, that we wanted to compute factorials by following the definition. In this case we could write a subroutine FACT(N) which calculates the factorial of N:

```
        FUNCTION FACT(N)
        IF (N - 1) 1, 1, 2
   1    FACT = 1
        GO TO 3
   2    FACT = N*FACT(N-1)
   3    RETURN
```

The algorithm represented by this program is theoretically correct. It is clearly correct for FACT(0) and FACT(1); it is also correct for FACT(2), because statement 2 is in this case FACT = 2*FACT(1), and since FACT(1) is correctly calculated as 1, FACT, that is, FACT(2), will be correctly calculated as 2*1 = 2. But since FACT(2) is calculated correctly, so is FACT(3), and so on ad infinitum.

Nevertheless, in most programming languages—including FORTRAN II, in which this program was written—this algorithm will not work. In order for it to work, the routine must be coded as a **recursive routine,** using special techniques. The difficulty arises from the fact that the function calls itself; the expression FACT(N−1) occurs in the definition of the function FACT. A similar situation occurs if a function *ultimately* calls itself; if the function A calls the function B, which calls the function C, which calls A, then the function A is said to call itself ultimately.

To see where the difficulty arises, let us reprogram FACT(N) in machine language. For the sake of simplicity, we set it up without a calling sequence; FACT(N) is entered with n in the accumulator and exits with $n!$ in the accumulator. We assume that the instruction CA is a return jump, that is, CA   Y stores the return address at Y and transfers to Y+1. Our return instruction may now be explicitly specified as TR* Y . The routine is then:

```
   FACT CO    0
        ST    FD
        SU    L1
        TNZ   F2
        LD    L1
```

```
        TR   F3
   F2   CA   FACT
        MU   FD
   F3   TR*  FACT
   L1   CO   1
   FD   RE   1
```

This routine will then be called by a sequence of instructions such as

```
        LDI  2
   P7   CA   FACT
```

to calculate the factorial of 2. Let us trace this routine. The steps are as follows:

1. The accumulator is loaded with 2.

2. Control passes to FACT+1, and the address P7+1 is stored at FACT.

3. The accumulator is stored at FD; FD now contains 2.

4. The number 1 is subtracted from 2, giving 1.

5. The number 1 is not equal to zero, so transfer is made to F2.

What should happen at this point is that FACT is called with 1 in the accumulator, producing 1! = 1; this is multiplied by FD, giving 2; and control is returned to P7+1. What actually happens, however, is as follows:

6. Control passes to FACT+1, and the address F2+1 is stored at FACT.

7. The accumulator is stored at FD; FD now contains 1.

8. The number 1 is subtracted from 1, giving 0.

9. The accumulator is zero, so transfer is not made to F2.

10. The accumulator is loaded with 1.

11. Transfer is made to F3.

12. Transfer is made to the return address, which is F2+1.

13. The number 1 is multiplied by 1, giving 1. (This is the first sign that something is wrong; FD was supposed to contain 2 at this point.)

14. Transfer is made to the return address, which is still F2+1, since this address is still contained in the cell FACT. The computer therefore enters an endless loop, continually multiplying 1 by 1 and getting 1, and cycling back.

The difficulties which we encountered here are not resolved simply by changing to another form of instruction. If the call instruction leaves the return address in a register, the return instruction will still have the wrong quantity in the register when return is made the last time. If a calling sequence is used, the number n will have to be extracted from the calling sequence, but this does not affect the outcome. Nevertheless, there do exist ways to write recursive subroutines. In some list processing languages, *all* subroutines are treated as recursive; when subroutines are coded in machine language or in an algebraic language, it is usually advisable to use recursive subroutines only when necessary, since recursive programming uses both space and time.

7-7   Recursion Levels

One way to write a recursive routine is to use the concept of **recursion level.** The difficulty in handling the return addresses in our example stemmed from the fact that we needed *both* return addresses—once to return from the call at P7, at the "outer level," and once to return from the call at F2, at the "inner level"—and we had only one place to put them. Therefore, at step 6 in fact, one of the return addresses **overwrote** (or "clobbered") the other; the second return address was stored at FACT, and the first return address was lost. The problem with the data word FD was similar; we actually needed *both* values of FD, namely 1 and 2. If we were calculating FACT(3), we would need three values of FD, namely 1, 2, and 3; we would also need three return addresses, although two of them would be the same.

A recursion level is an integer which is increased each time a recursive subroutine is entered, and is decreased each time it exits. This integer is then used to index an array which contains all of the return addresses and recursive data. The amount of the increase and decrease is determined by the particular routine; it is the number of words of recursive data (one, in this case) plus one for the return address. The return address must be saved each time the routine is entered and restored each time it exits. Recursive data must be referenced by its position in the array. An array used in this way is called a **stack.**

To illustrate the use of a stack, we recode our subroutine. The stack, which is an array of 100 words, shall be called K; the recursion level is called LEVEL. When the routine is entered, it is assumed that LEVEL = 0.

```
LEVEL RE    1
K     RE    100
FACT  CO    0
      LX    LEVEL,1
      AX    L2,1
      SX    LEVEL,1
```

```
        ST    K,1
        LD    FACT
        ST    K-1,1
        LD    K,1
        SU    L1
        TNZ   F2
        LD    L1
        TR    F3
F2      CA    FACT
        MU    K,1
F3      LQ    K-1,1
        SQ    FACT
        AX    LM2,1
        SX    LEVEL,1
        TR*   FACT
L1      CO    1
L2      CO    2
LM2     CO    -2
```

Let us now trace this routine when called by the same sequence as before:

1. The accumulator is loaded with 2.

2. Control passes to FACT+1, and the address P7+1 is stored at FACT.

3. LEVEL (that is, 0) is placed in index register 1.

4. The number 2 is added to 0, giving 2 in index register 1.

5. The number 2 is stored as LEVEL.

6. The number 2 (from the accumulator) is stored at K+2.

7. The address P7+1 is loaded into the accumulator from FACT.

8. The address P7+1 is stored at K+1 (that is, K−1+2).

9. The number 2 (as originally entered) is brought back into the accumulator.

10. The number 1 is subtracted from 2, giving 1.

11. The accumulator is not equal to zero, so transfer is made to F2.

12. Control passes to FACT+1, and the address F2+1 is stored at FACT.

13. LEVEL (that is, 2) is placed in index register 1.

14. The number 2 is added to 2, giving 4 in index register 1.

15. The number 4 is stored as LEVEL.

16. The number 1 (from the accumulator) is stored at K+4.

17. The address F2+1 is loaded into the accumulator from FACT.

18. The address F2+1 is stored at K+3 (that is, K−1+4). Note that the addresses P7+1 and F2+1 have now both been saved, one at K+1 and the other at K+3. Similarly, the data items 1 and 2 have both been saved, one at K+2 and the other at K+4, instead of both being left in the cell FD as before.

19. The number 1 (which was in the accumulator at the start of this call) is brought back into the accumulator.

20. The number 1 is subtracted from 1, giving 0.

21. The accumulator is zero, so control does not transfer to F2.

22. The number 1 is loaded into the accumulator.

23. Transfer is made to F3.

24. The address F2+1 is loaded from K+3.

25. The address F2+1 is stored into FACT.

26. The number 2 is subtracted from 4, giving 2 in index register 1.

27. The number 2 is stored as LEVEL.

28. Control is transferred to the address in FACT, that is, F2+1.

29. The number 1, which was left in the accumulator from the previous call to FACT, is multiplied by 2, giving 2. (The number 2 was stored here at step 6.)

30. The address P7+1 is loaded from K+1.

31. The address P7+1 is stored into FACT. (Note that since a different address is stored into FACT this time, we avoid the endless loop which we encountered before.)

32. The number 2 is subtracted from 2, giving 0 in index register 1.

33. The number 0 is stored as LEVEL.

34. Control is transferred to the address in FACT, that is, P7+1, and the recursive routine has exited normally.

The condition that the level be zero when the routine is entered is actually unnecessary. The level may be any number small enough to insure that the stack does not overflow during the course of the routine. When the routine exits, the level will be the same as it was when it was entered.

In informal usage, the term "recursion level" is often used to denote the number of return addresses currently on the stack, irrespective of the recursive data.

7-8　Lists and Recursion

Recursive routines are widely used in programs which perform complex tasks. They effectively reduce the size of a program, since the same sections of code are used at various recursion levels. On the other hand, it is often possible to improve the speed of a recursive routine by rewriting it without recursion or with less recursion. Thus a faster factorial routine than the one of the preceding section might be written as follows:

```
FACT    CO    0
        ST    ANS
F1      SUI   1
        TZ    F2
        ST    FB
        MU    ANS
        ST    ANS
        LD    FB
        TR    F1
F2      LD    ANS
        TR*   FACT
ANS     RE    1
FB      RE    1
```

This takes 14 steps to calculate the factorial of 2, as opposed to 34.

Recursive routines are at a particular advantage when processing list structures, since the very definition of a list structure is recursive. In this case, in fact, the most elementary operations on list structures are most naturally coded as recursive routines. These include the following:

(1) *Equality test.* We have a routine, EQUAL, which compares two list structures to see if they are equal and returns 1 if they are and 0 if they are not. Two list structures are equal if they have exactly the same format and contain exactly the same elements. EQUAL proceeds by comparing the first element of the first list structure with the first element of the second. These must either be both sublists or both not sublists; otherwise, EQUAL returns 0. If they are both sublists, EQUAL calls EQUAL to compare the sublists. If the sublists are not equal, EQUAL returns 0; if they are, EQUAL proceeds to the next element of each main list. If the two original elements were both not sublists, EQUAL compares them; if they are not equal, EQUAL returns 0, and if they are equal, EQUAL proceeds to the next element. Upon proceeding to the next element, EQUAL may find that it has processed the last element of one or both main lists. If both, EQUAL returns 1; if one but not the other, EQUAL returns 0; if neither, EQUAL loops back to test whether these elements are sublists or not.

(2) *Printing.* We have a routine, PRINT, which prints a list structure as an S-expression. The routine first prints a left parenthesis. It then examines the first element of the list. If this is a sublist, PRINT calls

PRINT to print this sublist. Otherwise, PRINT prints the element, followed by a blank (or comma). It then proceeds to the next element; if there is no next element, it prints a right parenthesis and exits.

(3) *Reading.* The routine READ reads an S-expression and converts it to a list structure. If the S-expression was in proper format, READ returns a 1; otherwise, READ returns a 2, unless the "S-expression" consisted of a single right parenthesis, in which case READ returns a 3. READ starts by examining the first character read. If it is a left parenthesis, READ sets up a pointer to a sublist and calls RSUB to read this sublist. If it is a right parenthesis, READ returns a 3. Otherwise, READ continues to read characters, returning a 2 on any illegal character, until it encounters a blank or a comma; it then forms a list element with the given name and returns a 1. The routine RSUB calls READ to read the first element of the sublist. If READ returns a 3, RSUB exits. If READ returns a 2, RSUB gives an error exit; after READ has called RSUB it must return a 2 if this error exit was taken. If READ returns a 1, RSUB proceeds to the next element of the sublist. Note that neither READ nor RSUB calls itself, but READ calls RSUB and RSUB calls READ; therefore both routines must be written recursively. (There are several other methods of reading S-expressions.)

In all the above examples we have used the word "sublist" as short for "sub-list-structure." A sublist, in other words, may have sublists of its own; the fact that each of these routines processes an entire list structure implies that the sub-list-structures will be correctly processed.

List processing may also serve as an aid to recursion. In particular, a stack, which is an array, may be replaced by a list. One disadvantage of using a stack is that it may *overflow;* if the recursion level becomes high enough, there may not be enough space in the stack to hold all the data required. If a list space is already present, the stack may be kept in the form of a list, and the danger of overflow is reduced. A list used in this way is called a **push down list.** The push down list was developed by Allen Newell, who described it as being constructed "like a cafeteria well for holding plates—as each new plate is put in the top of the well, all the others are pushed down, so that the only apparent change is that a new plate sits on top. When this top plate is removed, the one just below it 'pops up' and becomes the new plate on top."

The top of a stack has index equal to the current recursion level, and is the highest order element currently in the stack. The top of a push down list is the *head* of the list; when a new element is added to a push down list, it is inserted at the head of the list as usual, and when an element pops up, the first element of the list is deleted. An apparent advantage of using stacks rather than push down lists is that more than one word at each recursion level may be referenced by using various addresses with the index register containing the recursion level; with push down lists the words must be used one at a time. However, this difficulty can usually be avoided by good programming.

7-9 Radix Exchange Sort

Recursion may be applied to the problem of sorting, to produce a core sort algorithm which is as fast as selection sorting—that is, it takes at most nk steps, where n is the number of items and k is the length of the key—and which has the additional advantage that it does not require any scratch memory. It is called the *radix exchange sort*.

The radix exchange sort operates on the individual bits of the sort key from left to right, in contrast with the standard selection sort, which operates on them from right to left. An array or a two-way list may be sorted, but not a one-way list, because processing in both directions is required. The first stage of the sort is as follows. Two pointers are initialized, one to the first element of the table, and one to its last element. The first pointer now moves down the table searching for an item which contains a one in the first bit position, and the second pointer moves up the array searching for an item which contains a zero in this position. When these two items are found, they are exchanged. Again the pointers move until two more such items are found, and they are likewise exchanged; the process continues until the two pointers meet.

The table is now "partially sorted" in that all items beginning with 0 are first and all items beginning with 1 are second. A sort on the second bit of the key over the *entire* table would destroy this partial sorting. However, if the items beginning with 0 could be sorted separately on the second bit, and similarly the items beginning with 1, then the table would be partially sorted on the first two bits. This process could then be continued until the table is completely sorted.

In the nonrecursive radix exchange sort, the ith pass is considered as a collection of (at most) 2^{i-1} sorting operations on various sections of the table. This requires that the starting and ending addresses of these portions be known. For a key length of k, there are k passes required; on the last pass, there are 2^{k-1} possible sections of the table, each of whose starting and ending addresses must be known. The starting address of each section is one greater than the ending address of the previous section, so that the maximum auxiliary storage required is 2^{k-1} cells.

In the recursive radix exchange sort, only $2k$ auxiliary cells are required for starting and ending addresses, and k more cells for return addresses; these are kept on a push down list or stack of maximum length

3*k*. Let us call the sort routine RRES; it then proceeds by (1) dividing the given table once, (2) performing one phase using the first bit of the key, and then (3) calling RRES separately twice, once on each section of the table, with a key which consists of the given key with its first bit removed.

We may contrast the recursive and nonrecursive radix exchange sort by considering the following example. Suppose that the table length is 16, the key length is 4, and the keys contain the integers from 0 to 15. Then, in the nonrecursive sort, the first phase sorts the entire table; the second phase makes 2 sorts, the third 4 sorts, and the fourth 8 sorts, for a total of 15 sorts. The recursive sort also performs 15 sorts, but in a different order, as follows:

	Nonrecursive sort			Recursive sort		
Phase	Lowest index	Highest index	Sort number	Lowest index	Highest index	Level
1	1	16	1	1	16	1
2	1	8	2	1	8	2
2	9	16	3	1	4	3
3	1	4	4	1	2	4
3	5	8	5	3	4	4
3	9	12	6	5	8	3
3	13	16	7	5	6	4
4	1	2	8	7	8	4
4	3	4	9	9	16	2
4	5	6	10	9	12	3
4	7	8	11	9	10	4
4	9	10	12	11	12	4
4	11	12	13	13	16	3
4	13	14	14	13	14	4
4	15	16	15	15	16	4

More precisely, the routine RRES, with parameters SA, EA, and KB, where SA is the start address of the table, EA is the end address of the table, and KB is the key bit (initially 1), proceeds as follows:

(1) The size of the table is checked; if it is small enough, other sorting methods may be used. This step is optional and works for arrays only.

(2) One phase is performed on the given table, exchanging elements and arriving at an address AM at which the pointers meet.

(3) If the item at AM contains a zero in position KB, set EA1 = AM. Otherwise, set EA1 = AM − 1 unless AM = SA, in which case skip

this step. Now perform RRES with parameters SA, EA1, and KB + 1.

(4) If the item at AM contains a one in position KB, set SA2 = AM. Otherwise set SA2 = AM + 1 unless AM = EA, in which case skip this step. Now perform RRES with parameters SA2, EA, and KB + 1.

(5) Exit. The sort is now complete.

PROBLEMS

1. A subroutine may have a variable number of parameters. If it does, the number of parameters is sometimes itself contained as the first parameter. Would it be possible for the number of parameters to be given as the *last* parameter? Why or why not?

2. When a program does not run properly and stops in the middle by mistake, it is customary to direct the computer to produce a memory dump, giving the contents of every cell in memory at the time of the stop. Suppose that a program contains several subroutines, and the programmer receives such a memory dump. What advantage does he now have if he has coded his subroutines with calling instructions which leave the return address in memory, rather than in a register?

3. In each of the following situations, state whether you would code the given subroutine as an open or a closed subroutine, and why. In some cases, the decision may not be clear cut; you should then state under what conditions you might take the other course of action.

   (a) A subroutine with three parameters, X, Y, and Z, multiplies X and Y, stores the result in Z, and returns.

   (b) A subroutine containing 15 instructions and no transfers, other than the return, is called from exactly two places. The subroutine has no parameters.

   (c) A subroutine has one parameter and is called from six different places, each time with a different parameter value. The purpose of the subroutine is to calculate the value of a polynomial of degree 12 in its parameter. All the coefficients of this polynomial are nonzero.

   (d) A subroutine tests whether the contents of the accumulator are negative; if so, a flag is set, and the contents of the accumulator are converted to positive. The flag is set in one instruction.

   (e) A closed subroutine A uses an open subroutine B exactly once. None of the parameters of A appear in B. The subroutine A is recoded as open. (The question here is, should the subroutine B remain open or be recoded as closed?)

4. In the following problems, use the machine language available to you.

   (a) Write a macro called FW which divides an instruction word into four fields of given length and places given data in them. For example, if the data words are of length 24, the line

FW   6,4,4,10,5,3,7,2

should divide the instruction word from left to right into fields of lengths 6, 4, 4, and 10, and place in these fields the numbers 5, 3, 7, and 2, respectively, producing the 8-octal-digit data word 05156002.

(b) Write a macro which removes a list element from a list of available space and attaches it to the head of a given list.

(c) Write a macro called MASK which produces a mask having specified left and right bit limits. All bits between these limits should be ones, and all bits outside these limits should be zeros. For the purposes of this macro, the bits of a word are numbered from 1 at the left to n at the right, where n is the length of the data words. For example, if $n = 30$, the line

MASK   3,17

should produce the 10-octal-digit data word 1777760000.

(d) Write a macro which calls another macro. Explain carefully what each one does.

(e) (Note: This part is to be done *only* if the macro facility in your machine language includes some method by which the number of parameters given on a macro line may be used by a macro with a variable number of parameters.) Write a macro called CALL, which calls a subroutine with a given calling sequence. Thus the line

CALL   INT,A,B,C

should call the subroutine INT with the parameters A, B, and C.

5. Which of the following instructions have relocatable addresses in a relocatable assembly with no absolute ORG statements?

(a) AXT 100,2 on the IBM 7094. Puts the number 100 in index register 2.

(b) SA7 Q8 on the CDC 6600. Puts the address Q8 in register A7 and stores the contents of register X7 in cell Q8. The symbol Q8 appears in the assembly line Q8 BSS 1, reserving one cell for a data word called Q8.

(c) AA,14 7,TBL2-TBL1 on the UNIVAC 1108. Using immediate addressing, adds the difference between TBL2 and TBL1 to accumulator 7. The statements TBL1 RES 100 and TBL2 RES 100 in this assembly reserve 100 cells each for arrays called TBL1 and TBL2.

(d) AD 0,Y-8 on the IBM 360. Adds the long (double precision) floating point number contained at Y-8 to floating point register zero. The symbol Y has been defined as equal to YB+200, where YB is an array of length 400.

(e) MOVEI 4,L on the PDP-6. The symbol L has been defined equal to 64; this instruction therefore places the number 64 in register 4.

6. The following procedure for calculating Y(I) from X(I), for I = 1 to 100,

has one mistake in it. Find the mistake and state what incorrect action the procedure would take if the mistake is not corrected. The formula according to which $Y(I)$ is to be calculated is

$$Y(I) = E^2$$

where

$$E = \begin{cases} D + 2.0 + 1.0/D & \text{if } D \leq 0 \\ \\ D + 1.0/D & \text{if } D > 0 \end{cases}$$

and where $D = X(I)^2 - X(I)$. The procedure is as follows:
1. Set $I = 1$.
2. Calculate $D = X(I)*X(I) - X(I)$.
3. If $D \leq 0$, set $K = 1$.
4. Set $E = D + 1.0/D$.
5. If $K = 1$, set $E = E + 2.0$.
6. Set $Y(I) = E*E$.
7. Add 1 to I.
8. If I is less than or equal to 100, return to step 2.

7. What would happen if a pair of co-routines were not initialized?

8. The ABRACADABRA puzzle involves calculating how many ways the word ABRACADABRA can be spelled from left to right in the following diagram (the italicized letters represent one possible way):

*A*BRACADABRA
B*R*ACADAB*R*
R*A*CADAB
A*C*ADA
C*A*D
A

Let NWAYS(I, J) be the number of ways in which a path may be traced from the "A" at the left of the diagram to a letter which is *i* positions to the right of, and *j* positions below, this "A." Thus NWAYS(5, 5), for example, is 1, since there is only one way of spelling ABRACA from the upper left-hand corner to the bottom of the puzzle. Also, NWAYS(10, 0) is the total number of ways of spelling ABRACADABRA. Describe how NWAYS(I, J) may be calculated by means of recursive subroutines.

9. The following procedure, called TOTAL, finds the sum of all numbers on a list structure and puts this sum in SUM, assuming that SUM has previously been initialized to zero:
    1. Set a pointer to point to the first element of the list structure.
    2. If the current element is a number, add it to SUM.

3. If the current element is a pointer to a sublist, call TOTAL with the pointer set to the first element of this sublist.
4. If there are no more elements on this list, return.
5. Otherwise, move the pointer to the next element on the list, and return to step 2.

Write similar procedures to manipulate list structures in the following ways:

(a) Print out a list structure as an S-expression.

(b) Determine whether a given list structure of numbers contains the number 1.

(c) Replace the number 6 by the number 7 whenever it occurs in the given list structure.

Chapter 8

CHARACTER STRINGS

8-1 Processes on Strings

Character strings are more difficult to work with than integers, floating point numbers, or even complex numbers, because of their variable length. Nevertheless, there are wide classes of problems in which the data is best represented by character strings. Computer translation of (natural) languages involves extremely large data bases of character strings; assemblers, compilers, and other processors work with the character strings which make up a source program; mathematical research involves formulas, which may be expressed as character strings. There are even character string processing languages, which perform most of the useful operations on strings. COMIT and SNOBOL are string processing languages. List processing and string processing are related—one can, for example, construct a list of strings—and several string processing languages have been written as extensions of the LISP list processing language.

The most elementary string-oriented subroutine may be called "extract-and-advance." A character string is assumed to be in memory at some location (in its usual form) and the subroutine loads an accumulator with one character and advances an internal flag or flags in such a way that the next time the subroutine is called it will load the next character. This routine may be coded as an open or a closed subroutine; the number of instructions involved is a good measure of the efficacy of character string processing in any given computer.

The IBM 360 has byte addressing, with one character per byte; extract-and-advance simply consists of loading an indexed word and adding 1 to an index register. The UNIVAC 1107 and 1108 have character loading instructions for each character in a word, plus automatic index incrementation; extract-and-advance is performed in one indexed execute instruction referencing an indexed character load, and two index registers are required to hold the pointers. The PDP-6 also requires only one instruction, called Increment and Load Byte. The IBM 1400 series resembles the IBM 360 in this regard. The IBM 7040 and 7044 have character loading instructions and can extract-and-advance in two instructions, using two pointers. The rest of the IBM 700 series, the CDC 1604, 3600, and 6600, the SDS 930, and many other computers have no character-oriented instructions, and perform extract-and-advance by means of closed subroutines which keep the word from which the current character is being extracted and circularly shift it each time, or else keep several masks and several shift counts; timing ranges from four to ten instructions.

Similar to this subroutine is one called "store-and-advance," which stores a character and advances an internal flag or flags so that it will store a new character next to it the next time it is called. Store-and-advance should take the same amount of time as extract-and-advance. On computers with no character handling instructions, there is an important difference. In extract-and-advance, the entire word containing the current character may be kept as a data word within the routine, in such a way that the current character is always at one end. This cannot be done in store-and-advance, because when the program stops storing characters, the last word of characters would still be embedded within the subroutine. Each character must thus be shifted to its proper position and inserted into the word.

A few computers have **insert** or **substitute instructions,** which insert certain bits from one word into certain positions in another word, leaving the rest of the other word as it is. Such an instruction requires three operands—one for a mask, one for the first word, and one for the second word. In the CDC 1604 and 3600 command Selective Substitute, these operands are, respectively, the Q register, the memory word, and the A register; the result is left in the A register. On any other computer, however, this operation can be performed in three instructions as follows, assuming that the second word is in an accumulator: "exclusive or" with the first word; "and" with the mask; "exclusive or" with the first word again. (Why does this work?)

Both extract-and-advance and store-and-advance may best be written as macros. Using such macros (here entitled EXCH and STCH, respectively) it is possible to write such routines as the one below, which moves a character string from one position to another in core:

```
        IEX    WPI,CP1
        IST    WP2,CP2
        LX     N,1
P1      EXCH
        STCH
        DCT    1,1,0,P1
```

Here WP1 and CP1 are the **word position,** or address, and **character position,** an integer which numbers the characters of a word, for the first character of the string; WP2 and CP2 are the word and character positions, respectively, for the first character of the string in its new location; IEX and IST are macros which initialize the extract pointers and the store pointers respectively; and N is the length of the string. This routine may easily be extended to form the **concatenation** of two strings, or the string obtained by placing one after the other. Macros may also be written to extract the current character, or the following character, without advancing.

8-2 Packing and Unpacking

Unpacking a word means extracting all its fields and placing each field in a separate word; **packing** a word means combining fields from separate words and forming a single word with fields. Packing and unpacking apply to any word with fields, not just to a word of character codes. For example, a floating point number may be unpacked into its exponent and fraction fields; some computers have unpacking instructions which do this.

Packing a word with n fields requires $2n$ instructions. Fields are entered from left-most to right-most; each field is added (or "OR"-ed)* into the word after the word has been shifted left by the length of the field, except for the first field; the $2n$th instruction stores the packed word. Unpacking a word with n fields requires $3n$ instructions, and two adjacent registers; the word is first loaded into the register at the right. Each field extraction involves clearing the register at the left, shifting both registers to the left, and storing the register at the left. To store the last field, the register at the right is circularly shifted by the field length and stored. On a computer with at least n accumulators, unpacking a word with n fields can be done in n accumulators using $2n + 1$ instructions. The word is first placed in accumulator 1; accumulators 1 and 2 are double-shifted right, leaving the first field in register 1. Registers 2 and 3 are now double-shifted right, leaving the second field in register 2, and the process continues until field $n-1$ is in register $n-1$. Register n is now single-shifted to position field n properly. The n registers are now stored. Of course, it is always possible to use fewer instructions if the given computer has instructions which load or store a specific field.

Sometimes it is desirable to unpack an entire array of character codes.

---

* Two numbers are added with an add instruction; two numbers are "OR"-ed with a logical OR instruction.

This is particularly true when the given computer has no character-handling instructions. If the characters have been read from cards or tape, they will be packed; but the extract-and-advance algorithm is made much easier if they are unpacked. Similarly, the store-and-advance algorithm will be very easy if unpacked characters are stored, but they must then be packed if they are to be output on cards, tape, or the printer.

The following code, written in our machine language, unpacks an array of character codes. The number of characters per word is CPW; the length of the array PA of packed character codes is PAL; and the number of bits per character is BPC.

```
UAL    EQU    PAL*CPW
PA     RE     PAL
UA     RE     UAL
START  LXI    0,3
       LXI    0,2
P2     LXI    CPW,1
       LQ     PA,2
P3     LDI    0
       LDL    BPC
       ST     UA,3
       AXI    1,3
       DCT    1,1,0,P3
       ICT    2,1,PAL,P2
```

Recall that the LDL instruction is a double logical shift.

The following code, written in our machine language, packs an array of character codes, under the same assumptions as above.

```
UAL    EQU    PAL*CPW
PA     RE     PAL
UA     RE     UAL
START  LXI    UAL,3
       LXI    PAL−1,2
Q2     LXI    CPW,1
Q3     AXI    −1,3
       LD     UA,3
       RDL    BPC
       DCT    1,1,0,Q3
       SQ     PA,2
       DCT    2,1,0,Q2
```

This packing algorithm loads the right-most character of a word first; therefore the loop has been carried out from the end of the array of un-packed character codes, UA. Another packing algorithm, which assumes more explicitly that the remainder of each unpacked character code word is zero, consists of loading the left-most character first, and shifting the accumulator left instead of right, adding in each new character. This algorithm would have been used from the front to the end of the array UA.

8-3   Patterns

The word **pattern** is used in computing in two different general senses. Some computers have input devices which are capable of scanning a picture; these may then be programmed to analyze patterns in the visual sense. For example, a digitized television picture may consist of gxy bits, where x and y are the raster dimensions and g is the gray-scale factor. This means that the picture consists of a two-dimensional array of dots, with x dots in each vertical column and y dots in each horizontal row, and these dots may be any one of 2^g colors, from black to white, where each color is represented by a particular g-bit code. These gxy bits may then be placed in a file, and programs written to determine what visual patterns are in the picture. The other meaning of "pattern" arose originally from linguistic analysis. Some of the earliest natural language programs were written to test whether a sentence corresponds to a certain configuration, or pattern, such as

```
THE _____ IS ON THE _____ .
```

Examples of sentences which would match this pattern are as follows:

```
THE CAT IS ON THE MAT.
THE MAN IS ON THE TELEPHONE.
THE TAPE IS ON THE COMPUTER.
```

By convention, the blank spaces may be filled with any character string, including possibly more than one word, so that the following sentences also match this pattern:

```
THE MAN IS ON THE TELEPHONE TALKING TO HIS WIFE.
THE CAT EATS THE MEAT WHICH IS ON THE DISH.
THE MAN SAYS THAT WHEN THE SWITCH IS ON THE BELL RINGS.
```

But the sentence THE CATS ARE ON THE MAT does not match this pattern.

How do we write a program to test whether a given string matches a pattern of this form? In the case of the pattern above, we can test the beginning of the string to see whether it starts with THE. Now we are allowed to have any characters before "IS ON THE." The next test, therefore, must be for the character I. However, we cannot be sure that any character I which we find is the beginning of IS ON THE; if it is not, we have to keep scanning. For example, if the input phrase were

THE TEST IS ON THURSDAY AND THE ASSIGNMENT IS ON THE BOARD.

then the test for I would be satisfied in the tenth character of the sentence; we would continue to look for IS ON THE, and would in fact find IS ON TH, but the next character is a U. This, however, does not mean that the sentence does not match the pattern; in fact, it does match the pattern, as we will find if we scan the sentence further.

There is one important theoretical difficulty with this algorithm. It does not arise for this pattern, but may arise for a general pattern. Suppose that the pattern to be matched is

IT _____ ON AND ON UNTIL _____ .

Thus a sentence such as IT GOES ON AND ON UNTIL IT STOPS may be matched without difficulty. However, suppose we are given the sentence

IT GOES ON AND ON AND ON UNTIL IT STOPS.

Now the matching proceeds as follows. The sentence starts with IT; there is an O in GOES, but the next character is an E, so this does not match. There is an O in the first ON, and we look for ON AND ON UNTIL and find ON AND ON followed by a blank, but the next character is an A, so there is no match. Now what happens if the search is continued from this point? The next O is in the third ON, and a search for ON AND ON UNTIL fails at this point; the program ultimately concludes that the sentence does not match the pattern, when in fact it does.

The difficulty is that we skipped over the place where the string ON AND ON UNTIL actually starts (at the second ON) while checking out another possible match. This cannot happen; the character scan after this match fails. After the A in the second AND, it must start over, not at this letter, but at the point where the character scan originally stopped— at the O in the first ON. This brings us to a technical problem. The algorithm as we have developed it so far can be programmed using only the basic extract-and-advance operation described in section 1. If we are to "back up and start over," however, this operation is not enough. One possibility is to actually backspace over the character string by the number of characters needed. However, this would require that we count the number of characters in each scan. There is a much simpler method: saving and restoring the pointers. At the beginning of each scan for a matching string, we save the pointer or pointers which denoted the character position to the extract-and-advance subroutine. If the match fails, we restore these pointers, so that the next extract-and-advance will extract the second character of the match that failed.

> The capability of saving and restoring sometimes puts extra requirements on the extraction routine. If characters are unpacked and stored one to a word, or if characters are addressable, there is exactly one pointer, which is kept in an index register and may be saved and restored very easily. In those extraction routines which keep two pointers in index registers, there is likewise no difficulty. If the words of character codes are taken from core and circularly shifted, however, the circularly shifted word in its current position, as well as the two pointers, must be saved and restored.

8-4   Frames

Instead of writing a routine for each pattern which tests whether a given character string matches the pattern, we may express the pattern itself as a character string and write a general routine for matching with any pattern. A pattern expressed as a character string is called a **frame.** The usual method of specifying blanks in a frame is by choosing some character which will never appear in the strings under consideration. If we use $ for this character, the frame for our example will be

THE $ IS ON THE $.

A routine may now be written to match any string against any frame. The string and the frame are compared; a $ in the frame causes the current character position in the string to be saved, and return is made to this point if the match fails.

Other routines which operate on frames may require a more complex format for a frame. For example, it may be necessary to extract the strings which fill the blanks and use them at a later stage. In this case, we will need to distinguish one blank from another if there are more than one. This may be done by numbering the blanks $1, $2, $3, etc. Thus if the pattern

THE $1 IS ON THE $2.

is being matched against the string

THE TEST IS ON THURSDAY AND THE ASSIGNMENT IS ON THE
BOARD.

then $1 is TEST IS ON THURSDAY AND THE ASSIGNMENT and
$2 is BOARD. If several strings and several patterns are being matched,
it may be necessary to distinguish these further, in which case we can give
them names. Thus the frame

THE *SUBJ* IS ON THE *OBJ*

gives the first of the above strings the name *SUBJ* and the other one
the name *OBJ*.

Names for strings are especially helpful in **pattern construction,** in
which a string is matched against a frame and a new string is simultaneously created, applying certain rules to the old string. One of these
rules is *replacement,* or substitution of one string for another. Thus a routine may be written to replace CAT by DOG if it appears in the string.
Applying this rule to THE CAT IS ON THE MAT produces THE DOG
IS ON THE MAT. The string CAT is searched as a frame (possibly
denoted by $ CAT $). Each character which does not match is copied
into the new string. When a match is found, the matched characters are
not copied; if the match fails, the search is restarted where it left off,
and copying proceeds as usual. If the match is successful, so that the entire string CAT is found, the characters in the new string, DOG, are copied into the new string, followed by the remainder of the old string.

Just as patterns may be represented as frames, so replacement rules
may also be represented as character strings, with some character (usually
=, if this character is not found in any string) between the old string and
the new string. A routine may be written to modify any string according to
any replacement rule.

The string processing languages COMIT and SNOBOL have pattern
matching and construction operations. If a process involves string manipulation almost exclusively, it may be written in such a language. If it involves list processing as well, it may be wiser to use CONVERT or FLIP,
which are string processing subroutines of the LISP list processing language. If both string manipulations and algebraic expressions are used in
the same program, string processing subroutines may be used, which are
called from a program in machine language or in an algebraic language.

Another well-known example of pattern construction occurs in the
editing instructions on the IBM 1400 series, the IBM 360, and elsewhere. These convert a character string consisting of digits to a character string containing dollar signs, decimal points, and the like, which
represents an amount of money. The specific type of conversion is

controlled by a frame called an **edit word.** Thus the string 00263548 is converted by the edit word $bbb,bbb.bb (where b stands for blank) into the string $002,635.48 ; the same initial string is converted by the edit word bbb,bb0.bb into the string 2,635.48 . Precise details of this form of pattern construction, on any computer, may be found in its operations manual.

8-5   Algebraic Expressions

Computer programs to calculate the value of an algebraic expression such as

TAU + B5 − (A12*4.0) + (D − (X − 3.5))

are used in assemblers. We shall now develop the theory of such programs.

It is assumed that the program has access to a table of symbols and their values. That is, when we load the symbol B in the above expression, we can look up the value of B. How this is done is immaterial: we may have an array or a list of two-word items, a hybrid hash table, etc., but we will assume only that there is a subroutine which is entered with a symbol and exits with the corresponding value.

Numbers present a special case. A number is not a symbol with a value; the value of a number is determined directly from its digits. The algorithm for determining this value is, fortunately, very easy:

1. Place the value of the first digit in cell NV.

2. Extract-and-advance one digit.

3. If this digit is not numeric, skip steps 4 and 5. NV contains the value of the number.

4. Multiply the contents of NV by 10 (or, for octal numbers, by 8; or, for numbers in any other radix *n,* by *n*) and add the value of the current digit, storing the result back in NV.

5. Go to step 2.

Operators of many kinds may be used. The simplest operators consist of one character, such as + or − or * or /. Note that we cannot tell what an operator applies to until we have read at least the next symbol. Thus, for an expression such as in +1, we save a code for "plus" somewhere in memory. After we have read the 1, we look at the code; if it is the code for "plus," we add the second operand, in this case 1. Another common type of operator consists of an alphabetic code surrounded by periods; thus .G. or .GT. or .GR. or .GRT. may mean "greater than"; .E. or .EQ. or .EQL. may mean "equal to," etc. When these symbols are used as logical operands, the result is a logical variable; "A .EQL. B" is equal to one or zero depending on whether A is or is not equal to B. In this case, we have a table of operators; when we load a period, we enter a section of code which loads alphabetic characters one after the other and accumulates a symbol until it encounters another period, at which point it looks up the operator in the table and treats it like any other operator.

Other kinds of operators include **, used to denote exponentiation (and also the less frequently used ++, ––, etc., found in some assemblers). If the operators * and ** are both admissible, then when the character * is loaded, we do not know whether or not it is part of **. If the next character is a *, we proceed to the next symbol by loading a character, storing it, loading the next, and so on. Otherwise, we must proceed to the next symbol under the assumption that the first character is already loaded. Thus we have two different assumptions about entry to the section of code which accumulates a symbol; these may be treated by two separate entry points, or starting locations, for this section of code.

Similar problems arise with *numerical conventions*. An octal number may be distinguished from a decimal number by adding B; thus 10000B means 10000 octal, or 4096. In this case, the value cannot be calculated as we have described above; instead, the numeric characters must be stored in an array, and the value calculated later. One assembler avoids this problem by stipulating that any integer beginning with a zero is octal, and all other integers are decimal. Numeric characters may also occur in symbols. If the language specifies that a symbol must begin with a letter, then symbols may be easily distinguished from numbers. Sometimes, however, this restriction is not made; such symbols as 56T4, 9CODE, and 1103A are perfectly valid symbols. In such cases we cannot be sure that we are actually dealing with a number until after encountering one or more numeric characters followed by an operator; these characters must be stored in an array as before. Floating point numbers are usually designated by numeric characters separated by a decimal point, such as 5.0 or 36.625; the integral part and the fractional part may be converted to floating point and added. If periods are also used for operators, however, our algorithms become more complicated; we cannot tell the difference between 5.0 and 5.EQL.X until we have encountered the character 0 or E.

Negative numbers such as −5 sometimes present a problem because they may appear anywhere, including after other operators; thus 5*−5 is perfectly legal and equal to 5*(−5) or −25. In fact, the minus sign may appear before any symbol or an expression in parentheses as a **unary operator,** which applies to only one symbol, in contrast to **binary operators,** which apply to two symbols. Care must be taken here that no composite operators end with −; or, if they do, some rule must be made to distinguish the unary minus, such as stipulating that it never occur after another operator except in parentheses. Thus 5*−5 will not in fact be legal, but 5*(−5) will be.

8-6 Syntax

The set of rules which determine how characters may be combined to form expressions, statements, etc., in a computer language is called the **syntax** of that language; the language itself consists of the symbols together with the syntax. This is in analogy with the idea of syntax in a natural language, according to which words can be combined to form phrases, clauses, and sentences.

The simplest forms of syntax are those in which each character has one well-defined use—letters for symbols, numbers for themselves, the symbols ($+ - * / =$) being used in the usual way, for instance. Syntax in computer languages, unfortunately, is almost never that simple. A single character may ordinarily be used in more than one way. We have seen several examples of this: numeric characters used in symbols and numbers; the period, used in floating point numbers and in operators; alphabetic characters, used in symbols and in operators; the asterisk, used to denote powers and multiplication. In each case, the algorithms which decode such expressions become more complicated if characters can have more than one meaning, since it must be possible to decide which meaning applies in a given situation. When the syntax of a new language is being designed, care should be taken that these algorithms can actually make these decisions—that is, that each expression can be constructed in only one way according to the syntactic rules. If this is not true, the language will be **ambiguous,** and cannot be completely analyzed by any computer program. (Several well-known computer languages actually have obscure ambiguities, or had them in proposed extensions which were later withdrawn.)

A simple example of ambiguity occurs with the use of the asterisk in an assembler to denote the current location. Thus

$$P5 \quad TR \quad *-6$$

is equivalent to

$$P5 \quad TR \quad P5-6$$

If the asterisk also denotes multiplication, there is still no ambiguity; $**5$ is the current location times 5, $***$ is the current location times itself, and even $********$ is the current location to the fifth power. The asterisk, however, cannot now be used to denote both multiplication (*) and powers (**). For we would then not know whether $******$ stood for

*		*		*		*		*		*		*
current location	times	current location	times	current location	times	current location

or

*		**		*		**		*
current location	to the power	current location	to the power	current location

There are thousands of other syntactic devices used in computer languages; all the others we have mentioned so far are unambiguous.

Parentheses present a unique problem in analyzing expressions. In an expression such as $A*(W-X+Y-Z)+B$, for instance, we do not know what to multiply A by until we have scanned all the way to the right parenthesis. The simplest solution, though not necessarily the fastest, is to treat an expression in parentheses as having a value, just like a symbol, and writing the expression analysis routine as a recursive subroutine. Such a routine will calculate the value of any expression in parentheses. If it encounters parentheses inside parentheses, it will call itself, calculating the value of the expression in the inner parentheses, and using it, just as it would use the value of any other symbol, to calculate the value of the expression in the outside parentheses. If the recursive subroutine is set up in this way, it will, however, assume that whatever expression it is asked to calculate is contained in at least one pair of parentheses, and steps must be taken to "fool" it in this regard. However, these steps are easy; we need only to insert one spurious left parenthesis at the beginning, and treat the end of the expression, however this is sensed, as if it were a right parenthesis.

Care must also be taken regarding blanks when syntax is being designed. Some languages ignore blanks altogether, but this produces ambiguities and "almost-ambiguities" very easily. For example, DO 5 I=1,7 is a valid statement in FORTRAN II; because blanks are ignored, it can be written as DO5I=1,17. The statement DO5I=1 is also legal; it sets a variable called DO5I to 1. There is no ambiguity here, but a difficulty in analyzing the expression; two syntactic constructions must be considered until the algorithm reaches the comma. A more reasonable rule is to demand blanks in some places, such as after the word DO, and forbid them elsewhere, such as between the letters of a symbol; but some assemblers, for the sake of faster processing, forbid blanks entirely in the variable field except preceding a symbol, and other assemblers do not admit even that exception.

8-7 Precedence

When an expression contains various operators, rules must be established as to the order in which the operations are performed. The easiest rule to implement is that in which operations are performed as they occur, from left to right; thus A+B−C*D/E is evaluated by taking A, adding B, subtracting C, multiplying by D, and dividing by E. This is not, however, the usual way in which such an expression is understood. In fact, A*B+C usually means (A*B)+C, but A+B*C usually means A+(B*C).

If we were to say in words how to evaluate such expressions, we would say, "Perform all the multiplications and divisions first, and then perform all the additions and subtractions." This does not need to be taken literally as a statement of what the computer does; the expression A*B+C*D+E*F, for example, would be interpreted as (A*B)+ (C*D)+(E*F), but it would probably be calculated, in our machine language, as

```
LD   A
FM   B
ST   T
LD   C
FM   D
FA   T
ST   T
LD   E
FM   F
FA   T
```

and the computer here does not perform all the multiply operations first. What we mean by the above statement is that two or more symbols connected by multiplication or division are to be *considered* as being combined into expressions which are then added or subtracted; we have marked this considering operation by the parentheses in (A*B)+ (C*D)+(E*F). We say that multiplication and division have a higher *precedence* than addition and subtraction.

Expressions may be evaluated under precedence rules by using a stack. Operations and operands are stored on the stack, and when each operation is found, a test is made to see whether there are any operations on the stack of equal or greater precedence. Any such operation is performed; the operation and its operands are removed from the stack and the result is placed on the stack. When there are no operations left of equal or greater precedence, the current operation is placed on the stack. The end of an expression is treated as an operation of the lowest precedence; then (for arithmetic operators) come + and −, followed by * and /, followed by the exponential operation if it is allowed. As an example, we list the actions performed by the evaluation routine on the expression A*B+C*D+E*F:

Symbol loaded	Action	Stack now contains
A	Placed on the stack	A
*	There are no operations on the stack at all, so this one is placed on the stack	*; A
B	Placed on the stack	B; *; A
+	The operation * is of higher precedence than +, so A*B is performed; A, *, and B are removed from the stack, and the result A*B is placed on the stack. The operator + is now placed on the stack	+; A*B
C	Placed on the stack	C; +; A*B
*	The operation + is of lower precedence than *, so the * is placed on the stack	*; C; +; A*B
D	Placed on the stack	D; *; C; +; A*B
+	The operation * is of higher precedence than +, so C*D is performed; C, *, and D are removed from the stack, and the result C*D is placed on the stack	C*D; +; A*B
	The operation + is of precedence equal to +, so (A*B)+ (C*D) is performed; A*B, +, and C*D are removed from the stack, and the result A*B+ C*D is placed on the stack	A*B+C*D
	The operator + is now placed on the stack	+; A*B+C*D

Symbol loaded	Action	Stack now contains
E	Placed on the stack	E; +; A*B+C*D
*	The operation + is of lower precedence than *, so the * is placed on the stack	*; E; +; A*B+C*D
F	Placed on the stack	F; *; E; +; A*B+C*D
End of expression	The operation * is of higher precedence than "end of expression," so E*F is performed; F, *, and E are removed from the stack, and the result E*F is placed on the stack	
	The operation + is of higher precedence than "end of expression," so (A*B+C*D)+(E*F) is performed; everything is removed from the stack, and the result A*B+C*D+E*F is placed on the stack	
	The operation "end of expression" is not placed on the stack; the result is now at the top of the stack	

Precedence also applies in logical operations. In an expression such as a ∧ b ∨ c ∧ d ∨ e ∧ f, the ∧ operations are considered by convention to be performed first, and then the ∨ operations. The question of whether arithmetic operations should precede logical operations is less clear, but experience suggests that they should. A language with precedence rules will express these by assigning to each operation an integer called its **precedence;** the collection of all the operators and their precedences is sometimes called the **operator hierarchy.**

8-8   Polish Notation

The general term **Polish notation** refers to the implications for computing of deep logical investigations into the properties of prefix, infix, and suffix notation made by the mathematician Łukasiewicz.

Operators in ordinary algebra are written in **infix notation,** which means that the operator is written between the two operands: A+B,

A*B, etc. There is also **prefix notation,** in which the operator is written first (+ A B) and **suffix notation,** in which the operator is written last (A B +). It was noted by Łukasiewicz that both prefix and suffix notation do away with both the major problems we have encountered: parentheses and precedence. For example, let us take the expression (A−B)−C; this would be expressed in suffix notation as (A B − C −), and the second minus sign has (A B −) and C as operands. The expression A−(B−C) would appear in suffix notation as (A B C − −); the second minus sign in this expression refers to the *first* minus sign in the original expression, which has as operands A and (B C −) or B−C. An expression under precedence rules is expressed in Polish notation by first inserting parentheses as dictated by the precedence rules, and then converting the resulting expression, which is independent of any precedence rules, to Polish notation. Thus, in the usual precedence rules for algebraic expressions, A*B+C becomes (A B * C +) in suffix notation, and A+B*C becomes (A B C * +). In prefix notation, A*B+C would be (+ * A B C), and A+B*C would be (+ A * B C).

   An algebraic expression can be converted to a string in suffix notation, called a **Polish string,** by a procedure which is not recursive, although it does use a stack. Operands are added directly to the Polish string. When an operator is read, any operators on the stack of equal or greater precedence are added to the Polish string in order; when there are none of these left, the operator is placed on the stack. The left parenthesis and the right parenthesis are treated as if they were operators with a precedence equal to "end of expression," except that no other action takes place when a left parenthesis is placed on the stack or removed from it, and parentheses are never added to the Polish string. Thus the stack contains only operators, not operands. As an example, we convert the expression A−(B+C*D)/E into its equivalent (A B C D * + E / −) in suffix notation:

Symbol loaded	Stack	String	Action
A	Void	A	Placed on the string
−	−	A	Placed on the stack
(	(, −	A	Placed on the stack (No other action takes place, even though the minus sign has higher precedence than the left parenthesis.)

Symbol loaded	Stack	String	Action
B	(, −	A B	Placed on the string
+	+, (, −	A B	Placed on the stack (Note that only the operator at the *top* of the stack is checked for precedence; thus no action takes place here, even though there is a − on the stack.)
C	+, (, −	A B C	Placed on the string
*	*, +, (, −	A B C	Placed on the stack (No other action takes place because + has a lower precedence than *.)
D	*, +, (, −	A B C D	Placed on the string
)	−	A B C D * +	The operators * and + are placed on the string from the stack in that order; the (is removed from the stack, since its precedence is equal to that of), but neither (nor) are placed on the string. The minus sign is not placed on the string, since its precedence is greater than)
/	/, −	A B C D * +	Placed on the stack (No other action takes place because − has a lower precedence than /.)
E	/, −	A B C D * + E	Placed on the string
End of expression	Void	A B C D * + E / −	The operators / and − are placed on the string from the stack in that order

The suffix string, or Polish string, which we have produced can now be evaluated using a separate routine in which the operands, rather than the operators, are placed on a stack. Each time an operator is encountered, two operands are taken off the stack, the operation is performed, and the result goes back on the stack. We illustrate this process as applied to the result of the preceding algorithm, (A B C D * + E / −):

Symbol loaded	Stack	Action
A	A	Placed on the stack
B	B, A	Placed on the stack
C	C, B, A	Placed on the stack
D	D, C, B, A	Placed on the stack
*	C*D, B, A	C and D are taken off the stack, multiplied, and
+	B+C*D, A	the result placed on the stack
		B and C*D are taken off the stack, added, and
E	E, B+C*D, A	the result placed on the stack
		Placed on the stack
/	(B+C*D)/E, A	E and B+C*D are taken off the stack, divided, and the result placed on the stack
−	A−(B+C*D)/E	A and (B+C*D)/E are taken off the stack, subtracted, and the result placed on the stack

The result of the entire calculation is now at the head of the stack.

Prefix and suffix notation are sometimes referred to as **forward** and **reverse** or **right-hand** and **left-hand** Polish notation respectively. Reverse Polish notation is the easier to work with; forward Polish notation, however, can be produced by scanning the characters of an algebraic expression backward instead of forward. Both types of Polish notation have a peculiarity when expressed as strings: symbols may occur next to each other, which is impossible in infix notation. The symbols in our example consisted of single characters, and so no confusion arose, but when a symbol may consist of more than one character, a separation character is needed. Thus the string (NA NB +) might be written as NA.NB+ , with the period as separation character; otherwise, it could be confused with (N ANB +). Note that the two processes described above can be combined into one process using co-routines; this process will then use two stacks, one for operators and the other for operands.

8-9   Recognizers

The use of Polish notation allows us to treat both parentheses and precedence rules without the explicit use of recursion. On the other hand, recursion may be explicitly used, not only for parenthesized expressions, as we have seen, but also to decode expressions under precedence rules. Recursive routines written in this connection are called **recognizers.**

A recognizer scheme is set up by defining various kinds of expressions, each of which is built up from the others by a particular type or types of operator. Corresponding to each of these kinds of expressions, there is a recursive routine which *recognizes* it and calculates its value or generates code. For example, using the standard precedence rules for arithmetic expressions, and using only the operators +, −, *, and /, we might define:

(1) A *term* as either a symbol or another term times or divided by a symbol.

(2) An *expression* as either a term or another expression plus or minus a term.

(3) A *symbol* as either a character string of a specified type (for example, either an alphabetic character or another symbol concatenated with an alphanumeric character) or an expression enclosed in parentheses.

This form of recursive definition is very common in formal descriptions of languages. Its consequences in this case are as follows. The symbol X is a term; X*Y is a term, since it is a term (X) times a symbol (Y); X*Y/Z is a term, since it is a term (X*Y) divided by a symbol (Z); and, in general, any character string consisting of symbols connected by * or / is a term, such as

```
A1*A4/X
A*B*C*D*E*F*G*H
TOTAL/DEDNSP
```

The symbol X, being a term, is also an expression; X+Y is an expression, since it is an expression (X) plus a term (Y); X+Y−Z is an expression, since it is an expression (X+Y) minus a term (Z); and, in general, any of the terms given in the example above, is converted to an expression by replacing * and / by + or −. However, more general kinds of expressions are constructed by using such terms in the definition of expression. Thus A*B+C*D is an expression, because it is an expression (A*B) plus a term (C*D); furthermore, the definitions imply that A*B+C*D is interpreted as (A*B)+(C*D), just as the precedence rules would. Similarly A*B+C*D+E*F is an expression (A*B+C*D) plus a term (E*F). In general, any character string consisting of symbols connected by +, −, *, and / is an expression, such as

$$A+B-C*D/E+F$$
$$W*Y+W*Z+X*Y+X*Z$$
$$P-Q$$

The general definition of a symbol, in which parenthesized expressions are used as symbols, now allows us to admit arbitrary parenthesized expressions. For example, $(W+X)*(Y+Z)$ is a term, since $W+X$ and $Y+Z$ are both expressions and therefore $(W+X)$ and $(Y+Z)$ are both symbols. Since $(W+X)$ is a symbol, it is also a term, and thus $(W+X)*(Y+Z)$ consists of a term times a symbol; therefore, it is a term (and thus an expression as well). Nested parentheses, of course, are also permitted; $((W+X)*(Y-Z))$, for example, is a symbol by definition, and therefore both a term and an expression. In general, any algebraic expression in the usual sense (excluding only numbers and functions) is an expression by these definitions.

The recognizers are surprisingly short. We entitle them RT, RE, and RS (for "recognize term," "recognize expression," and "recognize symbol"); each routine returns two parameters, the first of which is the value of the expression, and the second of which is the character which immediately follows the term, expression, or symbol.

A. RT(X, Y) (Recognize term with value X, terminated by character Y)
    1. Call RS(X1, Y1).
    2. If Y1 is *, go to step 5.
    3. If Y1 is /, go to step 8.
    4. Set X=X1, Y=Y1, and return.
    5. Call RS(X2, Y1).
    6. Set X1 = X1*X2.
    7. Go to step 2.
    8. Call RS(X2, Y1).
    9. Set X1 = X1/X2.
  10. Go to step 2.

B. RE(X, Y) (Recognize expression with value X, terminated by character Y)
    1. Call RT(X1, Y1).
    2. If Y1 is +, go to step 5.
    3. If Y1 is −, go to step 8.
    4. Set X=X1, Y=Y1, and return.
    5. Call RT(X2, Y1).
    6. Set X1 = X1+X2.
    7. Go to step 2.

8. Call RT(X2, Y1).

9. Set X1 = X1−X2.

10. Go to step 2.

C. RS(X, Y) (Recognize symbol with value X, terminated by character Y)

1. Set CC (the character count) equal to zero.

2. Set Y equal to the next character.

3. If Y is not alphanumeric, go to step 7 (also if CC = 0 and Y is not alphabetic).

4. Set CC = CC+1. (Optional: If CC is greater than the maximum length for a symbol, there has been an error.)

5. Store Y as character CC of the symbol.

6. Go to step 2.

7. If Y is a left parenthesis, go to step 9.

8. Look up the value of the symbol (with given length CC and given stored characters), set X equal to this value, and return.

9. If CC ≠ 0, there has been an error.

10. Call RE(X, Y1).

11. If Y1 is not a right parenthesis, there has been an error.

12. Set Y equal to the next character after the right parenthesis, and return.

We have, of course, presented the recognizers in the particular form in which they are used to calculate a value. Generation of code requires a different form of recognizer.

PROBLEMS

1. (a) A computer has 40 bits per word and 8 bits per character. The bits in the word are numbered from 1 at the left to 40 at the right. A character string starts in bits 17 through 24 of cell 17752, and is 24 characters long. Which bits of which cell contain the last character of this string?

(b) A computer has 42 bits per word and 6 bits per character. The bits in the word are numbered from 41 at the left to 0 at the right. A character string starts in bits 35–30 of cell 00773 and ends in bits 17–12 of cell 00776. How many characters does it contain?

(c) A computer has 25 bits per word and 5 bits per character. The bits in the word are numbered from 25 at the left to 1 at the right. A character string starts in bits 5–1 of cell 01634 and ends in bits 15–11 of cell 01636. This character string is moved to a new location so that it now starts in bits 20–16 of cell 10000. Where is the last character of the string located now?

(d) A computer has 35 bits per word and 7 bits per character. The bits in the word are numbered from 0 at the left to 34 at the right. The character string IMPROPER STATEMENT is contained in memory in such a way that the first character occupies positions 0–6 of cell 40235. What bits of what cell does the last character occupy?

2. Suppose that a given computer has all of the arithmetic instructions (add, subtract, multiply, and divide) in fixed and floating point, but no shift instructions, and no masking (or logical) instructions. Describe how a subroutine might be written which extracts a field from a word which extends from bit m at the left to bit n at the right, where both m and n are parameters to the subroutine.

3. Given the following three patterns:

> _____ LIKE _____ BUT NOT _____.
> _____ WENT TO _____.
> A _____ AND A _____.

Which of these patterns do the following character strings match? (Some strings may match more than one pattern.)

(a) I LIKE TO EAT STEAK BUT NOT EVERY DAY.

(b) A BOY AND A GIRL WENT TO SCHOOL.

(c) LIKE AN OLD CAMEL HE WENT TO WORK BUT NOT CHEERFULLY.

4. If a pattern matches a part of a character string, the pattern is said to match the string in "unanchored mode." Thus the pattern

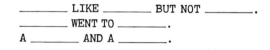

> YOU _____ BEANS _____ PEAS

matches the string IF YOU LIKE BEANS AND PEAS THEN COME TO DINNER in unanchored mode. To "anchor" a pattern matching process on the left (or on the right) means to insist that the left-hand (right-hand) end of the pattern corresponds to the left-hand (right-hand) end of the character string. Pattern matching routines are often written in such a way that the unanchored mode is normal, because most pattern matching in practice does not require matching of the entire character string. However, there is an argument against this, which is given by the answers to questions (b) and (c) below.

(a) For what general class of patterns does it make no difference whether matching is performed in unanchored mode, or anchored on both the left and the right?

(b) Suppose that it is normal for matching to be anchored on both the left and the right, in a given matching routine. Can unanchored matching be performed directly? Why or why not?

(c) Suppose that it is normal for matching to be unanchored, in a given matching routine. Can anchored matching be performed directly? Why or why not?

For the following strings, matching is to be performed against the three patterns of problem 3 above, in unanchored mode.

(d) WE WENT TO A MOVIE AND A PLAY.

(e) I WOULD LIKE A KNIFE AND A FORK BUT NOT A SPOON.

5. Character strings may be kept as lists. A character string of length n is treated as a simple list of n characters. If a second character string is now given as a list, these strings may be compared for equality in the same way that two simple lists are compared for equality; this process takes n steps. Now suppose that we are given k strings, each of length n, and we are to determine whether a given string matches any of them. If the given strings are simply compared one after the other (linear search), the process will take kn steps, or $kn/2$ if the list of strings is sorted. A special type of list structure may be formed, in such a way that one may tell whether the given string matches any of the k given strings in at most cn steps, where c is the number of bits per character. Describe this structure. (Hint: Suppose that some of the strings to be searched all begin with the same letter. To be specific, suppose that $n = 4$ and that ABFR, ALBR, AMAV, AMUN, and AXAA are among the strings to be searched. Then the list structure might contain the single letter A on a list with initial letters of other strings; associated with this letter might be a substructure representing the strings BFR, LBR, MAV, MUN, and XAA. This substructure would then have the same basic form as the main structure. Such a list structure is called a *search structure* for the given set of strings.)

6. Consider the following definitions:

An *alphabetic character* is A, B, C, D, E, F, G, H, I, J, K, L, M, N, O, P, Q, R, S, T, U, V, W, X, Y, or Z.

A *numeric character* is 0, 1, 2, 3, 4, 5, 6, 7, 8, or 9.

An *alphameric character* is an alphabetic character, a numeric character, $, or '.

A *symbol* is either an alphabetic character, or a symbol followed by an alphameric character.

Which of the following are symbols under this definition?

(a) 7
(b) S
(c) S6
(d) SR
(e) ABCDEFGHIJKLMNOPQRSTUVWXYZ0123456789
(f) $15
(g) $15.00
(h) TAX'RATE

7. Consider the following definitions, some of which refer to those made in problem 6 above:

A *symbol* is either an alphabetic character, or a symbol followed by a numeric character.

An *SLWP* is either a symbol, or an SLWP followed by a blank character followed by a symbol. (The letters SLWP stand for "simple list without parentheses.")

A *simple list* is a left parenthesis, followed by an SLWP, followed by a right parenthesis.

An *LWP* is either a symbol, or a simple list, or an LWP followed by a blank followed by a symbol, or an LWP followed by a blank followed by a simple list. (The letters LWP stand for "list without parentheses.")

A *list* is a left parenthesis, followed by an LWP, followed by a right parenthesis.

For each object given below, write "symbol," "SLWP," "simple list," "LWP," or "list," depending on the type of the object. Some objects may be of more than one type, or of none of these types.

(a) C21A

(b) G H J K L

(c) (G H J K L)

(d) (F1296 G4637 (H2094 (I9787 J3354) K6577))

(e) M12 P14 (C17 J18) X91

8. Recursive definitions of objects in languages such as the definitions of symbols, simple lists, etc., given in the preceding example, may be written in a symbolic notation known as BNF, which stands for Backus Normal Form or Backus-Naur Form, after John Backus and Peter Naur. Thus we might write the definition of symbol in problem 6 above as

$$<\text{symbol}> : := <\text{alpha-char}> \mid <\text{symbol}> <\text{num-char}>$$

This example illustrates the rules of BNF: objects are enclosed in angle-brackets $< >$; an object is defined by placing it to the left of the $: :=$ sign, and these definitions may be recursive, i.e., the object may appear in its own definition; if an object has several alternative definitions, these are separated by vertical lines $\mid$; if the definition of an object consists of the concatenation of several other objects, these objects are simply written one after the other without any intervening symbol or separated by a blank.

Rewrite all the definitions of the preceding two problems in BNF.

9. Suppose that the precedence of multiplication were *lower* than that of addition, rather than higher. Suppose also that subtraction has the same precedence as addition, and division has the same precedence as multiplication. What would then be the value of the expression

$$1 + 5 * 8 * 3 + 2 + 6 - 8 + 5 - 4 - 3 / 3 * 9$$

and how would it be derived?

Chapter 9

PROGRAMMING SYSTEMS

9-1 Types of Systems

Much of the work done by programmers consists, not in writing new programs, but in making modifications to existing programs. This is particularly true in the case of very large programs, which are continuously being enlarged and extended, and in which new errors are continuously being found and removed. Such programs are often called **programming systems.** The phrase "programming system" is quite loose; it has been applied indiscriminately to almost every large program, but should properly be applied to programs which admit a wide variety of *types* of input, rather than simply a very large input file. In addition, a program which, with its subroutines, takes up the entire time of any computer is properly called a programming system; included in such systems are the **monitor systems** or **executive systems** which control the order in which programs are run and provide for uninterrupted transition between one program and another. (The phrase "programming systems" is sometimes also used in a stricter sense, including *only* monitor or executive systems.)

There are several types of executive systems. In the simplest type of executive system, sometimes called a **batch-processing monitor,** the input card decks of several programs are collected in a batch and run through the card reader together. When one program terminates, control returns to the monitor, which transfers control to the next program. More complex monitors have a priority system; all runs are input and stored on drum or disk, and jobs are then read from the disk and run according to their priority and the amount of time they have waited. A **multiprocessing executive system** directs programs to be run either more than one at a time, on a computer with more than one processing unit, or on a shared basis—part of one program running first, then part of the next program, and so on. An **interactive monitor system** communicates between a computer and several typewriters, Teletypes, or other hand-operated input-output devices; an example of this type of system is an airline reservation system, in which reservation clerks in various cities have their own keyboards. A **time-sharing system** is a special type of interactive system in which each user at a typewriter or Teletype may direct his own programs, of whatever description, to be run; these programs are run on a shared basis as in a multiprocessing system.

Another type of programming system is the **language processor.** An assembler and an algebraic compiler are language processors. The phrase "language processor" has also been used very loosely; almost all programming systems have been called language processors at one time or another, since the input specifications of any routine may be called an input language. Among these are the processors for general-purpose programming languages: assemblers for machine languages, algebraic compilers for algebraic languages, business compilers for business languages, list processing systems, character string processing systems, and a great variety of hybrids of these. There are also other general-purpose languages, many of which are designed to help in formulating an arbitrary problem in a specific field. Thus there are general-purpose languages for simulation, for circuit design, for sorting, for symbolic algebraic manipulation, and so on. Each of these languages has its own processor, and sometimes several processors.

A programming system may have characteristics of both a monitor and a language processor. This is particularly true at a computer installation having a standard language, so that all programs (or at least all programs run between certain hours) must be written in that language. The language processor may then also serve as a monitor system; if the language processor remains in core while the programs which it processes are being run, it may remain in core at all times. An **operating system** is a collection of programming systems; it normally contains a monitor system and one or more language processors which are controlled by that monitor system.

Many programming systems perform file processing. Each complete file process with input and output files is known as a **pass,** and each programming system which processes files may be referred to as a **one-pass, two-pass,** etc., system. A two-pass assembler reads the source file on the first pass and builds a symbol table; then it reads the source file again on the second pass and, using the symbol table, constructs object code, which may be listed and/or punched as an object deck. A one-pass assembler or algebraic compiler usually produces its output in core, so that further operations, which otherwise would be done in a second or third pass, become loops over data in core. Such a processor will have a very stringent limit on the size of the object program it can produce. More powerful algebraic compilers have a large number of passes; the FORTRAN IV compiler for the UNIVAC 1107, for example, has six passes.

9-2 Computer Simulation

When a computer manufacturer introduces a new computer, a large collection of programs for it must be made available. Among these will be an assembler, one or more compilers, an executive system, and a library of subroutines for mathematical functions and input-output. Checking out these programs takes a large amount of time, and, if done on the new computer, delays the date on which it is usable. Therefore, such programs are very often checked out by *simulating* the new computer on an existing computer. Simulation of one computer by another is accomplished with a **simulation program.** The computer being simulated is called the **source computer;** the computer on which the simulation is actually run is called the **object computer.**

If the source computer and the object computer have the same word length, the program to be simulated, including instructions, data, and reserved areas, may be loaded directly into the memory of the object computer. The simulation program is also loaded. Simulation proceeds by executing each instruction word in turn, according to the operation code format of the source computer. An instruction word is loaded and unpacked; that is, each of its fields is placed in a separate memory word. We have already seen how to do this for character codes by shifting; the same procedure works even if the fields are of different lengths. For example, if the instruction word format specifies an operation code field of 9 bits, an A-field of 4 bits, an I-field of 1 bit, a B-field of 4 bits, and an address field of 18 bits, then these fields may be placed in the cells COC, CA, CI, CB, and CADDR in our machine language (assuming a 36-bit word) by the instructions

```
LQ    INSWD
LD    LO
LDL   9
ST    COC
LD    LO
LDL   4
ST    CA
LD    LO
```

```
LDL    1
ST     CI
LD     LO
LDL    4
ST     CB
LD     LO
LDL    18
ST     CADDR
```

where INSWD contains the 36-bit source computer instruction word and LO contains zero.

The effective address of the instruction word is now calculated. If the index and indirect address fields are both zero, the effective address is contained in the address field. If the index field is non-zero, the current contents of the given index register are added to the address field. The index registers of the source computer are represented by special memory cells within the simulation routine; the same is true, in fact, for any other source computer registers. If indirect addressing is specified, the contents of the word whose address is given in the address field are used as an address. For some source computers, the index and indirect address fields of this word must again be tested, so that more than one level of indirect addressing is possible. The section of the simulation routine which calculates an effective address will follow the effective address algorithm of the source computer.

Finally, the operation code is looked up in a table of operation codes and the corresponding operation performed. If the operation code field is small, there may be an array of transfers, one for each possible value of the operation code field; some of these may transfer to a section of code which prints the fact that an improper operation code has occurred. For a large operation code field, with relatively few of the possible operation codes actually used, there will be a sorted table of operation codes which may be binary-searched for the given code.

The operation which is performed must follow precisely the execution rules for the source computer. If the instruction loads a register, the memory cell involved is moved to the special memory cell representing that register. If the instruction stores a register, the reverse process takes place. Arithmetic operations such as addition and subtraction must be performed according to the integer representation (signed-magnitude, one's complement, or two's complement) of the *source* computer, rather than the object computer. For example, if the source computer has a signed-magnitude representation and the object computer does not, the simulation program checks whether the signs are alike and adds or subtracts accordingly. After each operation which is not a transfer, the "location counter," i.e., the cell in the simulation routine containing the address of the instruction currently being interpreted, is incremented by one. For a transfer, the effective address is stored in this cell. For a skip instruction, this cell is incremented by one or by two, depending upon the condition involved. Condition tests must also take into account the integer representation of the source computer. If the source computer has a signed-magnitude representation and the object computer has a one's or two's complement representation, or vice versa, then one negative number will be larger than another negative number on the object computer if and only if it is smaller than the other on the source computer.

There are many variations on the process of computer simulation. If the source computer has a smaller word length than the object computer, then each object computer word contains a source computer word either left justified or right justified. If the word length in the source computer is larger, direct correspondence of addresses becomes impossible and an address coding scheme becomes necessary. This means that the word in address a in the source computer actually appears at address $f(a)$ in the object computer, where f is a function appearing in the simulator (for example, to determine what word or words in the object computer are affected when a source computer instruction specifies a given effective address). If the source computer is binary and the object computer is decimal, or vice versa, a coding scheme must be used for the instruction and data words themselves. Input-output instructions are rarely simulated and usually cannot be, because they depend on the timing of the various input-output devices; instead, an entire input-output *subroutine* will be simulated, that is, its function will be performed by a subroutine for the object computer.

9-3   Interpretive Routines

An **interpretive routine** is a routine whose operation is similar to that of the computer itself. That is, it has its own instruction word format and its own location counter, which is kept in memory or in a register. The instruction word to which the location counter points is *interpreted* by the routine; that is, it is decomposed into fields, one of which is an "operation code" directing the interpreter to one of several open or closed subroutines. One of the fields is also usually an address field; that is, each operation is specified to act on some data word.

Routines for computer simulation are interpretive routines; the instruction word format in this case is the actual hardware format of some other machine. Another type of interpretive routine is the *interpretive out-*

put editing routine. This is most commonly used for the production by the computer of output to be printed. A typical printer produces 120 characters per line; these 120 characters must be in some array in memory in packed character-code format. This is not the format in which they are used in calculations; therefore, conversion routines must be written to form such character codes in one of several formats: decimal, octal, character string, instruction word, or floating point. There are two standard methods of converting a floating point number to a character string, namely, with the exponent or without it; the number 3000 might appear as 3000.000 in one format and .30000000E+04 in the other. When an interpretive output editing routine is used, there is an operation code which either specifies the type of conversion or signifies that the given line is ready to be output on the printer or a specified tape unit; there is an address field which specifies the data to be output; and there is a *print position field,* specifying the number (from 1 through 120, in this case) of the print position at which the data is to be aligned.

An excellent example of an interpretive output routine is DOUT, a standard routine for the IBM 700 series. The instruction word of this routine is a 36-bit word, with prefix (3 bits), decrement (15 bits), tag (3 bits), and address (15 bits), just as in the Type A instruction format of these machines. The address is the address of the data to be output. The print position is given in the decrement. The prefix specifies the operation code and may have any of seven values: decimal, octal, character codes, floating point with exponent, floating point without exponent, output this line, and termination.

An expanded version of this routine, which illustrates some of the other possibilities in interpretation, is available for the UNIVAC 1107 and 1108, and known as EOUT. The instruction word of this routine is a 36-bit word, with fields known as F (5 bits), T (7 bits), D (6 bits), Index (1 bit), Indirect Address (1 bit), and Address (16 bits). The print position is given in the T field; the address is given in the Address field. Any address will be indirect if the Indirect Address field is equal to 1. An internal "index register" is kept, which may be loaded by an interpretive instruction; the contents of this register are added to any address if the Index field of the corresponding instruction contains 1. The function code field F contains functions for decimal, octal, and binary conversion, floating point conversion with or without exponent, character code conversion by characters or by words, scale factors, binary points for fixed point numbers, arbitrary fields of words, output to one of various devices, and termination. There is also an interpretive transfer, whose address is taken as the next interpretive word, and an interpretive subroutine call and return. The D field has various meanings, depending upon the function code; for the octal conversion it gives the number of octal digits, for the character code conversions the number of characters or words, and for the output function a code for the output device.

The interpretive words in an output editing routine occur in an *array,* and are interpreted in sequence, except for an interpretive transfer in any form. Similarly, the interpretive words in a simulation routine are interpreted sequentially except for the transfers and conditional transfers. It is also possible for interpretive words to be in the form of a *list,* or a *list structure.* This is especially common in interpretive routines for list processing. Since such a routine will have a list space, this list space may contain not only lists of data, but also lists of interpretive words. The order in which such a list structure is interpreted is roughly the same as the order in which its elements occur in the S-expression for that list structure.

> The IPL-V list processing language for the IBM 700 series has an instruction word containing a P field (3 bits), a Q field (3 bits), a SYMB field (15 bits), and a LINK field (15 bits). The LINK is the address of the next interpretive word, so that interpretive words are normally kept in lists. The SYMB field usually denotes the list function to be performed, but it may, depending on the P and Q field contents, denote the start address of a new list of interpretive words. List structures of interpretive words may thus be built up.
>
> The LISP 1.5 list processing language for the IBM 700 series has an instruction word containing an address field (15 bits), a decrement field (15 bits), and a sign field (1 bit). The other bits in the word are not used, and the sign field is used only during garbage collection. The LISP interpreter determines whether the decrement field points to an element of a list, or to a sublist, by checking whether the contents of this field specifies a location within the list space. If it does not, it points to an item containing a name, which may be the name of a function to be performed. The address field always contains the address of the next interpretive word, so that interpretive words are normally kept in list structures.

It is now easy to understand why the large programs available on most computers are known collectively and informally as "software." A program consisting of instruction words to be executed in an indicated order may be so executed in two ways. A computer may be built which uses the format of the given instruction words as its instruction word format; this computer may then execute the given program directly. Or the instruction words may be loaded into *any* computer, and a program written which executes the given program interpretively. In the first case, the program is executed by the **hardware;** in the second case, it is executed by the **software.** Double precision on the UNIVAC 1108 is handled by the hardware; that is, this computer actually has double precision instructions. The instruction word format and instruction *repertoire* of the UNIVAC 1107 is the same as that of the 1108 in most respects, but here double precision is handled by the software; the instruction code for an 1108 double precision instruction causes the 1107 to call a subroutine (by performing an interrupt), and this subroutine performs the given double precision operation. Likewise, floating point operations on the SDS 930 are performed by the software.

9-4   Interpretation of Character Strings

There are several programming systems which scan a character string and interpret it. That is, certain characters or symbols are taken as "function codes," and these direct the program to take one of various actions. As an example, we take the FORTRAN format scan routine.

A format statement in FORTRAN is a character string, such as

$$(E10.4,2X,F9.6,5H \text{ AND } I5)$$

When a FORTRAN program is compiled, each format is placed in the object program as a character string. Each READ or WRITE statement corresponds, in the object program, to one or more calls to a subroutine which converts the data given in the READ or WRITE according to the given format. The conversion routines are essentially the same as in an interpretive output editing routine; but the interpretation is different. Interpretation in this case starts by extracting a one-letter function code, which may be E, F, I, X, H, and sometimes others. There are three ways to interpret such a function code:

(1) If there are only a few possible functions, a separate test may be made for each one. Thus if there are seven letters corresponding to function codes, then interpreting the function code requires a maximum of seven tests, or 14 steps.

(2) If there are a large number of possible functions, these may be kept, sorted, in a table. A binary search of this table now interprets the function code.

(3) If almost every possible character code corresponds to a function, a table of 2^n routine addresses (for an n-bit character code) may be formed. The character code is added to the first address of the table and the result is used as a transfer address. The address of an error routine is kept in each position in this table that does not correspond to a function. Methods such as this are often called **table lookup,** as opposed to calculation.

The routine for each function specifies further interpretation. Thus in this case the I format requires one integer; the E and F formats require two integers separated by a period. An integer, of course, may consist of more than one character. Whenever a given numeric character is followed by another, the current integer is multiplied by 10 and the integer given by the new character added. This process continues until a character is scanned which is not numeric—a comma, or a period, in this case. An integer may also precede the function code; thus we may have 2I4 or 3E12.6 or 7H ERROR . This means that a variable must be kept which is used as a count; this variable is set to 1 before the function code scan, and if the character in the function code position is numeric, an integer is extracted and the count variable is set to this integer.

The characters which are interpreted do not need to be all in core at once. They may consist of card images, for example, which are read from an input file; the interpreter is then known as an **input interpreter.** The first pass of any compiler is an input interpreter; it has separate actions for each statement type. Both passes of a two-pass assembler interpret the operation code and go to various open or closed subroutines depending on the code. As before, the routine for each operation code specifies further interpretation. For example, the variable field of an EQU instruction cannot contain a **forward reference**—i.e., a symbol which is defined later in the program being assembled. The subroutine which treats the operation code EQU must check for this possibility and flag it as an error if it occurs. Again, most operation codes correspond to a single instruction word, and the location counter variable, which specifies the current address, will be incremented after the instruction word is formed so that it points to the next instruction word position. But this is not the case for ORG or EQU, where it is not incremented at all; for reserving a block of storage (RE in our machine language), where it is incremented by the size of the block; or for a macro, where it is incremented possibly several times, once for each instruction word in the macro.

An **algebraic interpreter** also acts on character strings. This is a program which scans an algebraic statement, and then actually performs the indicated operation. An algebraic statement consists of a variable, a separator (such as =) and an algebraic expression. A search is made for the variable; if it is not in the table, it is placed in the table and a data word is reserved for it. The algebraic expression is now analyzed as in the preceding chapter, and its value is stored in the data word corresponding to the given variable. A subroutine along these lines is contained in most assemblers, for analyzing the variable field; the assembler may then fill the address field of the current instruction word with the value of the expression in this field.

9-5 Compilation

The computer time used by an interpreter may be divided into *interpretation* and *execution*. Total interpretation may take as long as, or longer than, total execution. In a **compiler,** on the other hand, the statements and subroutines to be executed are collected, or **compiled,** into an object program. The computer time used by a compiler may thus be divided into *interpretation* and **code generation,** or the formation of object code including instruction and data words; execution of the object program takes place at a later time.

If the source program contains no transfer statements, an algebraic interpreter is faster than an algebraic compiler. In this case, there is no need to collect the executable statements into an object program. However, most programs contain transfers, either in actual transfer statements or implied, as in iteration statements. It takes much less time to compile and execute a loop than it takes to interpret it and execute it. If a loop is compiled, each statement is interpreted only once; if it is interpreted, each statement is interpreted each time it is executed. It is chiefly for this reason that algebraic compilers are much more commonly used than algebraic interpreters. In interactive systems, such as time-sharing systems, it is useful to have an algebraic interpreter to check out programs in algebraic language that are later to be compiled.

There are two bases of comparison of algebraic compilers for the same language: **compilation time** and **execution time.** One compiler may run faster than another, but may produce poorer quality object code—that is, execution time is slower, whereas compilation time is faster. Which compiler is better for a given application depends on what percentage of the computer's total time is being used for compilation as compared with execution. Some algebraic compilers produce assembly language code as output, and this code must then be assembled; other algebraic compilers produce object code directly, giving a large improvement in compilation time. If assembly code is produced, it may be listed, allowing the algebraic language programmer to "see" his object program; for this reason, the best compilers produce both assembly code and object code simultaneously or in successive passes. The fact that the object code of a compiler is of the same format as the object code of some assembler is also an argument in its favor. Some compilers do not have this feature, and "exist only unto themselves," as it were—a user of such a compiler must write his entire program in the language of this particular compiler, a distinct lack of flexibility.

There are a great many different types of compilers besides the algebraic compilers. The object program is usually produced on a file, such as an object deck on a punched-card file, but it may simply be produced in core ready for execution; a compiler which operates in this way is called an **in-core compiler.** The object code consists of closed and open subroutines. Compilation is at its greatest advantage, compared with interpretation, when as many as possible of the subroutines are open. In an algebraic compiler the statement A = B may be compiled into two instruction words, one to load a register with B and the other to store it in A. In a list processing compiler, on the other hand, where B is an entire list structure that is to be copied into A, a statement corresponding to A = B may require a closed subroutine with A and B as parameters. Even in an algebraic compiler, closed subroutines are often used for such features as double precision or complex arithmetic.

9-6 Packages

A very few compilers produce calls to closed subroutines exclusively. If a programming system involves no open subroutines, a better way to implement it is to dispense with a compiler (or interpreter) altogether and design the system as a collection of subroutines for some special purpose. Such a collection is called a **package.**

The SLIP (Symmetric List Processor) system, which manipulates two-way lists, is an example of a package. Each function or operation which can be performed on a two-way list is coded as a subroutine, which may be called from a FORTRAN program. For example, NEWTOP(P, Q) inserts P at the top of list Q; NEWBOT(P, Q) inserts P at the bottom of list Q; NXTLFT(P, A) inserts P in a list, just at the left of the item whose address is A; and NXTRGT(P, A) inserts P in a list, just at the right of this item. In these subroutines, P may itself represent a list, so that sublists may be put on lists and list structures may be created. Pointers may be advanced right or left, or down (onto a sublist) or up (from a sublist), using other subroutines in the package. Each pointer is normally part of an item, called a "reader," which contains the name of a list, a pointer to an item on that list or some sublist (to any level), and the value of the level. Thus the reader R may be advanced to the right by ADVLWR(R, F) and to the left by ADVLWL(R, F); in either case F is a flag which is set non-zero if and only if the list reached the end. Every element of a two-way list in SLIP is either a name or not; there are other advance operations which keep advancing until a name is reached (ADVLNR(R, F), ADVLNL(R, F)) or until an element which is not a name is reached (ADVLER(R, F), ADVLEL(R, F)). The subroutine NULSTL(A, L) splits the list L into two parts at the point A by removing A and all elements to its left from L; the subroutine NULSTR(A, L) removes A and all elements to its right from L to create a new list. The function INITAS(SPACE, N) initializes the list of available space, assumed to have size N.

There are many other subroutines in the SLIP package. There are also certain FORTRAN functions, which return a value. Thus NAMTST(K) is zero if and only if K is a name; LSTEQL(LA, LB) is zero if and only if the list structures LA and LB are the same; LCNTR(R) is the subroutine level counter of the reader R; LOFRDR(R) is the list

name in the reader R; LSSCPY(L) is the name of a new list, formed by
the LSSCPY function (acting as a subroutine) as a copy of the list L.

Being able to write programs using subroutines and functions from
a package carries with it both an advantage and a disadvantage. On one
hand, any program which uses such subroutines can also contain any
other desired logic. Many special-purpose languages contain algebraic
features, but these features are normally not as extensive as those of an
algebraic language; especially if the object code of the special-purpose
language is not compatible, a user of it will be restricted in what else he
can do at the same time as he is using the features of that language. On
the other hand, special-purpose languages are often easier to learn and
use than general-purpose algebraic languages; everyone who uses the
SLIP language must already be a programmer, whereas this is not always
true with other special-purpose languages.

A package is, of course, much easier to write than an interpreter or
a compiler. In fact, any interpreter contains a package internally, and
the closed subroutines called by the object code of a compiler must be
coded as a package along with the compiler. For this reason, packages are
ideally suited to small scale computing efforts. They are also at an advantage when each subroutine is relatively long and has few parameters,
or when the computer being used has a small amount of memory.

Both the advantages of fast object code and simplicity of package
construction are provided by a **macro package.** Instead of a collection of
subroutines, we have a collection of macros for an assembler. However,
this scheme has two disadvantages: we must write our programs in assembly language, rather than an algebraic language; and, in all but the most
powerful assemblers, there is no efficient macro library facility, so that if
more than one assembly is involved, the entire macro package must be
included at the beginning of every assembly.

9-7   Code Generation

Object program generation, or **code generation,** from algebraic expressions, is performed in algebraic compilers. Instead of *performing* instructions on data to obtain a value, the compiler *inserts* these instructions
into an object program. For example, the algebraic expression

$$((A*B)-C+(D*E)) * ((W*X)+(Y*Z))$$

will be translated, in our machine language, into

```
LD    A
FM    B
```

```
FS    C
ST    TEMP1
LD    D
FM    E
FA    TEMP1
ST    TEMP1
LD    W
FM    X
ST    TEMP2
LD    Y
FM    Z
FA    TEMP2
FM    TEMP1
```

for floating point data. A code generator which handles both floating and fixed point data must have access to the data-type information for each variable. Sometimes it may have to compile object code to add a fixed point number and a floating point number. In this case, code must be generated to convert the fixed point number to floating point or vice versa. The same is true for other data types—double precision numbers, complex numbers, character strings, etc. The simpler algebraic compilers avoid the problem by specifying, in the corresponding algebraic language, that **mixed mode expressions**—such as $A+N$ where A is floating and N is fixed —are illegal.

A simple code generator produces the above machine language in the following way. A counter, which we will call TEMPC, is kept on temporary storage; it is initialized to 0. The given algebraic expression may be considered as converted to its Polish-string form, which in this case is

$$A \ B \ * \ C \ - \ D \ E \ * \ + \ W \ X \ * \ Y \ Z \ * \ + \ *$$

This string is scanned and the following action is taken:

1. The A, B, and * are scanned, and the code LD   A and FM B is generated. Since the LD is the first instruction in the program, no temporary storage takes place.

2. The C and the − are scanned, and the instruction FS   C is generated. This illustrates the general rule: When an operator is preceded by *one* operand, only one instruction is generated, namely the instruction which applies that operator (subtract) to that operand (C).

3. The D, E, and * are scanned. The * is preceded by *two* operands, and therefore a load instruction must be generated. In addition, whenever a load instruction is generated, *unless* it is the first instruction in the entire expression, the previous contents of the accumulator must be stored (oth-

erwise they will be lost). In this case we increase TEMPC by 1, producing 1, and compile a store instruction (ST) into temporary storage location 1 (that is, TEMP1) before compiling the LD   C   and the FM   D .

4. The + is scanned. This operator is preceded by *no* operands, and the rule in this case is that it is applied to the current temporary storage location, and TEMPC is decreased by 1. Thus we compile a FA TEMP1 , and TEMPC becomes 0.

5. The W, X, and * are scanned. Since * is preceded by two operands, a load must be generated, which in turn means that TEMPC is increased by 1, giving 1; the accumulator is stored at (in this case) TEMP1; and the entire sequence of generated instructions is thus ST TEMP1 , LD   W , and FM   X .

6. The Y, Z, and * are scanned. The result is much like the previous step except that TEMPC now becomes 2, so that storage is made into TEMP2. Thus the instructions generated are ST   TEMP2 , LD   Y , and FM   Z .

7. The + is scanned. As in step 4, this operator is applied to the current temporary storage location, or TEMP2, producing FA   TEMP2 , and TEMPC is set to 1.

8. The * is scanned, producing a * applied to TEMP1 (that is, FM TEMP1), and TEMPC is set to 0.

There is one situation which we have not treated. If an operator such as − or /, which is not commutative (i.e., P−Q and Q−P are not the same), appears with no preceding operands, we have effectively given the operation in the wrong order. In fact, as we know, even for a simple expression such as

$$(A+B)/(C+D)$$

the fastest code calculates the C+D first and then divides. In this case the Polish string is

$$A \ B + C \ D + /$$

and our code generation algorithm, before it encounters the /, has produced

```
LD    A
FA    B
ST    TEMP1
LD    C
FA    D
```

Now it cannot produce FD   TEMP1 , for this code would calculate (C+D)/(A+B) rather than (A+B)/(C+D). Code generators solve this problem in various ways. A code generator producing all code by a simple forward scan, as we have done so far, could proceed by generating ST TEMP2 , LD   TEMP1 , and FD   TEMP2 , although this would not be as efficient as possible. Other code generators rearrange their code in such a case.

9-8   Register Assignment

The instructions of our machine language do not take into account the possibility of the computer's having a quotient register, in which quotients are left and multipliers are expected. In this case, the object code will have to contain instructions which move the accumulator to the quotient register, or vice versa. There is, however, a simple way of deciding when to compile such instructions. A flag is kept by the code generator to determine whether the last instruction left its results in the quotient register or not; this flag is set or reset on each generated arithmetic instruction. Before each store instruction, it may now be determined whether the quotient register or the accumulator is to be stored. Before each arithmetic instruction, it can be determined whether the current result is in the right place, and if it is not, an instruction word can be generated which moves it there. When a load instruction is generated, the corresponding operand is checked to see which register is to be loaded. Similar methods may be used when there is more than one register for arithmetic operations, and two adjacent registers take the place of an accumulator and a quotient register.

When there are several arithmetic registers, code generation algorithms are quite different. In the first place, temporary storage is no longer required, unless the algorithm "runs out of registers" for some reason. Instead of a temporary storage counter, we have a register counter; each load instruction except the first causes the register counter to be increased and calculation to be performed in a new register, and each operator with no operands is applied, in the generated code, to the old and new registers. The result may be left in either register; it is normally left in the old one, except in the case of non-commutative operators, when it is left in the new one. Non-commutative operators in Polish strings with no preceding arguments may thus be treated in sequence, in contrast with the case in which there is only one register.

In computers in which there are many full-size registers, these are often usable for purposes other than arithmetic operations—as index registers, for example, or as base registers in a base addressing scheme. The **register assignment problem,** for any algorithm which generates code for such a computer, is the problem of using the available registers in the best possible manner. The availability of an extra accumulator may allow a certain saving of space in the object program, where its availability as an index register may allow a different amount of space to be saved, and these two amounts are, ideally, to be compared to find as good a register assignment as possible. For example, the code generation of the preceding section involved three store instructions, none of which would have been necessary had our machine possessed three arithmetic registers. Thus the 15 instructions which were generated there would have been reduced to 12. On the other hand, arithmetic statements or sequences of statements very often involve subscripted expressions in which the same subscripts keep recurring, and in this case it will save instructions if the subscript values are kept in index registers. In evaluating the sequence

$$
\begin{aligned}
P1 &= A(I) + B(J) + C(K) \\
P2 &= A(J) + B(K) + C(I) \\
P3 &= A(K) + B(I) + C(J) \\
Q1 &= A(I+1) - A(I) \\
Q2 &= B(J+1) - B(J) \\
Q3 &= C(K+1) - C(K)
\end{aligned}
$$

we would like to keep the values of I, J, and K in three index registers throughout, since then each of the first three statements requires only four instructions and each of the last three requires only three. (Remember that if K, for example, is in index register 3, then LD   C+1,3   loads $C(K+1)$.) If only one index register is available, each of the first three statements requires seven instructions and each of the last three requires five. Hence all six require 36 statements, as against 24 (including three load-index instructions) if three index registers are available.

The principal problem in register assignment is determining when a register can be released for further assignment. An index register can be released when it is no longer needed as a subscript, and may also be released when the variable with which it was loaded is changed. An accumulator can be released when it contains a temporary result that is no longer needed. If no register can be properly released, one may have to be released "forcibly" by storing its contents in a temporary cell. In deciding which register to release in this way, registers whose contents are needed a short time later in the object program should receive low priority.

The register assignment problem is a special case of the **optimization problem** for object code—that is, the problem of producing the "best" object code, in terms of execution time and space requirements. Code generators employ a wide number of forms of optimization. If a computer has add-to-memory instructions, such statements as A = A + B may be optimized by loading B and adding A to memory. If a computer has instructions with immediate addressing, these should be used whenever possible in object code; sometimes, however, they will not be possible, as in floating point operations, or when an integer to be used in an operation is too large to be kept in an address field. Arithmetic expressions involving numbers may be written in the source program and computed during compilation; thus the statement N = 36*36 is executed in the object program, not by multiplying 36 by 36, but by loading the number 1296 and storing it in N.

9-9   Common Subexpressions

One way of optimizing object code is by re-using the values kept by a computation in registers or temporary cells. For example, consider the expression

$$(A*B)+(C*D)+(A*B*C)$$

(We ignore for the moment the fact that this expression should probably have been written as $(A*B*(1.0+C))+(C*D)$, for floating point data. Programmers do write algebraic expressions in ways which do not lead a code generator immediately to the best possible object code, and the conversion of an expression by computer to such a form is difficult and time-consuming, although it has been done.) If object code is generated from this expression for a computer with at least two registers, so that A*B is calculated in one register and C*D in another, and the sum is formed in the second register, then the first register need only be multiplied by C to form A*B*C. A code generator can do this if it keeps current information as to what quantities are contained in what registers.

Should the object code, in fact, form the sum $(A*B)+(C*D)$ in the first or the second register in this case? That depends on the rest of the expression. The above expression contained A*B*C, and so A*B, which was left over in the first register after the sum is accumulated in the second, is now used to calculate A*B*C. If the expression had been

$$(A*B)+(C*D)+(C*D*E)$$

then it would have been better to form the sum in the first register so that C*D would be left over to form C*D*E. Some code generation algorithms make a through study of **common subexpressions,** such as C*D in this last example, which occur in two or more places within an expression. A common subexpression may be of any length. If there are several registers, common subexpressions are usually left in registers after they are calculated, for later use. If there is only one arithmetic register, a common subexpression may have to be stored, even though it would not otherwise have been. In the expression

$$(A*B*C*D) + (A*B*C*E)$$

the straightforward code would be (in our machine language)

```
LD    A
FM    B
FM    C
FM    D
ST    TEMP1
LD    A
FM    B
FM    C
FM    E
FA    TEMP1
```

for floating point data; but a code generator might produce

```
LD    A
FM    B
FM    C
ST    TEMP1
FM    D
ST    TEMP2
LD    TEMP1
FM    E
FA    TEMP2
```

in which the common subexpression A*B*C is stored at TEMP1, reducing the number of instructions from 10 to 9 and the number of multiplication from 6 to 4. One more temporary cell is required; this may, however, be needed anyway for other purposes.

It is sometimes possible to use subexpressions which are common to a series of arithmetic statements which occur in line. This fails if it is possible to transfer to a statement which uses a common subexpression calculated previously. Also, care must be taken if a variable appearing in a common subexpression occurs on the left of the equal sign. For example, in the sequence

```
X = A + B + C
B = B + 1
Y = A + B + D
Z = (A+B)*(A+B)
```

the expression A + B is common to the last two statements, but not to the first and the last, because B is re-evaluated by the second statement.

PROBLEMS

1. Some computers have two FORTRAN compilers. In some cases, this situation exists because there are two different operating systems with different formats for object code. But suppose that there is more than one compiler, each accepting exactly the same source language and each producing object code in exactly the same format. Can you think of an advantage in such an arrangement?

2. A routine is being written to simulate the UNIVAC 1108 on the IBM 7094. The 1108 is a one's complement machine; the 7094 is a signed-magnitude machine. Both machines have 36-bit data words, and on each machine the instruction words are the same as the data words. The 1108 has an instruction format consisting of 6 bits for the function code (operation code), 4 bits each for the J, A, and B fields, 1 bit each for the index incrementation and indirect address fields, and 16 bits for the address field. The 1108 has fifteen B registers, whose contents are kept in the 7094 during simulation in an array BREG (at BREG+1 through BREG+15). The 1108 also has sixteen A registers, whose contents are kept at AREG through AREG+15. These arrays overlap by four words to take account of the fact that the four A registers A0 through A3 also serve as B registers B12 through B15. The B field of an 1108 instruction is the index register field and designates a B register whose contents are to be added to the contents of the address field to produce an effective address, in the absence of indirect addressing. The location counter of the 1108 is kept as the variable LCTR in the 7094, and contains the value of the instruction being executed, even though the actual location counter register of the 1108 contains this value plus one. An 1108 program in the 7094 is assumed to be represented faithfully; that is, each word of the 1108 program occupies a cell in the 7094 whose address is the same as the address of that word in the 1108. The simulator places the various fields of the 1108 instruction word, right justified, into the cells FFIELD, JFIELD, AFIELD, BFIELD, XINCRF, INDADF, and UFIELD respectively, in the 7094. The simulator now uses the contents of FFIELD as a switch and transfers to one of various routines, each of which treats a specific function code. What should these routines do for each of the following 1108 instructions?

(a) An instruction to load A-register A6 from a location given in the address field. All other fields are zero.

(b) An instruction to add the contents of the location given in the address field to B-register B7. The J-field is equal to 4, which means that the left half of the memory word only is involved in the addition, and is considered as an 18-bit (signed) integer. All other fields are zero.

(c) An instruction to perform a logical AND operation on the contents of register A6 and a memory word, leaving the result in A7. The B field is set equal to 10. All other fields are zero.

(d) An instruction to transfer to the location given in the address field if register A0 does not contain zero. The J field in this instruction is part of the function code. All other fields are zero.

(e) An instruction to test whether the contents of register A15 are equal to the contents of the word in the address field. If so, the next instruction word is to be skipped. All other fields are zero.

3. The following routine may be considered as an interpretive routine. The data which it interprets is kept in the array K. What kind of data is it, what is its format, and what does the routine calculate?

```
            NV = K(1)
            I = 2
    100     GO TO (121, 101, 102, 103, 104), K(I)
    101     NV = NV + K(I+1)
            GO TO 111
    102     NV = NV - K(I+1)
            GO TO 111
    103     NV = NV * K(I+1)
            GO TO 111
    104     NV = NV / K(I+1)
    111     I = I + 2
            GO TO 100
    121     (next statement)
```

4. In each of the following cases, a computer with the given operation code characteristics is being simulated. State in each case which of the three methods of function code interpretation described in the text (a separate test for each code, a binary search, or a table lookup using the function code as index) would be most suitable. Assume that it is more important to save space than to save time.

(a) The operation code field is 6 bits long and there are 62 separate operation codes.

(b) The operation code field is 12 bits long and there are 278 separate operation codes, more or less randomly distributed.

(c) The operation code field is 5 bits long, but the only operation codes which are ever used are A, J, and M.

5. In some algebraic languages, conditional statements may contain parentheses. Thus the statement

```
  IF (A.EQ.B .OR. (C.EQ.D .AND. (E.EQ.F .OR. G.EQ.H))) RETURN
```

directs the program to return (presumably from a subroutine) if A equals B, or if C equals D and E equals F, or if C equals D and G equals H. In a certain algebraic compiler, such statements are handled in the following way:

Each condition, such as A.EQ.B , is treated as a logical variable which has the value 1 if the condition is true and 0 if it is false. These conditions are combined into more complex conditions by using .OR. and .AND. , which are implemented by using the logical OR and logical AND instructions of the computer.

For example, in the above case, suppose that $A \neq B$, $C = D$, $E \neq F$, and $G = H$. Then the code generated by this compiler would do the following: A zero would be generated for E.EQ.F , and a one would be generated for G.EQ.H . A logical OR instruction would be applied to this zero and one, giving a one. A logical AND instruction would be applied to this one and a one which is generated for C.EQ.D . Now a logical OR instruction would be applied to this one and a zero which is generated for A.EQ.B ; the final result would be one, signifying "true," and therefore the subroutine return would be made. Thus the object code generated for this statement would contain two logical OR instructions and one logical AND, as well as other instructions to compute the zeros and ones for the various conditions and to test the final result.

Although this method works, it produces much more object code than is necessary. Describe a better method of implementation of conditional expressions containing parentheses. (Hint: First try to efficiently hand-code the example above in machine language.)

6. In calculating the volume of a cube by the formula $V = 4\pi r^3/3$, a programmer writes

$$V = 4.0*3.1416*R*R*R/3.0$$

Suppose that this statement is being compiled. What can the compiler do to improve the speed of the object program? What should the compiler be able to sense in order to perform this operation?

7. Loops that are performed only a very few times are often better written out. For example, the FORTRAN loop

```
        DO 87 K = 1, 3
87      G(K) = 0
```

should probably be replaced by the equivalent statements

```
        G(1) = 0
        G(2) = 0
        G(3) = 0
```

This will always save time; it will also save space if the loop is executed no more than k times, where k is a certain cutoff value. Find this value in each of the following two situations.

(a) There are exactly two full-word registers, each of which can be loaded and stored in one instruction. Loading an index register takes one instruction; increment, compare, and transfer takes three instructions. All instruction words have the same length.

(b) There are five registers, each of which can be loaded in one instruction, and two other registers, each of which can be stored in one instruction. No register may be loaded and stored. The contents of any register may be moved to any other register in one instruction. Loading an index register takes one instruction; increment, compare, and transfer takes two instructions. All instruction words have the same length. (Note: This is roughly the situation on the CDC 6600. The fact that such loops may be optimized even further on this machine is to be ignored, as is the fact that some instruction words not used in this example have different lengths.)

8. Even when a loop is performed many times, it may be run faster if it is *partially* written out. Thus the FORTRAN loop

$$DO\ 89\ L = 1,\ 100$$
$$89 \quad C(L)\ =\ A(L)*A(L)$$

may be replaced by the equivalent loop

$$DO\ 89\ L = 1,\ 99,\ 2$$
$$C(L)\ =\ A(L)*A(L)$$
$$89 \quad C(L+1)\ =\ A(L+1)*A(L+1)$$

In each of the two situations of problem 7 above, calculate how much time is saved by this procedure.

9. In calculating monthly interest payments KI(I) for $I = 1$ to 100, where the principal in each case is KP(I), a programmer writes

$$DO\ 54\ I = 1,\ 100$$
$$54 \quad KI(I)\ =\ KP(I)*KR*KT$$

where KR is the rate and KT is the time. This loop will be performed faster if it is rewritten as

$$KRT\ =\ KR*KT$$
$$DO\ 54\ I = 1,\ 100$$
$$54 \quad KI(I)\ =\ KP(I)*KRT$$

Perform this type of optimization on each of the following FORTRAN loops:

(a)   V(1) = 2.0
        DO 27 N = 2, NN
        S = B*B − C*C
        U = 2.0*B*C
        W = (S + U)*(S − U)
27   V(N) = V(N−1) + 1.0/V(N−1) + 1.0/W

(b)   DO 179 J = 1, 12
       A(J) = 2*J
       B(J) = A(J)+5.0+W
 179 C(J) = B(J)+6.0+2.0*W+V
(c)   DO 699 I = J, N
       U(I) = A(I) + B(J) + C(J)
       V(I) = A(J) + B(I) + C(J)
 699 W(I) = A(J) + B(J) + C(I)

Chapter 10

INPUT-OUTPUT DEVICES

10-1 Devices and Media

Every computer has instructions for input and output (usually written as one word, **input-output,** and abbreviated I/O). These instructions control the transmission, by **input-output devices,** of information on **input-output media.** Cards and paper tape are examples of input-output media. Transmission of information from an input medium to the computer is known as **reading;** transmission of information from the computer to an output medium is known as **writing.** Cards are read by card readers and written by card punches; paper tape is read by paper tape readers and written by paper tape punches. Magnetic tape, on the other hand, is both read and written by the same device, namely, a tape unit. Thus we say that a magnetic tape unit is an input-output device, in contrast to input devices such as card readers, and output devices such as card punches.

Other I/O devices include the following:

(1) **Typewriters, Teletypes, and printers,** which write on ordinary paper.

(2) **Drums, disks, and other intermediate access units,** which read and write on an oxide-coated surface.

The range of existing I/O devices is very wide. We mention here some other devices, some of which are still in the experimental stage; a detailed discussion of these devices is outside the scope of this book.

(3) **Scanning devices,** which read characters from ordinary paper; the characters must normally belong to a fixed character set. In an **optical scanner,** these characters are read photoelectrically; in a **magnetic ink scanner,** it is assumed that the characters have been printed with a special ink which activates the reading mechanism. Such devices are used in banks, to read the account numbers printed on checks; they have various other commercial uses.

(4) **Plotters,** which form an arbitrary pattern. In a **mechanical plotter,** this pattern is formed with one or more pens on a sheet of paper; in a **microfilm plotter,** it is formed by an electron beam which traces the pattern on microfilm. Plotters have been used chiefly to write graphs; they can also write characters, and such characters often appear in graphs (such as "X" and "Y" for the two axes). Plotters may also be programmed to write special characters, such as Russian letters or script, or mathematical or musical symbols, or to draw pictures.

(5) **Other graphical input devices,** for example, digitized television input, which forms an array of bits representing a picture of something, or which can be directed to scan over such a picture and return one bit at a time representing the color at a certain point; and "tablets" which are flat and are covered with thousands of input sensors, allowing a picture that is drawn on them with a pencil or stylus to be input to the computer.

(6) **Display units,** which write on an oscilloscope or cathode ray tube. From the programming viewpoint, display units are similar to plotters, except that the output which they produce is not permanent; plotters, in fact, are sometimes called **hard copy display devices.** Some display functions, such as the display of characters from one fixed alphabet, may be performed by the hardware. It has been proposed to use a television screen for display, so that an ordinary television set may be adapted as an output device. Cathode ray tube display units have also been used for input, by means of a **light pen,** an electronic instrument which may be held on the face of the tube to sense a spot of light at any point on the screen.

(7) **Mechanical devices.** These are used in space vehicles; a computer-controlled camera, for example, might contain instructions for opening and closing the aperture, aiming the camera, snapping the shutter, developing a picture, etc. They are also used in **process control**—the operation of large-scale mechanical processes, such as those occurring in a factory, under computer control. Devices have also been constructed which pick up objects and manipulate them somewhat as a human hand does. One branch of the science of artificial intelligence, which studies the relation between computers and human beings, is the study of coordination between mechanical hands and mechanical "eyes" (such as digitized television) and its relation to coordination between human hands and eyes.

(8) **Analog input-output devices.** An analog input device registers the reading of a pointer, such as a voltmeter or a thermometer; an analog output device controls some quantity which is subject to continuous control, such as the speed of a motor or a voltage level. **Analog-to-digital** (A-D) **converters** are used for reading analog devices, so that the information which is read assumes the digital form required by the com-

puter. **Digital-to-analog** (D-A) **converters** are used for "writing"—that is, setting the given continuous quantity. Many mechanical devices use A-D and D-A converters for communication with the computer, although some do not—the taking of a picture by a camera, for example, requires only a single bit.

(9) **Terminals.** This term has been applied loosely to any input-output device, usually a typewriter, which is located in a different room or building from the computer to which it is connected; we refer here to devices which have buttons to push for input and lights to turn on for output, such as inspection data collection devices in factories, airline reservation devices, and the like.

10-2   Cards

Tabulating cards or **tab cards** (or, more informally, "IBM cards"), of the standard 80-column, 12-row format, and the less frequently used cards of 45 columns and 12 rows, known as "90-column cards" because of the method of data representation, may be read by a **card reader** and written (i.e., punched) by a **card punch.** In some small computers there is a single device which serves both as a reader and a punch. Card readers and punches may be modified to accept cards with fewer columns.

The simplest type of instruction for a card reader or punch is one which directly performs the "basic operations," as we usually think of them, associated with card I/O. One operation may read a card, another may punch a card; these are the direct operations. There are also other auxiliary operations, such as turning off the reader or the punch; directing that a card, after being read or punched, is to be stacked in one of two (or three) piles or **stackers** by the device; testing whether the reader or the punch is on, or whether a card is stuck (or "jammed") in it, or whether there are any more cards to be read or punched. Card punches have a **chip box** which slowly fills with waste cardboard chips the size of a punched-card hole; another possible test instruction would be to determine whether the chip box is full. More often, the various abnormal conditions (chip box full, card jam, no cards in hopper, overheating, etc.) appear as lights on the device; any such condition causes the device to be "not ready." If the instruction to read or punch is now given, the computer will halt until the device is ready.

Cards are coded in several ways. Two 36-bit words may be contained in each row, one in columns 1 through 36 and the other in columns 37 through 72. This coding method allows twenty-four 36-bit words to be contained on a card, and is known as **row binary.** In **column binary,** each 36-bit word is divided into three 12-bit sections, each of which is contained in one column. Thus three columns are required for each such word. Twenty-four 36-bit words can be contained in columns 1 through 72, or twenty-six in columns 1 through 78. Besides permitting usage of more space on the card, column binary may be generalized to 48-bit words, which use four columns each. Both of these methods provide closer packing than does the classical method, invented circa 1890 by Herman Hollerith and still known as **Hollerith (or decimal) code,** in which one column is used for each character; such cards must still be acceptable to computers because keypunch machines punch one character per column. If six characters are to be read into a 36-bit word, 78 columns will represent 13 words instead of 26.

The Hollerith code for alphabetic and numeric characters is as follows:

CHARAC-TER	CODE	CHARAC-TER	CODE	CHARAC-TER	CODE	CHARAC-TER	CODE
A	12-1	J	11-1	S	0-2	0	0
B	12-2	K	11-2	T	0-3	1	1
C	12-3	L	11-3	U	0-4	2	2
D	12-4	M	11-4	V	0-5	3	3
E	12-5	N	11-5	W	0-6	4	4
F	12-6	O	11-6	X	0-7	5	5
G	12-7	P	11-7	Y	0-8	6	6
H	12-8	Q	11-8	Z	0-9	7	7
I	12-9	R	11-9			8	8
						9	9

Each code represents the row or rows in which punches occur; the 12 rows are numbered, from top to bottom: 12, 11, 0, 1, 2, 3, 4, 5, 6, 7, 8, and 9. Blank is represented by no punch at all; slash (/) by 0-1; plus or & by 12; and minus by 11. Other special characters may be added, although the codes for most of these are not standard.

Card readers have various ways of determining what particular coding method is being used. Some admit only one coding method; others have an instruction which sets one code or the other for the cards to follow. A convention adopted by IBM for some of their card readers and widely copied dictates that a 7 and 9 punch in column 1 of a card signifies a (column) binary card; this does not correspond to any Hollerith code, and causes little disruption in most binary card codes, such as object deck codes. An advance read station in the card reader determines whether a card is binary or decimal before it is read, and turns on the internal flag causing the card to be read in the proper mode.

An important characteristic of any card reader or punch is its speed, usually measured in cards per minute. To find the number of bits per second, we multiply by $16 = 960/60$, since a card has $80 \times 12 = 960$ possible holes.

The IBM 1402 Card Reader-Punch reads 800 cards per minute (CPM) and punches 250 CPM; the card reader and card punch are contained in the same cabinet. The IBM 1442 Card Reader-Punch reads 400 cards per minute and punches 91 cards per minute; cards to be read and cards to be punched are placed in the same hopper. Punching speed increases if fewer than 80 columns are punched on a card; the maximum is 265 cards per minute, with 10 columns per card. The Burroughs B122, B123, and B124 Card Readers read 200, 475, and 800 CPM respectively; the B303 and B304 Card Punches punch 100 and 300 CPM respectively. The IBM 2540 Card Reader-Punch reads 1000 CPM and punches 250 CPM. The UNIVAC 1004 card readers read 400 and 615 CPM respectively; the CDC 405 Card Reader reads 1200 CPM; and the RCA 70/237 Card Reader reads 1,435 CPM.

Most card readers and card punches read into or write from an array in memory whose starting address is arbitrary; the words of such a **card buffer** must have sequential addresses. The address of the first word of the card buffer is specified by the instruction which reads or punches a card. A few computers, notably the IBM 1401, have a fixed address which is always used as the start of the card buffer; the same is also true for printing.

10-3   Magnetic Tape

The I/O device which presents information on magnetic tape, as an I/O medium, to the computer is called a **tape drive** (or **tape unit,** or **tape servo**). Tape drives may read and write tape, and are sometimes capable of reading in two directions. Instructions applying to tape units are more diverse than those which read and punch cards, because the data structures are more complex.

Bits or digits are recorded on magnetic tape with a packing density which is measured in bits per inch; standard densities are 200, 556, and 800 bits per inch (bpi). Data is written on tape n words at a time; these words have sequential addresses in core, but the number n may be arbitrary. However, when the data is read back in, all n words must be read at once. Such a group of n words is called a **record** on tape and a **tape buffer** in core. After a record has been written on tape, a blank space is written, called the **inter-record gap.** When one record is read, the tape unit stops in the inter-record gap; because of the momentum of the tape, a certain amount of blank tape, smaller than the length of the gap, passes the reading mechanism, or **read head,** before the unit stops. It is now ready to read the next record. When several records are read in order as fast as they can be read, some tape units are able to maintain speed through the inter-record gap; others stop in every gap. As words are grouped into records, so records are grouped into **files;** the end of a file is signified by an **end-of-file mark,** which is usually a word or series of words in a special format, but may be simply a blank space which is appreciably longer than the inter-record gap.

Magnetic tape deteriorates with time; the oxide coating may develop weak spots, and the tape itself may stretch or crimp. One of the most important properties of a tape drive is its ability to read and write tape that is in poor condition. When any record is written on tape, extra bits, known as **redundant bits** or **parity bits,** are written as well. These serve as an error checking device, on certain assumptions about how many errors the tape drive is allowed to make per record.

> The IBM standard tape format, which has been adopted by many other manufacturers, includes parity bits as follows. Each character is recorded as a vertical row, extending the width of the tape. These characters may have either 6 or 8 bits. An extra bit is recorded in the same row for parity purposes; the number of bits in every row, including the parity bit, is even (BCD mode records) or odd (binary mode records). At the end of each record, there is one entire row of parity bits; each bit in this row is a parity bit for all bits in the corresponding bit position of each character of the record. That is, the record may be thought of as a rectangular array of bits on tape, in which the number of bits in each row and each column is even (BCD) or odd (binary).

The direct operations on a tape unit include: reading one record, writing one record; backspacing one record, in which the tape moves back to the preceding record without any data transfer; rewinding, or moving the tape back to the beginning; positioning the tape forward by one record without reading, which is the opposite of backspacing; writing an end-of-file mark; "reading part of a record," in which only the first n words are actually placed in core, although the tape is positioned to the next complete record; reading backwards, available on a few types of tape unit; and searching, an automatic operation which usually consists of repeatedly positioning the tape forward or backward until the first word of a record matches a certain word in memory. As with card devices, these can all be given by single instructions. Other auxiliary tape instructions include testing whether the tape unit is ready; whether it is positioned at the beginning of the tape, or at the end of the tape, or at an end-of-file mark; or whether the parity bits have indicated an error. Parity checking may also, in fact, be used in reading cards, but is ordinarily done by the program; a word on the card called the **check sum** contains check bits for the entire card.

Tape operations are subject to certain restrictions owing to their design. The read and write heads are normally separate, and are spaced as much as four inches apart. In addition, changing from write to non-write operations may destroy information on tape. This means, for instance, that a record in the middle of the tape cannot be rewritten safely. The speed of a tape unit is usually measured in characters per second; to find the number of bits per second, we multiply by 6 (for six-bit characters). In addition to this amount of time per character (called the **character transfer rate),** tape units take a certain amount of extra time per record. If the tape motion is continuous, this is simply the amount of time it takes to pass the inter-record gap; otherwise, it is the **start-stop time,** or the total time taken in stopping and restarting. The speed of a tape unit is also sometimes given in inches per second; the character transfer rate can now be found by multiplying inches per second by characters per inch (200, 556, or 800), and the time between records may be found by dividing the length of the inter-record gap in inches by the tape speed in inches per second. Note that bits per inch and characters per inch are the same, because "bits per inch" is a *linear* dimension; an inch of tape containing 7 columns of bits at 200 bits per inch actually contains 1400 bits. **Incremental tape units** are capable of reading and writing at variable speed; such a unit has a rated *maximum* speed, in inches per second, and a corresponding maximum character transfer rate.

The IBM 729 tape units have speeds of 36, 75, and 112.5 inches per second, depending on the model number; the inter-record gap is 0.75 inches long. The highest character transfer rate—112.5 in/sec at 800 char/in—is thus 90,000 characters per second (known as "90 KC-characters" or simply "90 KC"). The RCA 70/432 and 70/442 tape units have speeds of 37.5 and 75 inches per second respectively, with an 0.6 inch gap. The Burroughs B422 tape runs at 90 inches per second, 555.5 characters per inch. The UNIVAC tape unit known as UNISERVO VI-C runs at 42.7 inches per second; the gap length is 0.75 inches in 7-track mode (6-bit characters) or 0.60 inches in 9-track mode (8-bit characters). The DEC Type 555 Tape Unit, which runs on the PDP series of computers, has a packing density of 375 bpi and a maximum transfer rate of 90,000 bits per second. Unlike most other tape units, the Type 555 is addressable; records anywhere within the tape may be written at any time without destroying adjacent information. The Honeywell tape units are available with 1/2 inch tapes at 550 characters per inch, or with 3/4 inch tapes at 800 characters per inch; tape speed in both cases is 150 inches per second.

Magnetic tape is ordinarily much faster than reading or punching cards. Since the amount of time taken by a computer to run a program which reads many cards is often limited by the speed of the card reader, many computer installations which have large computers also have small computers which read cards and transfer the information to tape; this tape is then read by a large computer. Instead of punching cards, the large computer writes tape, which is later read by a small computer and its information punched on cards. A card reader or card punch used with a small computer, or, formerly, with special-purpose "card-to-tape" or "tape-to-card" equipment, in this way, is called an **off-line device,** as contrasted with a device which communicates directly with a large computer, or an **on-line device.**

10-4 Printers

The **line printer** is an output device which uses continuous paper forms as an output medium. It prints one horizontal line at a time, either by using separate type bars or type wheels for each print position or by using a continuous horizontal chain of characters together with a complex timing device. The standard paper size is $11'' \times 15''$, although many other sizes, including continuous card forms which may be separated into cards, have been used. The number of print positions on one horizontal line is usually 120, 128, 132, 136, or 144.

If input-output instructions on a machine are designed in the straightforward manner we have described, the basic operation on a printer is to print one line from a memory array called the **print buffer.** Among the auxiliary operations, the most important are those which control spacing. The printer may double-space, triple-space, or not space at all, causing overprinting. It may also skip to the top of the next page, called **page ejection,** or to a particular place on a page. Spacing is controlled by a paper tape loop which is continuously read by the printer. This loop has one column, containing 12 holes, for each separate horizontal line on the given form; each hole may be punched or not, depending on whether a skip is to be made to this line. An instruction to the printer causes the printer to skip to the first line whose column on the tape contains a hole at position i. If the column corresponding to the first line on a page, and only this column, has a hole at position 1, for example, then page ejection is accomplished by skipping to channel 1.

From the programming viewpoint, spacing is most often controlled by using a **carriage control character,** normally the character in position 1 of the print line. This character simply does not print, but controls the spacing.

The printer, like other devices, may be tested to see whether it is ready, using an instruction; the printer will not be ready if it is out of paper or out of ribbon, or has been opened up to change the paper. Printer speeds are measured in lines per minute. A printer may be connected to a small computer which is programmed to print out the information on a tape; use of such an **off-line printer** allows the large computer to write tape, rather than writing directly to an **on-line printer**. In practice, an on-line card reader or card punch is often unnecessary, but on-line printers are more often used, usually for messages to the computer operator. The characters in a printer buffer, as in a card buffer, are assumed to extend from left to right in each word and then to the next word; such a buffer, in particular, is usually a forward array, even on computers with subtractive index registers.

> The IBM 1403 printer, Model III, prints at 1100 lines per minute. This illustrates a general tendency to improve the characteristics of an input-output device without changing its generic number (1403 in this case); the improved devices are given model numbers. The IBM 1443 printer prints 150 lines per minute (Model 1) or 240 lines per minute (Model 2) with the standard character set; with larger or smaller character sets, this speed may vary from 120 to 600 lines per minute. For a small character set, the print chain may include each character more than once; this accounts for the higher speed in this case. The Honeywell printers use a revolving drum instead of a print chain. The Burroughs B321 printer operates at 700 lines per minute; the UNIVAC 1108 printers, 700 and 922 lines per minute; the CDC 501 printer, 1000 lines per minute; and the RCA 70/242 and 70/243 printers, 625 and 1250 lines per minute.

Any input-output device, including the printer, may be **simultaneous** or **non-simultaneous.** In a non-simultaneous printer, for example, the instruction which prints a line waits until the line is printed; the computer then executes the next instruction. If the printer is simultaneous, the instruction which prints the line causes printing to be started; the computer can then proceed to the next instruction while the print operation is completed. Since instruction execution is so fast, in comparison with the speed of an I/O operation, simultaneous I/O can allow many programs to run much faster than they would under non-simultaneous I/O.

When a simultaneous device is referenced by an instruction, it may be **busy**—that is, still processing the last card (or line, or record). In some computers, if an instruction accesses a busy device, the computer simply waits until the device is not busy. The result of this can be almost as bad as using non-simultaneous I/O, and therefore use is made of a **busy test,** an instruction which tests if a certain device is busy.

Care must be taken with buffers when using simultaneous input-output. After a print operation is started, the contents of the printer buffer are still being transferred to the printer; the next print line may be completely different, but the words of the printer buffer cannot be changed until the print operation is finished. To avoid this difficulty, some programs have two print buffers, which are used alternately. Simultaneous card readers are even more complex in this regard; after a card read instruction, the card buffer does not contain all the information on the card until the operation is finished. One way of reading cards simultaneously consists of reading the first card separately; the card reading operation then consists of the following steps:

(1) Testing whether the card reader is busy.

(2) When it is not busy, transferring the data in the card buffer to a separate card buffer.

(3) Starting to read the next card.

This sequence is logically equivalent to reading a card into the second buffer from a non-simultaneous card reader. The same operation in reverse may be used with a printer. When a printer is non-simultaneous, double buffering is not required; if one buffer is used repeatedly, it may be cleared (set to all blank characters) immediately after each print operation.

10-5 Other Sequential Devices

Typewriters and **teletypewriters** (or **Teletypes)** are much slower than line printers. They produce one character at a time, normally at a rate of 10 characters per second; as input devices, they accept characters as fast as a person can type them, up to a maximum of ten per second. The typewriter is the ideal device for communication between the computer and its operator, if the messages are not too long. Instructions for a typewriter or a Teletype often refer to only one character, instead of an entire line. One such character, the **carriage return** character, positions the typewriter or Teletype to the beginning of the line. Usually this is the beginning of the *next* line, although on some Teletypes it is the beginning of the *current* line, allowing overprinting; a carriage return and a **line feed,** which spaces one line, are necessary to start the next line. The carriage return and, if necessary, the line feed must in any event be specified explicitly for each new line; this distinguishes programming for these devices from programming for a printer. There are also characters for backspace, tab, shifting, and sometimes even for changing the color of the ribbon.

Several typewriters or Teletypes may be connected to one computer, and data may be collected in this way from several locations. An airline reservation system using typewriters, for example, may continuously interrogate all its typewriters and send information back to those typewriters that request it. There are also computers on which several programs, one for each typewriter or Teletype, may be run simultaneously or sequentially by a very complex programming system. Each program can provide output to, and receive input from, a user at its typewriter or Teletype. This is called a **time-sharing system.** Other types of terminals, including display units, may be used with a time-sharing system. Checkout of a program is much faster on a time-sharing system than on an ordinary computer, because a user, sitting at his terminal, may run his program as many times as desired with different input conditions, correcting errors as he goes.

Paper tape is the least expensive, per square inch, of all the input-output media, by a factor so large that its deficiencies are often forgiven. The number of bits per inch that may be recorded on paper tape is so small that magnetic tape actually costs less per bit than paper tape. A punched paper tape consists of several rows of holes; the number of rows is the **level** of the tape. Thus we speak of 5-level, 6-level, 7-level, and 8-level paper tape. Each "column," consisting of one hole in each row, now represents a 5-bit, 6-bit, 7-bit, or 8-bit character, respectively. Paper tape reading and punching instructions, like those for the typewriter, may specify a single character or an entire array.

Paper tape may be produced directly by a Teletype with the proper attachment. Accuracy is essential, however, since it is difficult to alter a paper tape once it has been punched. One error correction method which has found favor is the **rubout character,** consisting of all one-bits, so that every hole in a given column is punched. If a character is punched in error, it is rubbed out by punching all the rest of the holes. The program which reads the paper tape now ignores all rubout characters. In another variation, the rubout applies to the *preceding* character, so that several rubouts may erase several characters; the paper tape input program must now be slightly more complex.

Paper tape is normally read by a **paper tape reader** and written by a **paper tape punch;** the speeds of these devices are measured in characters per second.

> Typewriters for computer input are made by IBM (Model 1052) and many other companies. Teletypes (Models 33 and 35) are available from the Bell System and Western Union. The Model 35 Teletype is also available with a paper tape attachment which can be connected to the keyboard or to the computer; thus the computer may read or punch paper tape at 10 characters per second. Other paper tape readers and punches are much faster than this. The CDC 3694 Paper Tape Reader-Punch reads at 1000 characters per second (CPS) and punches at 110 CPS; the DEC Type 761 Paper Tape Punch writes 63.3 CPS; the DEC Type 760 Paper Tape Reader reads 400 CPS; the UNIVAC 1004 paper tape equipment reads 400 CPS and punches 110 CPS; and the RCA 70/221 Paper Tape Reader-Punch reads 200 CPS and punches 100 CPS.

10-6   Channels

The part of a computer which reads each instruction, interprets it, and executes it, is called the **central processing unit** (or **CPU**). The central processing unit is usually contained in one cabinet, the core memory in another. Each input-output device is connected to the CPU by a bundle of wires, known as an **I/O bus,** and associated encoding and decoding circuits at each end, all of which is known collectively as a **channel.** Because channels are expensive, most computers group their devices in such a way that one channel serves several devices. From the programmer's viewpoint, this means that, for a computer with n channels, no more than n input-output devices can be transferring data simultaneously, even though there may be more than n available devices.

As an example, we consider a computer with 28 tape units, of which eight are connected to channel A, eight to channel B, six to channel C, and six to channel D. Only four tapes can now be read at once, one on each channel. It is possible, on some channels, to write the *same* information on more than one device at the same time on the same channel; duplicate tapes might thus be written on each of the four channels simultaneously, for a total of eight tapes. When the device connected to a channel is both an input and an output device, as in this case, the channel must be capable of transferring data in both directions. If data can move in both directions at the same time, the channel is called a **duplex** or **full duplex channel,** and is logically equivalent to a pair of channels. A **half duplex channel** is constructed in such a way that data can be transferred in either direction, but not in both directions simultaneously. For devices such as a card reader or printer, only one data transfer direction is necessary, and a **unidirectional channel** may be used.

A channel may be considered as a "primary input-output device" with various "subdevices." That is, the channel has its own instructions; there will be instructions, for example, to turn on and turn off a given channel, and, in the case of a half duplex channel, to select reading or writing as the current mode of operation. There will be an instruction to test whether a channel is busy, or whether it has been turned on. A device cannot operate unless its channel has been turned on, although sometimes channel and device can be activated with a single instruction. Also, a device may continue to operate even after its channel is no longer transmitting; thus we may start data transmission to a new device on the same channel. Instead of testing each device to see whether it is busy, we may test whether the channel is busy. It is also possible for error conditions in a device to be transmitted to the channel, so that each device does not have to retain error flag registers accessible by special instructions.

Each channel has associated with it one or more **channel registers,** which contain the address of the word in core which is currently being read or written, and some information as to how much further the operation has to go—either a count, which may be positive or negative, or the address of the last word of the memory block, or this address plus 1. These registers may either be special core locations, which may be loaded into an accumulator in the normal fashion, or they may be special registers with their own loading and storing instructions. Among the channel registers are also to be found the flag registers, which specify whether the channel is ready or busy, whether error conditions have occurred, etc. These may be accessible through test instructions, or they may actually be bits in a register which can be stored and tested in the usual way.

It is perfectly possible for a computer to have more than one processing unit; thus there may be two separate location counters, with two instruction sequences in different parts of memory being executed at the same time. Several experimental machines, in fact, have two central processing units, whereas one large commercial system has one central processing unit and ten subordinate or **peripheral processing units.** Each processing unit has its own registers, error flag mechanism, and instruction decoding mechanism, all of which may be active simultaneously. Different processing units may have completely different instruction formats. One small-scale example of more than one processing unit is very common; in it, there is a processing unit for channel operations, and instructions for this unit determine the locations of arrays which are to be read from a channel or written to a channel. Each instruction specifies either that the channel processing unit pass to the next channel command in sequence, or that it stop, leaving only the central processing unit functioning. The channel processing unit is in turn started or restarted by an instruction in the CPU.

10-7   Interrupts

An **interrupt** or a **trap** is a call to an **interrupt subroutine** whose start location, the **interrupt location,** has a fixed address, usually small, determined by the hardware; it is caused by an **interrupt condition** (or **exception**) which may be an illegal instruction, an arithmetic fault, or an input-output condition.

The interrupt subroutine must save and restore all registers which it uses. In particular, the call itself must store the return address in memory, not in a register. If the hardware transfers to the interrupt location, this location contains a transfer to the interrupt subroutine. Sometimes the hardware does not transfer to the interrupt location, but instead effectively performs an **execute instruction** addressing this location. This instruction, found on many computers, treats its effective address as the address of an instruction word to be executed. The execute instruction itself does not alter the value of the location counter; indeed, this is the only way in which an execute instruction differs from a transfer instruction. Of course, if the executed instruction is a transfer, it alters the location counter.

If a given computer has a subroutine call instruction which stores the return address in memory, this instruction may be kept at the interrupt location; the interrupt itself then does not need to store a return address.

Illegal instruction interrupt conditions may include the following:

(1) Illegal instruction code. A particular value of the instruction code field may be either completely meaningless or "illegal in context"; some computers, for example, have an internal flag which suppresses all input-output instructions, causing them to be trapped.

(2) Illegal address. The address may not exist in the machine at all; this may happen if the memory is not full size. Some computers have **memory protection registers** which permit access only within a part of memory; any access not in this part of memory is trapped. There also exist traps on addresses whose low-order bits are improper; it may be required, for example, that the effective address of a double precision arithmetic instruction be even.

(3) Special conditions depending on the instruction code. On the IBM 360, for example, an attempt to perform an execute instruction on an execute instruction produces an interrupt.

Arithmetic fault conditions may include the following:

(1) Overflow. The sum of two integers is too large to fit into an accumulator; or, more generally, a "carry" into the sign bit.

(2) Divide check or divide fault. Either an attempt was made to divide by zero, or the quotient is too large to fit in a register.

(3) Floating point errors. The exponent, or characteristic, of the result of a floating point operation is too large (overflow) or too small (underflow) for the computer, or an attempt was made to do a floating point division by zero.

The action taken by an interrupt subroutine depends on the type of interrupt. For an illegal instruction, the error cannot be corrected, and the subroutine, after noting the fact of the error, either stops or returns to the monitor. For an arithmetic fault, the error is correctable and the interrupt routine may return to the program, which will still run although its output will probably be bad. In division by zero, for example, the quotient may be set to zero, and similarly for floating point errors, whereas on arithmetic overflow the result may be truncated to fit the size of the register. These actions, in fact, may be performed by the computer itself rather than the interrupt program (i.e., by the hardware rather than by the software); the interrupt program may now do other things such as counting the number of interrupts. Other interrupt conditions are found on some computers; an interrupt condition may not be an error condition at all, such as the transfer trap on the IBM 700 series, which, in a certain mode, interrupts on every transfer. An instruction may even be provided which always causes an interrupt.

Most interrupts may be **disabled** by an instruction; when an interrupt is disabled, interruption does not occur. A flag register within the computer records the fact that the interrupt condition has occurred; this flag may be tested by an instruction, or the interrupt may be **enabled,** or made operative, causing interruption to occur immediately. If the arithmetic interrupts are disabled, it is possible, for example, to test for overflow immediately after an instruction where overflow is suspected; on some computers, the overflow test turns the overflow indicator off again.

Two or more interrupts may have the same interrupt location. In this case, the interrupt subroutine must decode the interrupt before deciding which action to take.

The IBM 1401 has no interrupts. The Honeywell 200 series have interrupt facility available at extra cost. The IBM 360 interrupts store the entire 64-bit "program status word" (PSW) containing not only the location counter, but also the interrupt disable bits, an interrupt type code, and other flags. At the same time, a new PSW is loaded. On the CDC 6600, this exchange process includes the contents of the 24 registers as well, and is performed by an instruction known as Exchange Jump. The IBM 7094, which has no subroutine call instruction storing the return address in memory, uses two cells for each interrupt, one to store the return address and one to which to transfer. The transfer trap uses 0 and 1; the floating point trap uses 0 and 10; the STR, an instruction which always causes an interrupt, uses 0 and 2. Interrupts on Channel A use 12 and 13; interrupts on Channel B use 14 and 15, and so on. There is a compatibility mode which allows the 7094 to run IBM 704 programs; since the IBM 704 I/O instructions are not found on the 7094, they are trapped, and the two locations used for this purpose are 40000 and 40002. In addition, the 7909 Data Channel has its own location counter and its own set of commands, which may themselves be interrupted; the interrupt locations for this purpose are 42 and 43 for Channel A, 44 and 45 for Channel B, and so on.

10-8   Input-output Interrupts

The use of an interrupt to signify that an input-output operation has been completed is one solution to a problem that always arises with simultaneous input-output. Suppose than an I/O operation has been given, and while it is proceeding, the computer performs other instructions. It may now test the device or the channel to see whether it has finished. But how is it to know the exact moment at which the operation is complete? If it is known when one operation is complete, the next operation can be started immediately. If the operations are under the control of a channel processing unit, the problem can sometimes be solved by using several channel instructions in sequence. But now another problem arises: it may not be desired to start the next channel operation until the central processing unit is ready for it. For example, we may wish to read several records into the same core buffer; one record cannot be read in until the preceding one is moved somewhere else. For this reason, it is usually better to use interrupts.

When an input-output operation is complete, an interrupt occurs and an interrupt routine is called. This routine checks the error flags to see if any errors have occurred in the I/O operation; a tape may have been read with parity error, for example, in which case it has to be backspaced and read again. The interrupt routine also determines whether a new operation is to be started; this may be denoted by a flag which is stored in memory by the main program and tested by the interrupt routine, or by the status of a list of I/O operations to be performed. If a new operation is to be started, it is started by the interrupt routine, which then returns.

Care must be taken that the interrupt routine is not itself interrupted unless it provides for this eventuality. The easiest way to do this is for the computer to have an internal flag which denotes that it is now processing an interrupt routine; when this flag is on, no further interrupts can occur. However, interrupts may now be lost if several types of interrupt are operative at once. Also, input-output operations are slowed down if the interrupts which signify that an I/O operation is complete are delayed unduly. A more complex method of handling several types of interrupt is by using **interrupt priorities.** Each type of interrupt receives a priority, which is a small integer; higher priority interrupts may interrupt lower priority interrupt routines, but not vice versa. Thus a high-speed I/O device, for which timing is not essential, will not have its interrupts unduly delayed by interrupt routines for other devices which may take more processing time.

It is possible to specify that an interrupt routine do nothing at all. In fact, if the interrupt executes an instruction at a fixed location, this instruction may either be a NOP, or, on computers which disable the interrupt when interruption occurs, a single instruction which re-enables the interrupt. Of course, if this is desired, a better solution is probably to disable the interrupt in the first place.

Interrupts may also be used by each of two processing units, or each of two computers, to communicate with the other. Thus a large computer may send information directly to a small computer serving as a remote terminal; the two computers communicate by interruption. The running of a single program by two CPU's simultaneously sometimes has theoretical advantages. Suppose, for example, that we have two subroutines at our disposal, called S1 and S2, which perform the same function. If we could give these to two CPU's at the same time, processing might proceed as follows. The first CPU interrupts the second CPU, directing it to start subroutine S2. Meanwhile, the first CPU starts subroutine S1. If S2 finishes first, the second CPU interrupts the first, directing it to stop S1 and use the results of S2. If S1 finishes first, the first CPU interrupts the second, directing it to abandon S2, and proceeds. This would be particularly useful when each of the subroutines is very fast in many of the cases where the other one is slow.

10-9 Intermediate Access Units

Drum and disk units differ from almost all tape units in that they are addressable—each separate word has an address which may be referenced by input-output instructions. Given the address of a word on the unit, the time that it takes to reference the word at this address is called the **access time.** As soon as the word has been read, successive words can be read at a much higher rate, called the **transfer rate** (in bits, characters, or words).

The access time is not a constant, and a meaningful comparison of the access times of two units depends on detailed knowledge of their design. On a drum unit, the entire drum is in constant rotation at, let us say, r revolutions per second. The read and write heads are fixed. The access time is thus the time taken by the referenced word on the drum to revolve back to the appropriate head; this varies between 0 and $1/r$ and is, on the average, $1/2r$. On a disk unit, the entire disk is in constant rotation, but the read and write heads are not fixed; they move over the surface of the disk. Therefore, the access time may be divided into two portions. A certain amount of time is taken for the head to move to the proper position, and then more time is needed for the referenced word on disk to rotate into position. On some other intermediate access units, the entire unit is not in constant rotation but consists of data elements, such as magnetic cards or magnetic tape loops, which are selected and then read or written. The access time for a word on such a data element may likewise be divided into two portions—one to select the data element and one to access the given word once the element has been selected.

Data in an intermediate access unit is organized hierarchically. Words on a disk, for example, may be grouped into tracks, the tracks grouped into sectors, the sectors grouped into cylinders, and the cylinders into Disk Packs. It is often possible to increase program speed by organizing files so that they fit naturally into the available substructures within the unit. The movable head on a disk unit, for example, may take a much smaller amount of time to move from one position to the "next" position, as the unit is organized, than to move from one arbitrary position to another. Therefore, programs should be organized whenever possible so that the total distance moved by the head is minimized. Knowledge of the organization of a unit is also important if it imposes restrictions on write operations. A magnetic card or a magnetic tape loop must usually be written as a unit; in order to change an individual word or words, the entire data element must be read in, the words altered, and the entire element written out again. Similarly, on a disk unit, the write instructions may be such that only an entire track, or an entire sector, can be written at once.

The input-output medium—that is, the actual oxide-coated surface or surfaces—in an intermediate access unit is sometimes interchangeable. A **disk pack** is a memory module which may be inserted and removed from a disk unit, just as a tape may be mounted or unloaded from a tape unit. Thus each installation may keep as many disk packs as it needs, one for each current file or system. On most intermediate access units, however, this cannot be done; the unit has a finite memory size, or capacity, and is in this way more similar to a core memory than to a tape unit.

Addresses in most drum units and some disk units are similar to addresses in core. If a unit has n memory words, the addresses range from 0 to $n - 1$, although some of these addresses may not be usable for device design reasons and others may be used exclusively by the input-output programming system. There are also intermediate access units in which addresses are not in sequence from 0 to $n - 1$, but derive from the hierarchical organization of the device. In a disk unit, for example, each track, sector, and cylinder may have an address, and the number of words per track or tracks per sector is not necessarily a power of 2 (or a power of 10, for a unit with decimal addressing). This does not cause trouble if files are made to correspond with the organization of the device; but this may not be possible or desirable. Address coding schemes have therefore been devised to translate an address lying within the range 0 through $n - 1$ into an actual drum or disk address. Another solution is to use a programming system in which all files are referenced by name. Subroutines are provided to create new files; the system keeps track of all unused space on the unit and assigns space for a new file or further space for an existing file, or releases space used by a deleted file, as directed. This frees the programmer from any reference to drum or disk addresses at all.

If the capacity of an intermediate access unit is larger than that of the (full size) core memory of a given computer, an address within this unit will be too large to fit in the address field of an instruction word. Hence instructions which specify disk addresses must use either indexing, on a computer with full-word index registers, or indirect addressing. In practice, most drum and disk instructions are much more complicated than this. If data are being read from disk or written to disk, both a core address and a disk address must be given, together with a count, or the last core or disk address involved. The easiest way to do this is to specify the start address in core and either the count or the end address in core in the same way as they would be specified to a tape unit, and to specify the start address on disk separately. If an entire track is being read or written, the track address is specified separately.

PROBLEMS

1. The DEC Type 340 Display Unit is a typical cathode ray tube display device, which may be connected to a PDP-6 computer. This display unit may be programmed, using the memory of the PDP-6, and uses 18-bit instruction words in various formats. One such format is the "increment mode." In this mode, each instruction word is broken up as follows:

Bit 1	End flag ($= 1$ for last increment mode word)
Bit 2	Intensity bit
Bits 3–6	First move instruction
Bits 7–10	Second move instruction
Bits 11–14	Third move instruction
Bits 15–18	Fourth move instruction

   It is assumed that a picture is being drawn by a spot of light on the tube. Each move instruction is four bits long and directs the spot of light to move one position (approximately 1/100 of an inch) in any of various directions. The directions are coded as follows, in octal:

2—UP	12—RIGHT AND UP	16—LEFT AND UP
3—DOWN	13—RIGHT AND DOWN	17—LEFT AND DOWN
10—RIGHT	14—LEFT	0—NO MOTION

   It is sometimes necessary to turn off the spot of light as it is being moved; this is analogous to lifting a pen off the paper. This is done by means of the intensity bit (bit 1). If this bit is zero, the spot is turned off; if it is one, the spot is turned on. The spot remains off or on for the next four move instructions; if fewer than four instructions are desired, the last few should be coded as 0 (no motion).

The PDP-6 computer has a 36-bit data word, which can contain two increment mode words. These are executed by the display unit in normal sequence, as if they were instruction words. The scale, or position size (1/100 of an inch in the above example) may be changed by a display instruction word of a different format.

Five sets of 36-bit words are given below in octal. Each is to be considered as if it were being executed by this display device. In each case, state what character or figure has been coded. (The first one, for example, is the letter A.) Note: The motion indicated by a move instruction is made *before* the spot is intensified. If an increment mode word is given with the intensity bit off, then the position at which this word leaves the spot is not illuminated by a succeeding increment mode word with the intensity bit on, unless the first move instruction in this word specifies "no motion."

(a) 201042225253; 331463230000; 147000764200.
(b) 201042227340; 104210607400.
(c) 125252021000; 201463231474; 346342724200.
(d) 221042224210; 301463636314.
(e) 200000020000; 221252766317.

2. For each of the following input-output devices, write the following code letters if applicable:

    I—Used for input
    O—Used for output
    U—Unit record; a record read or written by the device always has the same length
    V—Variable length record; a record read or written by the device does not always have the same length
    D—Destructive; the device destroys the input-output medium, so that it cannot be erased and used again

(a) Card reader
(b) Card punch
(c) Paper tape reader
(d) Paper tape punch
(e) Typewriter
(f) Magnetic tape unit
(g) Drum
(h) Plotter
(i) Line printer

3. (a) A computer has 24 bits per word and 6 bits per character. A subroutine, CRD (X, N), reads a card into the array X of length N. Assume that the entire card is read in Hollerith format and converted to the character code of this computer. Where is the character code representing the character in column 27 of this card?

(b) A computer has 32 bits per word and 8 bits per character. A subroutine, CPU(X, N), punches a card from information in the array X of length N. Assume that the entire card is punched in Hollerith format from the character codes in the array X. Where is the character code which is punched in column 61 of the card?

(c) A computer has 30 bits per word and 5 bits per character. A subroutine, PRINT(X, N), prints a line from character code information in the array X of length N. It is desired to print the letter A in print position 42. Where, in the array X, should the character code for the letter A be placed?

(d) A computer has 36 bits per word. A subroutine, CRB(X, N), reads a card in column binary format into the array X of length N. Assume that a card has the *Hollerith* characters ABC in columns 31, 32, and 33. Which word of the array X will this information appear in, and what will be the contents of this word, expressed as 12 octal digits?

(e) A computer has 48 bits per word. A subroutine, CPB(X, N), punches a card in column binary format into the array X of length N. Suppose that the first word of array X (the word with address X) contains the octal number 4004201020104040. What will be the contents of columns 1, 2, 3, and 4 of the punched card, in Hollerith format?

a label, consisting of a character string, is punched on the tape in such a way that it can be read. The figure below shows a paper tape which has been labelled in this way:

4. When punching paper tape it is helpful to be able to label the tape. That is,

Describe how you might write a subroutine PTC(X, NC) which, given a character string starting at X and containing NC characters, labels a paper tape with this string. Assume that the computer has 36 bits per word, 6 bits per character, and that 7-level paper tape is used, with each character taking up 5 frames of tape.

5. (a) The RCA 70/432 tape unit has a speed of 37.5 inches per second, with an 0.6-inch inter-record gap. How long does it take for this tape unit to read ten 1380-character records at 8 bits per character and 200 bits (or characters) per inch?

(b) The Burroughs B422 tape runs at 90 inches per second, 555.5 characters per inch. It reads one record in 0.3 seconds. How long is this record, in characters?

(c) The CDC 501 printer operates at 1000 lines per minute. How many full pages of 66 lines each can it print in 20 seconds?

6. A file processing routine reads and punches cards. One card is punched for every card read. Processing time for each card read and punched is 120 milliseconds. The card reader reads 1000 cards per minute and the card punch punches 250 cards per minute. Processing, reading, and punching all take place simultaneously.

(a) How much extra time would it take to read and punch 100 cards if reading and punching could take place simultaneously with each other, but not simultaneously with processing?

(b) How much extra time would it take to read and punch 250 cards if reading, punching, and processing could not take place simultaneously?

7. A file processing routine is being programmed. It will read one tape file and write one tape file. Both files are made up of 417-word logical records. The tape unit being used is the RCA 70/442, which reads and writes at a speed of 75 inches per second, with an 0.6-inch gap; recording density is 556 characters per inch at one character per word. Assuming that the tape motion is continuous, how much time is taken to read 500 logical records, if

(a) the physical records are the same size as the logical records?

(b) each physical record contains 4 logical records?

(c) each physical record contains 20 logical records?

8. The CDC 1604 has several interrupts, all of which use location 7 as in interrupt location. What are the advantages and disadvantages of this design?

9. In some situations, it is useful for the programmer to be able to specify that a subroutine, which he has coded, is to be executed upon each occurrence of an interrupt of a specific type. For example, he might want to count the number of times that he attempted to divide by zero; or he might want to call a dump routine with his own specifications if an interrupt of a special type occurred. How might a monitor or executive system be constructed so as to give its users this facility? Assume that the monitor system includes interrupt routines for all possible types of interrupt.

Chapter 11

INPUT-OUTPUT
PROGRAMMING

11-1 Input-output Subroutines

It is by now conventionally assumed, except on the smallest computers, that machine-language programmers do not write their own input-output instructions. Instead, they call input-output subroutines which are supplied as part of the system for the computer. The construction of such subroutines is a major part of the work of the systems programmer. A standard input-output subroutine must be very thoroughly checked out, since it will be called by a large number of programs. Some types of input-output routines, particularly interrupt routines, are very hard to check out, since their operation depends on the timing of the various devices. In addition, input-output routines are generally among the first routines to be checked out, at a time when hardware errors are still possibly present.

A subroutine which transfers the words in an array to an input-output device, or which reads an input-output device into an array, will have two parameters: the starting address of the array, and either its last address or its length. An array constructed for input-output purposes is called a **buffer.** For example, an 80-column binary card may be read into a 27-word buffer in a computer with a 36-bit word, since three columns of the card represent the 36 bits. The starting address of this buffer and the number 27 may be given as parameters. For some devices the length of the buffer is constant and does not need to be supplied as a parameter; for others it is not. Records written on a tape unit may be of any length; records punched on a card may be of variable length up to the maximum number of words that can be contained on a card.

Such subroutines must communicate with the various interrupt routines if the computer uses interrupts to monitor input-output. When an interrupt occurs, the interrupt routine performs whatever action is necessary and returns. Input-output subroutines may keep and update a list of input-output operations to be performed; when one such operation is finished, the interrupt routine removes it from this list and proceeds to initiate the next, if there is one. Interrupt routines also may check for errors—if a tape read operation has produced an error, the tape is backspaced and read again.

Buffers may be of various sizes, depending on the characteristics of the devices. Sometimes conversion must be made from one buffer size to another. Files may be grouped into "records" for programming purposes in such a way that the "records" have no connection with the actual record structure of the device on which the files are contained. These two kinds of records are called **logical records** and **physical records,** respectively. A logical record may take up several physical records; or it may end in the middle of a physical record, and the next one may take up the rest of that physical record. Manipulation of logical and physical records and changing buffer sizes is performed by **buffering routines.** Buffering routines also allow two or more buffers to be used alternatively, so that one buffer can be read or written while the next one is being used or formed.

Print buffers present a special problem. The data to be printed consist of a packed array of character codes. The data to be printed, however, are very often not in character-code format; they may consist of integers, floating point numbers, double precision numbers, amounts of money, etc. Therefore, such data must be converted to character-code format before being printed. Routines to perform this conversion are called **formatting routines.** Records on tape, if they are to be printed later, may also be formatted; so may records to be punched, if punching is to be done in Hollerith format. When cards are read in Hollerith format, the formatting problem occurs in reverse; the character codes on the cards must be converted to one of various internal data representations. In this case, we simply speak of **formatted input,** as opposed to **formatted output.**

11-2 Formatted Output

Formatted output routines may be combined with character string interpreters (as in FORTRAN) or with instruction word interpreters; however, we shall consider only problems of formatting here.

(1) **Decimal integers.** On a decimal computer, an integer such as 269 can be easily converted to the character codes 2, 6, and 9, since the

individual decimal digits of 269 are accessible. On a binary computer, however, 269 becomes 100001101, and there is no separate access to the digits 2, 6, and 9. These digits may be calculated by successively dividing by 10 and taking remainders; thus

$$269 \div 10 = \quad 26 \text{ , remainder } \quad 9$$
$$26 \div 10 = \quad 2 \text{ , remainder } \quad 6$$
$$2 \div 10 = \quad 0 \text{ , remainder } \quad 2$$

The process terminates when the quotient is zero. It does not work for negative numbers, since (at least on some computers)

$$-269 \div 10 = -27 \text{ , remainder } \quad 1$$

for example. Therefore, negative numbers must be converted to positive and the sign added later. The remainders must now be converted to the corresponding character codes, except on the IBM 700 series and a few other computers, where each integer is its own character code.

(2) **Binary integers.** Conversion of integers in any number system other than the decimal system may be done by changing the number 10, in the above process, to the base of the given number system. However, when the base is a power of 2, there is a much easier way—the bits are simply read off, one at a time (for binary), three at a time (for octal), or four at a time (for hexadecimal).

(3) **Floating point numbers.** The floating point exponent corresponds to a power of 2 (or, on the IBM 360, to a power of 16), whereas the exponent to be printed corresponds to a power of 10. By the properties of logarithms, one exponent is a constant multiple of the other (approximately, since the exponents are integers). The exponent of a floating point number, after the bias is removed, should be multiplied by $\log_{10} 2$ or $\log_{10} 16$, as the case may be, to obtain the exponent to be printed. This exponent may be too large or too small by one position, but a special-purpose test for this is easily made. The fractional part of the floating point number may be converted to n decimal places by multiplying it by 10^n and treating the result as in integer. Another method is to successively multiply by 10 and subtract the greatest integer in the result; this method is slightly slower because it takes longer to find the greatest integer. Thus

$$0.269 * 10.0 = 2.69 \text{ , minus } 2.0 \text{ leaves } 0.69$$
$$0.69 \ * 10.0 = 6.9 \ \text{ , minus } 6.0 \text{ leaves } 0.9$$
$$0.9 \ \ * 10.0 = 9.0 \ \text{ , minus } 9.0 \text{ leaves } 0.0$$

Any number to be converted should first be normalized, either by adding zero or by a special normalize instruction. A special test must be made for zero. Any floating point number with a zero fraction is treated as zero, regardless of the value of the exponent, which must then be ignored. As before, negative numbers are changed to positive before conversion, and the sign added after conversion.

(4) **Character codes.** These can be inserted in an output buffer by an extract and store loop. If there are a large number of them, time can sometimes be saved by inserting whole words. Two words are placed in two registers, which are then shifted left by xc bits, where c is the number of bits per character. The register at the left is then stored; the two registers are shifted left by yc bits, where $x + y$ is the number of characters per word; a new word of character codes is loaded into the second register; and the process continues. The values of x and y indicate the offset of the character codes in the output image; if $x = 0$, then word boundaries in the characters being inserted in the image correspond to word boundaries in the image.

(5) **Instruction words.** This form of conversion is most commonly found in dumps and other debugging programs. Two tables are required, an operation code table and a symbol table. The operation code is extracted and the corresponding mnemonic is found in the table and converted as a character string. The address field conversion may be done by keeping the symbol table sorted by addresses; an arbitrary address field is now looked up in this table by a binary search, and if it is not found, a symbol which is in the table, plus or minus a constant, is inserted in the print image. If the symbol table contained

SYMBOL	ADDRESS
P1	25207
P2	25216
P2A	25231
P3	25237

then an address field of 25207 would be converted as the symbol P1; an address field of 25234 would be converted as P2A+3 (that is, the characters "P," "2," "A," "+," and "3"). The address field 25236 might be converted as P2A+5, or as P3−1.

11-3 Formatted Input

When input character strings are being converted to internal representation, the type of conversion may be determined by the form of the input string. For example, a convention may be made that a symbol starting with a number is an integer, unless it contains a period, in which case it is a floating point number; that a symbol enclosed in quotes is to be taken as a character string; or that a symbol starting with a letter is to be looked up in a table. Also, the positions of characters to be converted do not have to be fixed. An input record can, for example, contain data items separated by commas. An input formatting routine can read this data, convert it, and store the converted data as directed by its calling sequence. For these reasons, formatted input routines are much more diverse than formatted output routines. Again, we shall consider only problems of formatting, using the standard FORTRAN input formatting conventions in which data types are specified in the calling sequence, rather than by the form of the data itself, and positions of data in input records are similarly so specified.

(1) **Decimal integers.** A decimal integer, when scanned from left to right, may be "accumulated" by keeping a trial value of the integer; each time a new digit is encountered, the trial value is multiplied by 10 and the new digit is added. The same process works for numbers in any other base, with the value of the base substituted for 10. It may be terminated by a count, or, in more general situations, by the occurrence of a non-numeric character.

(2) **Floating point numbers.** Floating point input conversion is much easier than output conversion. The integer part (to the left of the decimal point) is treated like a fixed point integer and converted to floating point. The fractional part is treated like a fixed point integer, converted to floating point, and multiplied by 10^{-n}, where n is the number of decimal places. The integer part and the fractional part are now added in floating point. If an exponent is given, the corresponding power of 10 may be calculated or looked up in a table and multiplied by the given number. A positive integer less than 2^f, where f is the number of bits in the fraction part of a floating point number, may be converted to floating point in one instruction by inserting an exponent of $b + f$, where b is the standard bias. The result is not normalized, but it may easily be normalized in one more instruction.

In both integer and floating point input formatting, some convention must be specified to cover the possibility that the given field of the input record might contain blanks. The best procedure is to treat blanks as if they were zeros. The same is true, when reading data separated by commas, if two commas occur in succession; the data item after the first comma is assumed to be zero. If a minus sign is the first character of the item, this fact is saved and the integer or floating point number changed to its negative after input conversion.

(3) **Character codes.** The same processes may be used here for input as for output conversion.

(4) **Symbols with operators.** Some input formatting routines also allow character strings to represent symbols, whose values are looked up in a table; and these symbols may be connected by operators, such as $+$ and $-$. Such routines form a gray area between input conversion and analysis of algebraic expressions, which we have already examined.

11-4   Block Buffers

The basic direct input-output subroutine for a magnetic tape unit or an intermediate access device, which writes (or reads) an array of any length, is often a block buffering routine, which prepares physical buffers that are **blocks,** or groups, of logical buffers. The following routine, written in FORTRAN, writes the array A of length N on tape. It calls the subroutine BLKWR, which writes the array B of fixed size LENBL (the length of the block, assumed to be elsewhere defined) on tape.

```
      SUBROUTINE TWR(A, N)
      DIMENSION B(LENBL)
      DO 3 I = 1, N
      IF (NCT-LENBL) 2,1,2
   1  CALL BLKWR(B)
      NCT=0
   2  NCT=NCT+1
   3  B(NCT)=A(I)
      RETURN
      END
```

This routine assumes that NCT has previously been initialized to zero. This may be done by making NCT a common variable, or, in some versions of FORTRAN, by compiling the subroutine at the same time as the routine that calls it, so that both routines use the same variables. Also, BLKWR must be called once at the end of the file to be written, since the block buffer B is partly full and thus still contains information which has not been written. We say that this buffering routine, or alternatively the file which it writes, is **opened** by setting NCT to 0 and **closed** by calling BLKWR.

The following routine, written in FORTRAN, reads tape and places the words which it reads into the array A of length N. It calls the subroutine BLKRD, which reads tape into the array B of fixed size LENBL.

```
          SUBROUTINE TRD(A, N)
          DIMENSION B(LENBL)
          DO 3 I = 1, N
          IF (NCT−LENBL) 2,1,2
     1    CALL BLKRD(B)
          NCT=0
     2    NCT=NCT+1
     3    A(I)=B(NCT)
          RETURN
          END
```

This routine also assumes that NCT has been initialized to zero. We say that this buffering routine or its file is *opened* by performing this initialization. Closing of a read file is normally determined, not by the program, but by the form of the data. As soon as the file has been read completely, the routine BLKRD will make an abnormal exit of some sort; no further information is on the file to be read. The program may, of course, stop reading the file before it reaches the end of file.

Both of these routines may be speeded up by testing only once to see if the current array fits in the current block, rather than once each time a word is transferred to or from the block. If it will not fit, the current block is completed and written (or the data from the end of the current block is transferred and a new block is read) and the remainder of the buffer is treated as being located at the beginning of the next block. The routines will take more space in this case because there are more distinct cases to be covered—for example, the case in which one logical buffer is contained partially in more than two blocks or physical buffers. On the other hand, sometimes the convention is made that each logical buffer is contained in one and only one block. The blocks are now of variable length. This convention is useful in processing magnetic tape, for example, where the length of each block does not matter as long as it is not less than a certain minimum size, so that start and stop time does not become too large in relation to data transfer time. In this case, each buffer is tested to see whether it will fit into the current block. If it will not, the length of the current block is stored as the first word of the block; the block is written; and a new block is started (at the second word). If a buffer is larger than block size, it is itself written as a block; this assumes that every such buffer has an extra word at the start, denoting its length. When a file written in this way is read, the first word of each new block is taken as the block length, and as each buffer is read out, the position of the last word of the current buffer is incremented and compared with this block length.

There is another type of block buffering routine in which the buffers are not moved from or into separate arrays, but stay within the block. The routine returns a parameter which points to the starting location of the current buffer. In machine language, this will be an address field which may be placed in an index register by the calling routine for later reference. The convention that each physical buffer must be contained in one and only one logical buffer should be observed; otherwise the burden of switching buffers is thrown on the calling program. To write a buffer in this way, we may write (in FORTRAN)

```
      SUBROUTINE TWRX(N, INDEX)
      DIMENSION B(LENBL)
      IF (NCT—LENBL) 1, 1, 2
  1   CALL BLKWR(B)
      NCT=1
      GO TO 3
  2   NCT=NCT+NPREV
  3   NPREV=N
      RETURN
      END
```

assuming that NCT has initially been set to 1 and NPREV to 0. Here INDEX is the index within the block B at which the new buffer starts. Words are written by the object program directly into the buffer. The same routine, with BLKRD substituted for BLKWR, will serve for reading buffers; the first word read is pointed to by INDEX.

11-5 Double Buffers

The routines of the last section do not take advantage of the capability, present on all large computers and many smaller ones, of performing input-output and processing (i.e., instruction words) simultaneously. Thus, in TWR, the routine BLKWR is called to write the buffer B, and TWR must now wait until the write operation is completely finished before it can continue. This is true even if the write operation proceeds from the beginning to the end of the buffer and the next buffer is filled from beginning to end. Attempts have been made to keep a pointer, set by the hardware, to the word currently being written, and to arrange processing so that no word past this pointer is ever destroyed as the subsequent buffer is filled. These attempts have always failed, if for no other reason than that input-output operations are always subject to error. If the output record has not been written successfully, as indicated by a parity check or otherwise, then it must be rewritten; and it cannot be rewritten if it has meanwhile been overwritten.

A better solution to this problem is to have two buffers. (The word "buffer" in this section means what the word "block" did in the last— i.e., a physical buffer that may contain several logical buffers.) When one buffer is full, a write operation is started on it, and attention shifts to the other buffer. When this buffer is full, a test is made to see if the output device is still busy processing the previous record. As soon as the device is no longer busy, a write operation is started on the second buffer and further data is placed in the first buffer. The following routine is an alternate version of TWR which uses two buffers B1 and B2, and which also follows the suggestions of the last section for improving speed.

```
      SUBROUTINE TWR(A, N)
      DIMENSION B1(LENBL), B2(LENBL)
      N2=0
1     IF (NCT + N - N2 - LENBL) 8, 8, 2
2     IF (KFLAG) 3, 5, 3
3     DO 4 I = NCT + 1, LENBL
      N2 = N2 + 1
4     B1(I) = A(N2)
      CALL BLKWR(B1)
      GO TO 7
5     DO 6 I = NCT+1, LENBL
      N2 = N2 + 1
6     B2(I) = A(N2)
      CALL BLKWR(B2)
7     KFLAG = 1 - KFLAG
      NCT = 0
      GO TO 1
8     IF (KFLAG) 9, 11, 9
9     DO 10 I = N2+1, N
      NCT = NCT + 1
10    B1(NCT) = A(I)
      RETURN
11    DO 12 I = N2+1, N
      NCT = NCT + 1
12    B2(NCT) = A(I)
      RETURN
      END
```

This routine is opened by setting NCT to zero and setting KFLAG to either zero or one, depending on which buffer it is desired to start with.

It is closed by calling either BLKWR(B1) or BLKWR(B2), depending on the value of KFLAG.

Double buffering routines use more space and less time than single buffering routines. The time saved, however, is worth much more than the space wasted; therefore double buffers should always be used unless there is absolutely no space for them or unless the input-output is non-simultaneous, in which case they are not necessary. Double buffering may be used on input as well as output, and double buffering routines may be written to return a parameter giving the address of the current logical buffer within one of the two physical buffers.

11-6 Multiple Buffers

When the amount of time taken by the computer to process the data in each incoming buffer or to produce the data for each outgoing buffer is constant, two buffers are all that is needed. If this time is less than the time taken by the input-output operations, the program will be **I/O limited**; a certain constant amount of time will be spent waiting for an I/O operation to finish before processing can continue. Otherwise, the program will be **computation-limited**; its speed will be limited by speed of computation rather than by speed of input-output. In this case, input-output operations do not take place continuously; after each operation, a certain constant amount of time elapses before the next operation is started.

In practice, this is almost never the case. Certain parts of a computation will be computation-limited and other parts will be I/O-limited. In order to balance out the time taken by input-output operations and to decrease waiting time, more than two buffers may be used. The exact optimum number of buffers for a given situation is difficult to determine; however, if the computer is not multiprogrammed or time-shared, all of the unused core memory may be used for buffers.

Let us assume initially that there is only one type of input-output operation taking place within a program, using n buffers. In this case, pointers to these buffers may be kept in a circular list. Two special pointers to items within this circular list, which we shall call IOPTR and INTPTR, are kept by the input-output routine and its associated interrupt routine, respectively. The buffer which the input-output routine considers to have just been input or output is pointed to by IOPTR; the buffer which is actually being input or output is pointed to by INTPTR, and is modified by the corresponding interrupt routine. Initially, IOPTR and INTPTR are both set to point to the first buffer to be input or output.

For multiply buffered output, IOPTR "runs ahead of" INTPTR; the actual output operations do not, in general, keep up with the formation of new output buffers. As the output routine is called, it advances IOPTR and returns the item in the circular list to which IOPTR now points; this will be the location of a buffer which may now be filled by the calling routine. Alternatively, the output routine may fill the current buffer from an array given as a parameter, advance IOTPR, and exit. As each output operation is completed, an interrupt occurs, and control transfers to the interrupt routine. This routine compares INTPTR with IOPTR. If they are the same, no more operations need be performed and the interrupt routine terminates; otherwise, INTPTR is advanced and an output operation started on the buffer pointed to by the item to which INTPTR now points. In this way the output routine may stay a maximum of n buffers ahead of the hardware. This routine must also compare the two pointers after IOPTR has been advanced; if they are equal, all the buffers are full and the output routine must wait.

For multiply buffered input, INTPTR runs ahead of IOPTR; actual input operations produce new buffers in advance of the time at which they are actually used by the calling program. As each input operation is completed, the interrupt routine advances IOPTR and compares the new value with INTPTR. If they are equal, all buffers are full, and the sequence of input operations must wait. Otherwise, a new input operation which references the next buffer is initiated and the interrupt routine terminates. As the input routine is called, INTPTR is advanced. If it is now equal to IOPTR, the input routine waits until the current input operation is complete. The routine either returns a parameter giving the location of the new input buffer as indicated by IOPTR, or moves this information to a buffer given to it as a parameter.

Instead of a circular list, these routines may use a "circular array," which is actually an ordinary array together with a method of advancing any pointer to the array. The method consists of proceeding to the next item of the array unless the pointer points to the last item of the array, in which case it is reset to point to the first item. In this way, any array may be made to behave like a circular list.

A closely related construction is the **ring buffer,** used for typewriter and Teletype input-output when this is done on a character-by-character basis. The ring buffer is a circular array containing characters, which may be packed; two pointers to a character in this array are used, as above. The character which has just been typed in or typed out is pointed to by INTPTR, whereas the character which has just been made accessible to the routine which inputs a character or which has just been specified to the routine which outputs a character is pointed to by IOPTR. For packed characters, these pointers must of course give both word and character positions. The interrupt routines insert a character in the buffer on input and remove a character on output; the input routine removes a character from the buffer and returns it to the calling program, whereas the output routine accepts a character from the calling program and places it in the buffer. The entire procedure, in fact, is analogous to the multiple buffering procedure described earlier, except that the actual data, rather than pointers to the data, are kept in the ring buffer.

Finally, we consider the general case, where several I/O operations are proceeding at once. It is, of course, always possible for each I/O operation to have its own circular list of buffers, and its own IOPTR and INTPTR. This will work, but it is very wasteful for space, particularly buffer space. If the buffer size of several input-output operations is the same, it would be useful for them to have access to the same buffers. This leads to the concept of a **buffer pool.** A buffer pool may be considered as a list space in which every item contains or points to an entire buffer. Each input-output device using the pool has associated with it a list of buffers assigned to it; these take the role of the buffers between IOPTR and INTPTR in the previous example. There is also a list of available space, consisting of all buffers which are currently unassigned. When the input interrupt routine is entered, a new buffer is added to the end of this list. This buffer is found by removing a buffer from the list of available buffers. When the input routine is entered, the buffer at the beginning of the list is removed from the list and placed on the list of available buffers; and the new beginning of the list becomes the current buffer and is made available to the calling routine. The reverse procedure takes place on output. Using a buffer pool, it is not necessary for input or output operations to wait unless the *entire* pool is filled, although sometimes a **lookahead factor** will be specified as a maximum length of each of the lists of assigned buffers.

Ring buffers, circular lists, and lists of assigned buffers as above, have also been called **FIFO lists.** FIFO means "first in, first out"; the first item to be inserted in the list is the first to be removed from it. In contrast, push down lists and lists of available space are **LIFO** (last in, first out) **lists.**

11-7 Push Down Buffers

When a push down stack is kept on tape, drum, or disk, a certain amount of the stack should be in core—namely, the top of the stack, together with a certain (minimum) number of words below the top. If the stack is divided into buffers, and one buffer is kept in core at all times, then time must be spent waiting for each buffer to be written out or read back in. The solution to this difficulty seems to be double buffering of the push down stack. Actually, *triple* buffering is required. We now show intuitively why double buffering is not sufficient.

Suppose that there are two buffers, B1 and B2. As B1 becomes full, an output operation is started on it, and B2 starts filling up. But now suppose that, after the first item is pushed down into B2, this item is popped up, another item is popped up (from B1), and finally a new item is pushed down (into B1). Now buffer B1 has been modified and has to be written all over again. If this process (of two push-downs followed by two pop-ups) takes place several times, buffer B1 must be rewritten repeatedly, causing repeated waiting for I/O operations. A push down algorithm may resolve this problem by not starting to write B1 until B2 is half full. However, in this case each half of B2 (and of B1) is effectively a separate buffer, so that there are four buffers which are read or written in pairs.

The three buffers used in a push down buffering routine may be thought of as "the current buffer," "an extra buffer for forward motion," and "an extra buffer for backward motion." We shall call the buffers B1, B2, and B3. As items are pushed down into B1, filling B1, buffer B2 is started. When B2 is filled, an output operation is started on B1 (*not* on B2) and B3 is started. As each buffer is filled, an output operation starts on the preceding buffer, and the following buffer is started (by convention, B1 follows B3). The reverse procedure is followed for popping up. As buffer B2 is popped up, so that it is now "empty," an input operation of the previously written data is started into B3, and the next item is popped up from the end of B1. When the pop-ups reach the beginning of B1, a test is made to ensure that the previous input operation was completed; a new input operation is started into B2; and the next item is popped up from the end of B3.

Push down and pop up operations which are more thoroughly intermixed cause other problems. Let us call *either* a push down operation when the current buffer is full, *or* a pop up operation when it is empty, a *buffer change operation;* these two types of buffer change operation will be denoted by F (forward) and B (backward), respectively. It is clear that, if F and B operations alternate, no input or output operations need be started. However, if a set of F-B pairs is preceded and followed by two F's, the result is the same as if there were three F's in a row—that is, an output operation is started after a test has been made that the preceding output operation is complete. When a set of F-B pairs is preceded and followed by two B's, the result is the same as if there were three B's in a row—an input operation is started after a test as before. If two F's are followed by two B's, no operation is started at the first B, and, at the second B, the previously started output operation is abandoned and an input operation in the reverse direction is started. The same is true of a set of F-B pairs preceded by two F's and followed by two B's. Finally, if two B's are followed by two F's, then no operation is started at the first F, and the previously started input operation is abandoned and an output operation in the forward direction is started; this is also true of a set of F-B pairs preceded by two B's and followed by two F's. These being all the cases, we have a total of six, which may be shown to be as follows:

Case number	"F" and "B" sequence
1	F-F
2	F-F-B-F, F-F-B-F-B-F, F-F-B-F-B-F-B-F, etc.
3	F-F-B, F-F-B-F-B, F-F-B-F-B-F-B, etc.
4	B-B-F, B-B-F-B-F, B-B-F-B-F-B-F, etc.
5	B-B-F-B, B-B-F-B-F-B, B-B-F-B-F-B-F-B, etc.
6	B-B

These six cases are represented by the six states of a switch. That is, there is a variable, which we shall call MASTER, and which takes any value from 1 to 6, depending on the case as above. Each time a new F or B operation is performed (where we recall that these are *buffer change* operations, that is, push down or pop up operations which actually pass buffer boundaries) the value of MASTER is changed, and other action is taken, according to the following table:

Old value of MASTER	New value of MASTER after F	Action taken after F	New value of MASTER after B	Action taken after B
1	1	WO	3	N
2	1	WO	3	N
3	2	N	6	I
4	1	O	5	N
5	4	N	6	WI
6	4	N	6	WI

where the actions to be taken are coded as follows:

N—No I/O operation is started.

WO (Wait and Output)—When the last output operation is complete, a new one is started (in the forward direction).

WI (Wait and Input)—When the last input operation is complete, a new one is started (in the reverse direction).

O—An output operation is started. If a previous input operation was in progress, it is abandoned.

I—An input operation is started. If a previous output operation was in progress, it is abandoned.

11-8   Input-output Errors

The internal electronic operations of a computer may be assumed to be free from error. Any errors which occur are either corrected automatically, without program intervention, or are not, in which case the machine is presumed to be out of order. Input-output operations, however, are mechanical, and are subject to intermittent errors. These errors may be sensed by instructions, but must be corrected by the program. Among them are the following:

(1) **Parity errors in reading.** When a drum, disk, or magnetic tape is read, and often when a paper tape is read, parity bits which have been inserted when the tape was written are checked. An error in the parity bits indicates that either the record was originally written incorrectly, or it is now being read incorrectly. This condition may be sensed by the computer, which has instructions such as "transfer on parity check." If a parity error has occurred, the program should read the record again. For a tape, this means backspacing the tape by one record (for a forward read) or positioning it forward by one record (for a backward read) and then restarting the read. For an intermediate access device, the record is merely reread from its starting address (on the device). Some routines perform this reread operation only a certain maximum number of times, after which they assume that the record is unreadable—either by returning to an error return, for a read subroutine, or by printing "ERROR" together with a description of the error and either stopping or returning to the executive system.

(2) **Comparison errors in writing.** To decrease the number of records written incorrectly, a record which is written onto a magnetic tape, drum, or disk unit may be simultaneously read, and the data which is read may be checked against the data which is written. If the two do not match, the record may be rewritten. The same type of check may be made for paper tape, punched cards, or the printer, although in this case the erroneous record cannot be erased. Again, some routines perform the rewrite operation only a certain maximum number of times. However, if a record cannot be written properly, the write routine has one more recourse. It may be that the error is caused by a "bad spot" on the input-output medium rather than by internal trouble in the device. Magnetic tapes, drums, and disks can all develop "bad spots," since the oxide coating which has

the necessary magnetic properties may become scratched or may wear, or, in the case of a magnetic tape, it may twist or crimp. The write routine therefore spaces the device forward by some fixed amount, hoping to bypass the bad spot, and tries again to write.

(3) **Not ready conditions.** Originally, a device was "not ready" if it had not been turned on, and programs made routine checks of the ready status of each device before reading or writing, or else the first read or write operation was automatically delayed by the hardware until the device was ready. It was then discovered that a large collection of internal device errors could be treated by programs as if the corresponding device were not ready. Among these are card reader jam (card stuck in the mechanism); card punch jam; printer out of paper, or out of ribbon; no more cards in the hopper of the card reader or punch; card punch chip box full; overheating of any device; or even a parity error in a device which cannot be "backspaced," such as a card reader. In each case the program stops (if the computer is multiprogrammed, it passes to another program) until the operator corrects the condition. In some systems, one on-line typewriter or printer is reserved for messages to the operator, and thus the computer can inform the operator which device is not ready (unless it is the on-line typewriter or printer itself).

(4) **Timing errors.** The hardware of a computer regulates its own timing; but if mechanical failure prevents an operation from being completed, a program may sense this fact and act on it. Timing errors are normally found in the loop which tests whether a device or a channel is busy and delays until it is not busy. If there is no timing check in this loop and mechanical failure occurs, so that the busy flag stays on, the loop becomes endless. Usually some very large amount of time (such as one second) is chosen as the maximum time that a channel can take to read or write one record. When the busy flag is first sensed, the real time clock is read; each succeeding time that the busy flag is sensed, the value of the real time clock is compared against this initial value. When a timing error is finally recognized, a message may be sent to the operator as before.

(5) **End conditions.** On write operations, end conditions are not errors, but, like errors, they are sensed and acted upon by input-output programs. For a tape, the end condition is end-of-tape. For an intermediate access unit, there may be various end conditions, depending on the internal structure of the unit, which have names such as end-of-track, end-of-sector, end-of-cylinder, and so on. At any end condition, if further data is to be written, the output routine must find space for it somewhere else. On a tape unit, this implies sending a message to the operator to mount a new reel of tape. On intermediate access units, a new track or

sector or cylinder is usually easy to find, unless the unit is completely full, in which case the end condition is truly an error. End conditions are also sensed on read operations, and produce similar actions by the input routine; input routines, however, can also sense *end-of-file* conditions, implying that there is no more information to be read, which cause abnormal exit from the input routine. Some computers allow several tape reels to be mounted at once, so that there is no need for the routine to wait while a tape is changed.

A computer can also check for input-output *programming* errors of various types. If a data channel has its own instruction word format, there may be improper instruction codes which are sensed. Some computers are even capable of sensing an improper *order* of input-output operations. A write operation on disk, for example, cannot immediately follow a read operation unless the appropriate codes are inserted in the sequence of channel commands to enable the disk unit to switch over from reading to writing. Generally, however, if the channel command codes are proper but the addresses are wrong, data will be read into, or written from, the wrong area of core.

11-9   Input-output Programming Systems

A programming system for input-output purposes may be written either as a package or as a compiler.

Input-output packages are generally contained as part of the executive system of a computer. In this capacity they may remain in core at all times; this depends on the structure of the monitor system. If a large collection of routines remains in core at all times, this leaves less space for the user's routines. Therefore, some executive systems treat input-output packages just as any other subroutines. The only routine which must be in core at any time, in such a system, is a routine (often called EXIT) which reloads the executive system from tape, drum, or disk. When the executive routine has the next routine ready, it calls a subroutine, either at the beginning of core (**lower loader**) or at the end of core (**upper loader**), which reads this routine and its subroutines, including the EXIT routine, into core, perhaps overwriting the rest of the executive routine. Such a system is at an advantage if intermediate access storage is used; but if the executive routine must be reloaded from tape, an intolerable amount of time may be spent in this process.

Block buffering and editing on formatting packages are considered to be distinct from the "basic" input-output packages (containing the actual input-output instructions) and are only loaded when needed. In fact, as we have seen, a formatting package may be written as an interpretive routine.

A disadvantage of the use of packages for basic input-output is that most loaders will either load the entire package at all times, which may take up very large amounts of space, or at any rate it will load many more routines than are actually needed in any given situation. Along with any routine which is loaded, all its subroutines are loaded. But if any one of these subroutines is never called in a given situation, then it and all *its* subroutines (and all their subroutines, ad infinitum) are unnecessary. There do exist very powerful loaders, however, which do not necessarily load the subroutines of a loaded routine. Each call to such a subroutine is sensed by the loader and replaced by a call to the loader with the given subroutine name as a parameter; the loader then loads the subroutine while the program is in progress. In this type of system, the *loader* remains in core at all times, and may itself require a large amount of space.

Compilers for input-output accept a source language containing a complete description of the input-output situation in a given program, and output an object program containing only those portions of the standard input-output packages which are needed in this situation. Such compilers accept the following as input:

(1) A description of the computer itself: how many tape units it has, what channels they are on, what model they are, and the same questions for disk or drum units, card readers, card punches, printers, etc. This is important because the input-output equipment available for a given computer differs widely, depending on the particular installation. Also, one installation may have several similar computers with different configurations, and compilations may be performed on one computer for execution on another. (Since each additional input-output device or channel adds significantly to the cost of the computer, organizations which buy or rent computers tend to be very careful that only those input-output units are ordered which are actually needed.)

(2) A description of each file involved in the given input-output situation: what its name is, whether it is for input or output or both, what device it is on, how long the records are (if the device permits a variable record length), whether records are blocked or unblocked, and, if they are blocked, how long the blocks are; whether there are labels, and if so, what format they are in, and whether or not they are to be checked; and so on.

The Input-Output Control System (IOCS) written by IBM for its 1400 series is actually an input-output compiler which communicates with the AUTOCODER assemblers for this series by means of macros. It provides a great flexibility of input-output operations for these small computers. As presently constituted, its disadvantages are that compilation is very slow (this is a general problem with compilers and assemblers for this series) and that the input-output situation must be completely described, once and for all, in the source language, and cannot be modified at execution time. There is also a program for the IBM 700 series called Input-Output Control System or IOCS, which combines an input-output compiler communicating with assemblers through macros, with a package of subroutines. Both of these programs handle block buffering as well as basic input-output.

PROBLEMS

1. (a) Describe a formatted input procedure for integers in an arbitrary radix (number system base) according to the following format: the standard radix is 10; two integers separated by either R or X denote a radix, less than or equal to 10, and an integer in that radix, respectively; in addition, when the character X is used, the given radix becomes the new standard radix for all succeeding integers. Thus:

   2R101 denotes 5 (decimal);

   8R101 denotes 65 (decimal);

   5X40, 30, 2R1000, and 200, in that order, denote 20, 15, 8, and 50 (decimal) in that order;

   8X70, 3R22, 12R71, and 200, in that order, denote 56, 8, 71, and 128 (decimal) in that order.

   (b) How would this procedure be modified if a radix were restricted to be less than or equal to 36, with the 36 digits being 0 through 9 followed by A through Z in natural order?

   (c) Suppose that integers as in part (b) were to be combined, in algebraic expressions, with symbols containing alphanumeric characters and starting with an alphabetic character. What convention or conventions would have to be made about these integers to prevent syntactic ambiguity?

2. A recurring problem in program design is that of specifying maximum lengths for arrays. Sometimes the length of an array will be implied by the problem statement, but more often the array will be needed for intermediate results in a program and its length is determined by factors which are not easy to evaluate. As an example, consider the convention, made in many languages, that a numeric character string followed by the letter B is to be treated as octal. Assume that numeric character strings are being converted to multiple precision integers, where the precision of a given integer may be variable.

   (a) What problem arises in writing a formatted input routine to read such integers, that does *not* arise if octal numbers are preceded by 8R (see problem 1 above)?

   (b) How might this problem be solved if every integer must be completely contained on one card?

   (c) How might this problem be solved if there is a specified maximum precision for integers to be converted?

(d) How might this problem be solved if the formatted input routine is contained in a program which utilizes a list space?

3. A certain computer has fixed point addition and subtraction, and floating point addition, subtraction, multiplication, and division, but no fixed point multiplication or division. Describe how decimal integer formatted input and output might be performed on such a computer.

4. The following rounding algorithm is part of a formatted output routine for FORTRAN format expressions of type $Fn.m$; it assumes that the unrounded floating point number is already in the output buffer as a character string. For example, if the format is F8.4 and the number to be printed is $\log_{10} 5$ ($\cong 0.69897$), then the characters bb0.6989 (where b stands for blank) are in the output buffer. This number is now to be rounded to m decimal places, for the format $Fn.m$, and thus in this case the characters in the buffer are to be changed to read bb0.6990 (the correct rounded result). A character pointer CP is assumed to be pointing to the last character in the string representing the number. The algorithm proceeds as follows:
1. Examine the character to which CP points.
2. If it is a 9, proceed to step 4.
3. Add one to the character pointed to, store it back at the same position, and stop.
4. Store a zero character in the position to which CP points.
5. Set CP to point to the previous character.
6. Go to step 1.

This algorithm works for the example given above. For a general format of type $Fn.m$, however, this algorithm has one important omission. What is it? How should the algorithm be changed to take account of it?

5. (a) A computer has 48-bit data words; there are 8 bits per character. A card input buffer is 432 words long. At one character per column, how many 72-column card images can it contain?

(b) A computer has 60-bit data words; there are 6 bits per character. A card output buffer contains twenty-five 80-column card images at one character per column. How many words long is it?

(c) A computer has 36-bit data words; there are 6 bits per character. A printer buffer contains the images of 20 print lines; it is 400 words long. How many characters are contained in each print line?

6. As described in the text, a buffer pool is a list space of buffers. This list space uses a list of available space. Why is it impossible to use an array of available space?

7. In each of the following input-output programming situations, state whether you would use single, double, or multiple buffering, and why.

(a) A card reader reads 400 cards per minute; processing time varies from

40 to 120 milliseconds per card. Processing and card reading may take place simultaneously.

(b) A tape reads 90,000 characters per second, and another tape writes at the same rate. Input records are 840 characters long; output records are 600 characters long. At most, one output record is produced for every input record. Processing time varies from 400 ms to 1.1 second per record. The two tapes are on different channels; reading, writing, and processing take place simultaneously.

(c) A printer produces 1000 lines per minute. Processing time varies from 60 to 150 ms per line. Printing and processing do not take place simultaneously.

(d) A card punch produces 200 cards per minute. Processing time for each card is between 30 and 60 ms. Every ten cards, there is an additional amount of processing which takes 2 seconds. Card punching and processing take place simultaneously.

8. (a) A 32K computer contains a program, which, with its subroutines, uses 23,000 (octal) words. A total of 427 (octal) words are used by the loading routine, which remains in core with the program. The remainder of core is to be divided up into I/O buffers. Each buffer contains 288 (decimal) words of data and two pointers, which can both be fitted into a single data word. How many such I/O buffers can be formed? Give your answer in decimal.

(b) A 64K (byte) computer contains a program, which, with its subroutines, uses 3800 (hexadecimal) bytes. A total of 193 (hexadecimal) bytes are used by the loading routine, which remains in core with the program. A common area of 100 (hexadecimal) full words, each of which is four bytes long, is used by all the subroutines. The remainder of core is to be divided up into I/O buffers. Each buffer contains 256 (decimal) full words of data and four pointers, each of which takes two bytes. How many such I/O buffers can be formed? Give your answer in decimal.

9. The integer variable M is to be considered as an amount of money expressed in cents, which is greater than 10^n and less than 10^{n+1}. This variable is to be printed as an amount of money, with dollar sign, period, and commas if necessary. Give a formula for the total number of characters needed, in terms of n.

Chapter 12

INSTRUCTION THEORY

12-1 Set Theoretical Prerequisites

Instruction theory is the mathematical theory of computer instructions. A computer and its instructions are described in set theoretical terms, and theorems are then developed and proved. Like any mathematical theory, instruction theory depends upon set theory. We shall give a review of that portion of set theory which is necessary to understand instruction theory.

An **element** is any object which can be used in a mathematical context. Elements are grouped into **sets.** An element is either *in* a set, or not. A set may be *finite* or *infinite;* it is finite if and only if it has n elements in it, where n is a natural number—that is, a positive integer or zero. (The set of all natural numbers, as a set, has a precise definition which is extensively examined in set theory.) The word "set" is treated, in set theory, as undefined; it is a primitive, just as "point," "line," and "plane" are primitives in plane geometry.

If an element a is in a set A, we write a ϵ A (or "a is in A"). If every element in A is also in B, we write $A \subseteq B$ (or "A is contained in B"); or we write $B \supseteq A$ (or "B contains A"). If $A \subseteq B$ and $B \supseteq A$, then $A = B$. If it is not true that $A = B$, we write $A \neq B$. If $A \subseteq B$ but $A \neq B$, we write $A \subset B$, or $B \supset A$. If a is not in the set A, we write $a \notin A$.

Sets may be specified in various ways. The set containing exactly one element x is written $\{x\}$; the set containing exactly two elements, x and y, is written $\{x, y\}$. The set consisting of the n elements $x_1, \ldots, x_n$ may be written $\{x_1, \ldots, x_n\}$. A set may also be specified as containing all elements of another set which have a certain property. If Z is the set of all integers, then $\{x \epsilon Z: x > 5\}$ is the set of all integers greater than 5; $\{x \epsilon Z: x > 5, x < 10\}$ is the set of integers greater than 5 and less than 10, that is, $\{6, 7, 8, 9\}$.

If A and B are sets, then $A \cup B$ (or "A union B," or "the union of A and B") is the set of all elements which are in either A or B, or both. The phrase "or both" will be implicit whenever we say "or." If A and B are sets, then $A \cap B$ (or "A intersect B," or "the intersection of A and B") is the set of all elements which are in both A and B; and $A - B$ (or "the difference of A and B") is the set of all elements which are in A but not in B. The set of no elements is called the **null set** and is denoted by $\emptyset$; thus, in particular, $A - A = \emptyset$ for any set A. There is no such thing as the set of *all* elements; this implies a logical paradox. However, it is often the case that there is some set U, called the "universe," containing all elements that can possibly be under study in the current situation. In this case, for any set $X \subseteq U$, the set $U - X$ is called the **complement** of X and is written $\overline{X}$.

A **function** is a rule which assigns, to every element of one set, an element of another set. These two sets are called, respectively, the **domain** and the **range** of the function. If the domain of a function f is A and its range is B, we write $f: A \rightarrow B$. If $C \supseteq B$, it is permissible to write $f: A \rightarrow C$; strictly speaking, however, an element x is in the range of f only if $f(a) = x$, for some a in the domain of f. A function may also be called a **map** or a **mapping.** The function $f: A \rightarrow B$ is **one-to-one** if $f(a_1) = f(a_2)$ implies $a_1 = a_2$, for all $a_1, a_2 \in A$; it is **onto** (or "onto B") if B is its actual range, i.e., for each $b \in B$ there exists a $\in A$ such that $f(a) = b$.

Let $f: A \rightarrow B$ be a function and let A' be a subset of A. We define a new function $g: A' \rightarrow B$ as follows: if $a' \in A'$, then $g(a') = f(a')$. The function g is different from the function f, because its domain is different. It is called the **restriction** of f to A', or $f|A'$. The function $h: A \rightarrow C$ defined by $h(a) = g(f(a))$, where $f: A \rightarrow B$ and $g: B \rightarrow C$ are given functions, is called the **composition** of f and g, and is written $f \circ g$.

Let A and B be sets. The set of all ordered pairs (a, b), where $a \in A$ and $b \in B$, is called the **product** of A and B, and is written $A \times B$. The map $f: A \times B \rightarrow A$, defined by $f(a, b) = a$, is called the **projection map** of $A \times B$ onto A. The product of a space with itself, such as $A \times A$, can be viewed as the set of all maps $f: \{0, 1\} \rightarrow A$; an element (a_1, a_2) corresponds to the map f such that $f(0) = a_1$ and $f(1) = a_2$. Note that these elements are *ordered pairs;* that is, (a_1, a_2) and (a_2, a_1) are different elements of $A \times A$. The set of all ordered n-tuples $(a_1, \ldots, a_n)$, where A_1, $\ldots, A_n$ are sets with $a_1 \in A_1, \ldots, a_n \in A_n$, is called the *product* of the sets $A_1, \ldots, A_n$, and is written $A_1 \times \cdots \times A_n$. This product may be viewed as the set of all maps $f: \{1, \ldots, n\} \rightarrow A_1 \cup \cdots \cup A_n$ such that $f(i) \in A_i$ for $1 \leq i \leq n$. More generally, if M is any set, and to every element $x \in M$ there corresponds a set B_x, then the set of all maps $f: M \rightarrow B$, where B is the union of all of the B_x, such that $f(x) \in B_x$ for each $x \in M$, is the *product* of the B_x, and is written $\Pi_{x \in M} B_x$. The set M in this connection is called an **index set.**

12-2 The Computer

A precise definition of a computer as a mathematical object must cover decimal as well as binary computers. The development of this definition is slightly easier to understand if a decimal computer is taken as an example.

Let us consider one digit of one word of a decimal computer. In one sense, such a digit is an *element;* that is, an element of the set of all digits in all words of the computer. In another sense, a digit is a *set.* By a digit we mean, not a particular integer such as 3, but a digit *position* in a computer word, which is capable of holding the integer 3 as well as any other integer. The set in question is then the set of all possible integers (or "digits" in the nontechnical sense) which can be in this digit position. This situation is common in set theory; a set may be an element of another set, which is then often called a **class** of sets. In this case, each digit is a set B, and the class M of all digits of the computer is called the **memory** of the computer.

A bit, or binary digit, is a special type of digit; it contains only two elements, 0 and 1. A decimal digit contains the ten integers 0 through 9. On some computers, a decimal digit may contain 16 elements; since such a digit always uses at least four bits in binary logic, some other characters, such as plus, minus, and blank, are sometimes allowed as digits. On still other computers, a "digit" is indistinguishable from a character. There is nothing in theory to prevent an entire character from being treated as a digit. There may be 32, 64, 128, or 256 elements in such a digit, depending on whether it is a 5-bit, 6-bit, 7-bit, or 8-bit character. Or the hardware of the computer may specify that some character codes are illegal, so that even if there are 6 bits per character, for example, there may effectively be fewer than 64 elements in the given character position.

We shall refer to elements of the memory M as *bits, digits, characters,* etc., indiscriminately. It is evident that any given computer may be modeled in more than one way. If the characters consist of 8 bits, we may think of M as the set of all its characters, each of which is a set of order 256; or we may think of M as the set of all its individual bits, each of which is a set of order 2. Larger "elements," such as instruction words, data words, or items, may be thought of as elements of M. If a word of 32 bits is an element of a memory, it is a set of size 2^{32}. In general, each different way of laying out the elements of what is essentially the same memory M is called a **memory structure** for M. In mathematical terms, a memory structure of M consists of a decomposition, or partition, of M into disjoint sets whose union is M, together with a specification, for each element of the decomposition, of its status as a set, that is, of its component elements.

A **state** of memory M is a specification, for each element $B \in M$, of an element of B. A state is an instantaneous description of the contents of the entire memory. If every element B of M is the same in some sense, then a state is a function from M into B. For example, on a binary computer whose memory structure consists of individual bits, B is the set [0, 1], and a state is a function from M into [0, 1]. In the general case, we must make a different construction. Let us consider the *product* of all the elements of M. In order to do this, we need a different notation for an element B as an element of M and as a set; let us denote a typical element of M by x, and this same element, considered as a set, by B_x. The product of all elements of M is now equal to

$$ \mathcal{S} = \Pi_{x \in M} \, B_x. $$

An element of $\mathcal{S}$ consists of a function which assigns to each $x \in M$ an element of B_x. Thus the set $\mathcal{S}$ is precisely the set of all possible states of the computer. In addition, $\mathcal{S}$ has the following fundamental property:

If all mathematically possible states are allowable, the set $\mathcal{S}$ defined above is independent of memory structure; that is, for every possible structure of a given memory M, the sets $\mathcal{S}$ obtained from these structures will be the same.

Let us prove this statement. Suppose that M is decomposed into sets $D \in \mathcal{D}$, where $\mathcal{D}$ is a decomposition of M. The set $\mathcal{S}$ obtained from a memory structure based on this decomposition will have the form

$$ \mathcal{S} = \Pi_{D \in \mathcal{D}} \, B_D $$

where, for each $D \in \mathcal{D}$, B_D is the set of all elements corresponding to the digit D. If all mathematically possible states are allowed, B_D will be precisely the set of all states of D, considered by itself as a memory; i.e.,

$$ B_D = \Pi_{x \in D} \, B_x $$

and the set $\mathcal{S}$ will thus be equal to

$$ \Pi_{D \in \mathcal{D}} \, (\Pi_{x \in D} \, B_x) $$

An element of this set is a specification, for each $D \in \mathcal{D}$, of a specification, for each $x \in D$, of an element of B_x. Every $x \in M$ is a member of exactly one such set D, and thus each element of the above set is also, in a natural way, a specification, for each $x \in M$, of an element of B_x, i.e., an element of

$$\Pi_{x \in M} B_x$$

In fact, it may be rigorously proved that the above two products are *canonically homeomorphic;* there exists a natural one-to-one correspondence between them. Now the double product is dependent on memory structure, but the single product is not; thus any two memory structures will produce two double products which are the same because each is the same as the single product. This completes the proof.

DEFINITION. A **computer** (with finite memory) is a product $S = \Pi_{x \in M} B_x$, for some finite set M and collection of sets B_x. The set M is called the **memory** of the computer, and the sets B_x are called the **base sets.** The elements of S are called **states.**

It is assumed that each base set B_x consists of at least two elements. If a base set contains no elements, the entire computer is void. If a base set contains exactly one element, it may be eliminated from the product without changing the nature of S. The assumption that each B_x contains at least two elements is used in some of the later theory. We shall treat the case of infinite memory in a separate section.

12-3 Subsets of the Memory

The definition of a computer includes various degenerate cases. If B_x is a base set, then B_x may be considered to be a computer, that is, a product over a memory M which consists of exactly one element x. A state of this computer is an element of B_x. Every state $S \in S$, where S is a given computer, determines a state of x, where x is an element of the memory M of S. This state is in fact a *coordinate* of S. In the special case in which there is only one base set B, and each state is a function from M to B, a "coordinate" of S is actually the image, in B, of some element $x \in M$ and is denoted by $S(x)$. We shall continue to refer to the coordinate of S at the element $x \in M$ as $S(x)$, even though S is no longer regarded as a function.

A coordinate of a state is the state of a single bit, digit, character, or other element of M. This concept may be extended to the state of an arbitrary *subset* of a memory M. If M' is a subset of M, consider the product

$$S' = \Pi_{x \in M'} B_x$$

for the base sets B_x of the computer S. The set S' is also a computer; it may be called a **subcomputer** of S.

Each state $S \in \mathcal{S}$ determines a state $S' \in \mathcal{S}'$ in a natural way. If $x \in M'$, then $S'(x) = S(x)$. This completely defines S', because S' is defined if each coordinate of S' is defined. The state S' gives the contents of M', if the contents of the entire memory M are given by S. The map which assigns to each state S the corresponding state S' is known, in set theory, as a **projection map;** the state S' may be written as $\Pi_{M'}(S)$, where $\Pi_{M'}$ is the projection map corresponding to the subset M'. (The projection maps $\Pi_{M'}$ are actually defined as applying to *subsets* of $\mathcal{S}$; we use them here as they apply to single elements of $\mathcal{S}$, which may be considered as one-element subsets.) We shall use a different notation for the set S', based, again, on the case in which there is only one base set B. In this case S' is a function from M' into B, defined by $S'(x) = S(x)$, where $x \in M'$. Such a function is known in set theory as the **restriction** of the function S to M', and is denoted by $S|M'$. We shall continue, in the general case, to refer to the projection of the element S of the product space $\mathcal{S}$ onto the space $\mathcal{S}'$ defined by a subset M' of M as $S|M'$.

12-4   Instructions and Programs

An **instruction** on a computer $\mathcal{S}$ is a function $I: \mathcal{S} \rightarrow \mathcal{S}$.

The word "instruction" has been used in at least three distinct senses in computing. An **instruction word,** containing operation code, address, and various other fields, may be said to correspond to an instruction. Clearly such an instruction is a function from $\mathcal{S}$ into itself. For every state $S \in \mathcal{S}$, that is, for every complete description of the contents of memory before the instruction is executed, there is a new complete description $I(S)$ of the contents of memory after the instruction is executed. This does not depend on what actual word or words of memory contain the given instruction word, or on whether the instruction word is contained in core at all or is simply entered on the console switches and executed, as is possible on some computers.

An instruction may also be thought of as the action corresponding to an operation code alone. In this case the contents of memory after the instruction depend on the value of the effective address. However, such an instruction is still a map $I: \mathcal{S} \rightarrow \mathcal{S}$, if the location counter (or program counter) is considered to be part of the memory M. Given any state in which an instruction word with the given operation code is in memory and the location counter gives the address of this instruction word, the contents of memory after the instruction are uniquely determined. If the state S is such that the given instruction word is not contained anywhere in memory, $I(S)$ is not defined, but for the purposes of instruction theory we may always define $I(S) = S$. The instruction I

for which $I(S) = S$ for all $S \in \mathcal{S}$, i.e., the identity mapping, is, of course, the instruction commonly known as NOP.

There is still another meaning for the term "instruction." If the contents of memory, including the location counter, are known, and the location counter references an instruction word containing *any* legal instruction, the contents of memory after this instruction is executed are uniquely determined. In this sense, a computer may be said to have a single "universal" instruction, which it executes over and over. Even when the instruction word is improper, the result of executing it is still uniquely determined in terms of certain internal flag registers; an improper operation code may, for example, cause an interrupt or a halt.

It is clear that the memory M of a computer must be taken to include the registers if the description of an instruction is to be meaningful. It is not so clear, however, that the internal registers, such as the effective address register, which contains the effective address of the current instruction word, or the instruction register, which contains the entire current instruction word, need be included in the model. The description of an instruction will be different in different models; however, in most cases, it will be clear which model we are discussing. In any instruction which is not a transfer, for example, the location counter will be incremented; it will cause no confusion if this fact is ignored and we speak of an addition instruction, for example, as taking place in a memory word and an accumulator.

A **program** is also a function $I: \mathcal{S} \to \mathcal{S}$. Here the memory of the computer is assumed to exclude the memory taken by the instructions and constant data of the stored program. For every state of the memory, there is a new state after the program is run. In one sense, this simply means that subroutines and instructions are in some sense identical in function; anything which can be proved about a sequence of instructions can be proved about such a sequence in which some of the instructions are subroutine calls. A simple open subroutine with no transfers is executed in sequence, and this corresponds to *composition* of mappings. If $I_1: \mathcal{S} \to \mathcal{S}$ and $I_2: \mathcal{S} \to \mathcal{S}$, then $I_1 \circ I_2 = J: \mathcal{S} \to \mathcal{S}$ is defined by $J(S) = I_2(I_1(S))$. This is the result of performing the instructions I_1 and I_2 in order; this statement immediately generalizes to an arbitrary sequence of instructions $I_1, I_2, \ldots, I_n$.

Most instructions, as mappings, are not *permutations;* that is, they are not one-to-one onto. For example, a load, store, or arithmetic instruction is not one-to-one, because there are many states S with the same $I(S)$. A load or store instruction is not onto because the contents of one memory word and one register must be the same in any state $I(S)$; an arithmetic operation is not onto for a similar reason. However, there are some instructions which *are* permutations. The identity instruction, NOP, of course, is one. If the computer s is finite, any mapping $I: \mathrm{s} \rightarrow \mathrm{s}$ will be a permutation if and only if some power of it is the identity—that is, the result of applying it n times, for some n, in sequence is the identity. From this it can be seen that a circular shift (though not an arithmetic or logical shift) and an exchange instruction are permutations.

12-5 Instruction Definitions

We now have a rigorous mathematical method of describing any instruction on any computer, and thus defining it. As an example, we define the instruction $I = \mathrm{CLA} \qquad Y$ (Clear and add Y) on the IBM 7094 computer. The elements of the memory M which are relevant to this definition are as follows:

Y—The core cell Y
AAC—The arithmetic accumulator (the sign bit and bits 1–35)
P—The P bit of the accumulator
Q—The Q bit of the accumulator
LC—The location counter

Note that these are being considered as *elements* of the memory, not as subsets; we may, of course, structure our memory in such a way that any given disjoint subsets are considered as elements. The definition of $I = \mathrm{CLA} \qquad Y$ is now:

$$I(S)(z) = S(z) \qquad\qquad z \neq Y, AAC, P, Q, LC$$
$$I(S)(Y) = S(Y)$$
$$I(S)(AAC) = S(Y)$$
$$I(S)(P) = 0$$
$$I(S)(Q) = 0$$
$$I(S)(LC) = S(LC) + 1$$

This is precise but somewhat lengthy compared to the usual informal definition, which might read as follows:

$$(\mathrm{CLA} \quad Y\,) \quad Y \rightarrow AAC; \quad 0 \rightarrow P, Q$$

We shall now develop a terminology in which we may consider such "shorthand" definitions to be just as precise as the functional definition.

In the first place, let us assume that each definition begins with a specification of the form $I(S)(z) = S(z)$ for $z \notin M'$, where M' is some subset of M. The subset M' includes all elements of M which are mentioned on the left side of the equal sign in the remainder of the definition. The first statement of the definition is therefore entirely redundant, and may be omitted. In the second place, if the location counter LC of a computer is not explicitly mentioned, we may assume that it is advanced by 1, i.e., $I(S)(LC) = S(LC) + 1$ (if the computer is assumed to have a location counter at all).

Now suppose that there is an element $x \in M$ such that $I(S)(x)$ is constant, i.e., independent of S. In this case we write $c \to x$, where c is the constant. Thus "$0 \to P, Q$" (an obvious shorthand for "$0 \to P$, $0 \to Q$") shows that the P and Q bits are elements of M such that $I(S)(P)$ and $I(S)(Q)$ are constant.

Again, suppose that there are two elements $x, y \in M$ such that $I(S)(x) = S(y)$. In this case we write $y \to x$. Thus "$Y \to AAC$" is short for $I(S)(AAC) = S(Y)$.

Finally, let there exist elements $x, y_1, y_2, \ldots, y_n$, such that $I(S)(x)$ is a function of $S(y_1), S(y_2), \ldots, S(y_n)$. In this case we write $f(y_1, \ldots, y_n) \to x$ as a shorthand for $I(S)(x) = f(S(y_1), S(y_2), \ldots, S(y_n))$. These functions need not be written in functional notation; thus, for an add instruction, we may write "$y + AAC \to AAC$" as a shorthand notation for $I(S)(AAC) = S(Y) + S(AAC)$. The addition operation in this case, however, must itself be rigorously defined, because its domain is not the set of all integers; it must be apparent from the definition what happens in case of overflow. For a two's complement, binary computer, addition takes place in the ring of integers modulo 2^x, where x is the number of bits per word.

12-6 Regions

With every instruction I on a computer S, there are associated various subsets of the memory M of S. Two of these, the **input region** and the **output region,** are especially important. They consist, respectively, of that part of the memory which can affect the instruction and that part of the memory which can be affected by the instruction.

If we neglect the internal registers, such as the various error flag registers, the effective address register, and the location counter, which form part of the input and output region of almost every instruction, the regions of the common instructions are small and may easily be deduced from an informal description of the instruction. Thus, in our machine language, the input region of the instruction LD   X is the memory cell X, and its output region is the accumulator. The input region of ST   X is the accumulator, and its output region is X. The input region of AD   X is $X \cup AC$, where AC is the accumulator, and its output region is AC. For a circular shift of a register, that register is the input and the output region. To describe the regions of a transfer instruction, we must admit the location counter. The output region of an unconditional transfer is the location counter; its input region is the null set. This last statement implies that no part of the memory affects the instruction. The same applies to a "store zero" instruction, or to loading a register with immediate addressing.

We now give precise definitions of the input region $IR(I)$ and the output region $OR(I)$ of an instruction I. An element $x \in M$ is affected by the instruction I if its contents before and after the instruction I are different, i.e., $S(x) \neq I(S)(x)$. To say that x *can* be affected is equivalent to saying that there exists such a state S; i.e.,

$$OR(I) = \{x \in M: \exists\ S \in \mathcal{S}\ \text{with}\ S(x) \neq I(S)(x)\}$$

An element $x \in M$ is in the input region $IR(I)$ if it can affect the instruction I—that is, if the value of $S(x)$ can make a difference. By changing the value of $S(x)$, we arrive at a new state S'. The condition that *only* the value of $S(x)$ has been changed may be written

$$S(z) = S'(z)\ \text{for}\ z \neq x$$

To say that this "makes a difference" means that $I(S)$ and $I(S')$ must be somewhere different. Of course, they will always be different at x, unless x is part of the output region $OR(I)$. Hence it is improper to require only that they differ *somewhere*. On the other hand, if $OR(I) = \{x\}$, then $I(S)$ and $I(S')$ may differ *only* at x: so it is just as improper to require that they differ somewhere other than x. The only definition that makes sense is that $I(S)$ and $I(S')$ must differ *somewhere in the output region*. That is, there exists $y \in OR(I)$ such that

$$I(S)(y) \neq I(S')(y)$$

Again, to say that all this *can* happen is equivalent to saying that there exist such states S and S' and such an element $y \in OR(I)$; i.e.,

$$IR(I) = \{x \in M: \exists\ S, S' \in \mathcal{S},\ y \in OR(I)\ \text{with}\ S(z) = S'(z),\ z \neq x,\ \text{but} \\ I(S)(y) \neq I(S')(y)\}$$

The reader should check that the input and output regions of the instructions mentioned above are actually, by these definitions, what they are claimed to be.

The output region of an instruction is the null set, if and only if the instruction is the identity. The input region of an instruction, however, can be the null set in other cases. If $I(S)$ is constant for all S, then clearly $IR(I) = \emptyset$; this is the case for an unconditional transfer or a store zero. Later we shall see that, if the computer has finite memory, this condition is necessary and sufficient.

12-7 Allowable States

In the definition of a computer, we have assumed that S is an *entire* product space. This amounts to including all mathematically possible descriptions of the contents of memory. In practice, some computers have states which are not allowable; thus it becomes necessary to restrict ourselves to subsets of S. We shall now show that any reasonable restrictions are in some sense not restrictions at all.

Let S' be any subset of a computer S with memory M. A subset $M' \subseteq M$ has the **patching property*** if, given any two states $S_1, S_2 \in S'$, there exists $S_3 \in S'$ with

$$S_3(x) = S_1(x) \qquad x \in M'$$
$$S_3(x) = S_2(x) \qquad x \in M - M'$$

If every subset of M has the patching property relative to S', then we say that S' itself has the patching property. The union of two sets with the patching property has the patching property; so does their intersection. If M' has the patching property, then so does $M - M'$.

THEOREM. If S' is a subset of a computer S with finite memory M, and S' has the patching property, then $S' = \Pi_{x \in M} B'_x$, where $B'_x \subseteq B_x$ for each $x \in M$.

This statement implies that S' is itself a computer. To prove it, we define, for each $x \in M$, $B'_x = \{b \in B_x : \exists\, S' \in S' \text{ with } S'(x) = b\}$. By definitions, $B'_x \subseteq B_x$ and $S \subseteq \Pi_{x \in M} B'_x$. Conversely, let $S \in \Pi_{x \in M} B'_x$; we must prove $S \in S'$. For each $x \in M$, let $S_x \in S$ be such that $S_x(x) = S(x)$. Since the memory is finite, and each set $\{x\}$ has the patching property, we may apply the definition of the patching property a finite number of times to deduce that $S \in S$

It is therefore true that subsets S' of a computer S which have the patching property are actually computers in their own right. There remains the case in which S' does not have the patching property. A subset S' of S has the patching property if and only if each of its one-element subsets has the patching property, if the memory is finite. Hence we are reduced to the case in which some one-element subset does not have the patching property. Such an element of memory is "dependent" in some sense; whether a state is allowable on it depends on the values of that state on other elements. This situation actually occurs in some computers. For example, if we are modeling a decimal computer in a binary manner, so that

---

* The phrases "patching property" and "finite support property" are due to James W. Thatcher.

each decimal digit corresponds to four bits, the left-most bit of any decimal digit can always be 0, but it can be 1 only if the other three bits are 000 or 001, corresponding to the decimal digits 8 and 9.

Such a model is unsatisfactory in many ways. On the other hand, the decimal digits in this case form a memory structure which is much superior to the binary structure. A given decimal digit has the patching property; and, considering it as a set of bits, no subset of it has the patching property. This is a general fact which may be expressed as follows:

The class of all subsets of M which have the patching property relative to S' consists of the members of a decomposition D of M, and their unions.

The proof of this statement depends only on the fact that this class is closed under unions, intersections, and complements. It is, in fact, a statement in lattice theory; we give a proof of it here. For each $x \in M$, let D_x be the intersection of all subsets of M containing x which have the patching property. There are a finite number of these, since M is finite, and thus D_x also has the patching property. If $y \in D_x$, then $D_x \cap D_y$ has the patching property, contains y, is contained in D_y, and is therefore equal to D_y, so that $D_x = D_y$. Hence the sets D_x are either equal or disjoint for various x, and their union is M; i.e., they constitute a decomposition of M. If M' is any set with the patching property and $x \in M'$, then $D_x \in M'$ by the definition of D_x; so that $M' \supseteq \cup_{x \in M'} D_x$; since each $x \in D_x$, we also have $M' \subseteq \cup_{x \in M'} D_x$. Therefore $M' = \cup_{x \in M'} D_x$, and every subset with the patching property is a union of members of the decomposition. This completes the proof.

We may therefore build a memory structure out of subsets of M which have the patching property. But, by the preceding theorem, S' will be a computer in its own right, with this memory structure or any coarser memory structure. We have therefore established the following principle:

For finite memory, it is sufficient, in developing the theory of sets of allowable states S', to develop the theory of computers S.

An element $b \in B_x$ which is not in B'_x, in the theorem above, is called an **unnecessary element.** It is unnecessary because there is no state $S \in S'$ for which $S(x) = b$. In practice, if any of the base sets B have unnecessary elements, these may be ignored. Note that an element is unnecessary relative to a particular B_x; even if all of the B_x are substantially the same, an element b may be necessary for some B_x, and not for others.

12-8 Infinite Memory

A subset $S' \subseteq S$ which has the patching property, and for which there are no unnecessary elements, is necessarily equal to S when the memory is finite. If we were to extend our definition of a computer without change to the case of infinite memory, this statement would have to be replaced by the following:

THEOREM. If S' is a subset of a product $S = \Pi_{x \in M} B_x$ for an infinite set M, and S' has the patching property, and none of the B_x contain elements which are unnecessary in S', then S' contains a set S'' of the following form: Let $S_0 \in S$; then S'' consists of all states $S \in S$ such that $N = \{x \in M: S(x) \neq S_0(x)\}$ is finite.

Proof: Let S be such a state, and let the elements of N be $x_1, x_2, \ldots, x_n$. Since there are no unnecessary elements in any B_x, there exist states $S_1, \ldots, S_n \in S'$, with $S_i(x_i) = S(x_i)$, $1 \leq i \leq n$. Applying the patching property a finite number of times, we may find a state $S' \in S'$ with $S'(x_i) = S(x_i)$ for all i, $1 \leq i \leq n$. Now, applying the patching property again to S_0 and S' on N, we see that $S \in S'$.

This is as far as we can go; the sets S'' which may be constructed in this way actually possess the patching property and admit no unnecessary elements. The theorem above is true under the weaker hypothesis that S' has the **finite patching property,** i.e., every finite subset of M has the patching property.

The construction of the class S'', given above, is a familiar one in set theory; it is, in fact, a **restricted product.** For example, the set formed by taking the product of an infinite (countable) number of copies of the real numbers may be regarded as the set of all infinite sequences $(a_0, a_1, a_2, \ldots)$ of real numbers. The subset of this set consisting of those infinite sequences with only a finite number of non-zero components will be a restricted product of a countable number of copies of the real numbers. This set may also be regarded as the set of all finite polynomials $a_0 + a_1 x + \cdots + a_n x^n$ in one variable x, for arbitrary n. Other restricted products may be formed of the set of all $p + q$, where p is such a polynomial and q is a fixed polynomial in x with an infinite number of terms. Any other set, such as the integers or the set $\{0, 1\}$, could be substituted in the above for the real numbers. In a computer, there is often a "zero" element in each base set, and the state S_0 may be taken as the zero state, i.e., the state with $S_0(x) = 0$ for all x.

DEFINITION. A subset S' of a product $S = \Pi_{x \in M} B_x$ has the **finite support property** if, given any two states $S, S' \in S'$, the set $N = \{x \in M : S(x) \neq S'(x)\}$ is finite.

COROLLARY. If, in addition to the hypotheses of the theorem, S' has the finite support property, then S' is equal to a set of the form described in the theorem, i.e., to a restricted product.

For clearly, any restricted product has the finite support property, whereas if S_0 is any element of S', then any element of S', by this property, must be in the restricted product relative to S_0.

DEFINITION. A **computer** (with infinite memory) is a restricted product of sets B_x, for $x \in M$, relative to some element S_0 of the (unrestricted) product of the B_x. The infinite set M is called the **memory** of the computer; the sets B_x are called the **base sets;** and the elements of $\mathbb{S}$ are called the **states.** It is assumed that each B_x contains at least two elements.

This definition needs some justification. The theorem which we have just proved shows that a computer must contain *at least* all the elements of a restricted product, if it is to have the patching property. We shall now show why it is unwise to admit any more elements, i.e., to give up the finite support property. The following proposition is fundamental to any further combinatorial instruction theory; and it holds uniformly (i.e., for every possible instruction I) on a set $\mathbb{S}$ if and only if the finite support property is satisfied.

PROPOSITION. Let S_1 and S_2 be any two states of a computer, with either finite or infinite memory, and let I be any instruction. If $S_1 | IR(I) = S_2 | IR(I)$, then $I(S_1) | OR(I) = I(S_2) | OR(I)$. Conversely, let $\mathbb{S}'$ be a subset of the (unrestricted) product $\mathbb{S} = \Pi_{x \in M} B_x$ for an infinite memory M, and let $\mathbb{S}'$ satisfy the patching property, but not the finite support property. Then there exists an instruction I and two states S_1, $S_2 \in \mathbb{S}'$ such that $S_1 | IR(I) = S_2 | IR(I)$, but $I(S_1) | OR(I) \neq I(S_2) | OR(I)$.

We prove the first part of this statement. Let $N = \{x \in M: S_1(x) \neq S_2(x)\}$. If M is finite, so is N; if M is infinite, the finite support property holds, and N is still finite. Let the elements of N be $x_1, \ldots, x_n$. We now define states $T_0, T_1, \ldots, T_n$ by the formulas

$$
\begin{aligned}
T_i(y) &= S_1(y) = S_2(y) &&\text{for } y \neq x_j, 1 \leq j \leq n, 0 \leq i \leq n \\
T_i(x_j) &= S_1(x_j) &&\text{for } i < j \\
T_i(x_j) &= S_2(x_j) &&\text{for } i \geq j
\end{aligned}
$$

so that $T_0 = S_1$, $T_1 = S_2$, and $T_{i-1}(z) = T_i(z)$ for $z \neq x_i$, but $T_{i-1}(x_i) = S_1(x_i) \neq S_2(x_i) = T_i(x_i)$ since $x_i \in N$. We now prove that $I(T_{i-1}) | OR(I) = I(T_i) | OR(I)$ for $1 \leq i \leq n$; this will in particular show that $I(T_0) | OR(I) = I(T_1) | OR(I) = \cdots = I(T_n) | OR(I)$, or $I(S_1) | OR(I) = I(S_2) | OR(I)$, as is to be proved. We apply the definition of input region to the states T_{i-1} and T_i. If it were not true that $I(T_{i-1}) | OR(I) = I(T_i) | OR(I)$, then we would have $x_i \in IR(I)$. But since $x_i \in N$, we have $S_1(x) \neq S_2(x)$, which contradicts the hypothesis.

To prove the converse, let S_1 and S_2 be any two states of $\mathbb{S}$ for which the set $N = \{x \in M: S_1(x) \neq S_2(x)\}$ is infinite. We define an instruction I as follows. Let $y \in M$, and set $I(S)(z) = S(z)$ for $z \neq y$. The set B_y contains at least two elements; let $p, q \in B_y$. We define $I(S)(y) = p$ if the set $\{x \in M: S_1(x) \neq S(x)\}$ is finite, and $I(S)(y) = q$ otherwise. Since $I(S_1)(y) = p$ and $I(S_2)(y) = q$, we have $y \in OR(I)$, and it then follows from the definition of I that $OR(I) = \{y\}$. Now let $x \in M$, and let $S_3, S_4 \in S$ be such that $S_3(z) = S_4(z)$ for $z \neq x$. It follows immediately from the definition of I that $I(S_3)(y)$ and $I(S_4)(y)$ are either both equal to p or both equal to q, so that in any event $I(S_3)(y) = I(S_4)(y)$. Hence $x \notin IR(I)$, and since this is true for arbitrary $x \in M$, we have $IR(I) = \emptyset$. Therefore, $S_1|IR(I) = S_2|IR(I)$ vacuously, but $I(S_1)|OR(I) \neq I(S_2)|OR(I)$. This completes the proof.

The considerations of the preceding chapter are still valid for infinite memory, under the finite support property. If S' has the patching property, or even the finite patching property, then S' is a computer in its own right. If S' does not have the finite patching property, but does have the finite support property, then it is still true that the intersection D_x of all sets containing x which have the finite patching property also has this property, since this is actually the intersection of a finite number of them due to the finite support property. The class of all sets with the finite patching property then consists of the sets D_x and their (possibly infinite) unions; and it is still true that the set S is a computer if M is given the memory structure induced by the decomposition $\mathcal{D}$ whose members are the D_x.

12-9 Files

It is remarkable that the same mathematical model may be used to describe both the internal memory of a computer, and the files, such as tape files, which it uses. In one case the set M is finite; in the other case it is infinite.

As a simple example of a file, let M have a subset Z, where Z is the set of all integers. Let H be an element of M not in Z. The instruction defined by

$$I(S)(n) = S(n+1)$$
$$I(S)(H) = S(0)$$
$$I(S)(z) = S(z) \qquad z \notin Z \cup \{H\}$$

may be regarded as a **file read instruction.** The set Z represents all possible positions on the (potentially infinite) file, which is sequential and may be called a "tape." The element H is the "read head"; after the instruction I, H contains the element which was currently in position to be read.

All the other elementary file operations may be represented as instructions in this way. A **file write instruction** with write head H is given by

$$I(S)(0) = S(H)$$
$$I(S)(n) = S(n+1), \quad n \neq 0$$

where we now assume that any element of M not appearing on the left side of the equal sign in the definition is not contained in the output region. The instruction

$$I(S)(n) = S(n+1)$$

is a **file position instruction**—in this case, position forward. It is a permutation, being one-to-one and onto; because the memory is infinite, it is not necessary, and in fact not true, that some power of it be the identity. The instruction

$$I(S)(n) = S(n-1)$$

positions the file backward. Similarly, one may read or write backward.

Such models may be used for any type of file. In the simple examples above, we have assumed that the file is infinite, or at least potentially infinite, in both directions. However, this assumption is not necessary. For example, for a tape file of length x positions, we may consider a subset T consisting of all integers n for $-x \leq n \leq x$. If the tape is positioned at the beginning, we assume that $S(i) = $ 'N' for $-x \leq i \leq 0$, where 'N' is a special element of B_i for each $i \in T$ signifying that the given position does not exist. We also assume $S(x) = $ 'N', since the existing positions run from 0 to $x-1$. A forward position instruction is now given by

$$I(S)(n) = S(n+1) \quad n \in T, n \neq x$$
$$I(S)(x) = \text{'}N\text{'}$$

In these models, each integer in Z or in T stands for the position on the file which has distance from the read or write head equal to that integer. Thus, when we position the tape forward, the position under the head, that is, $S(0)$, now contains the information that was formerly in the next position, that is, $S(1)$. In another model, which is simply mathematical and does not correspond to the operation of any computer, a counter is kept to denote the position of the head, which may then advance up and down the file. Thus a position forward instruction would be of the form

$$I(S)(C) = S(C) + 1$$
$$I(S)(H) = S(S(C))$$

where C is the counter and $S(C)$ is the contents of the counter. Such an instruction does not consider the entire file to be in its input and output regions.

The **theory of automata** treats mathematical models of very simple computers. For example, a **sequential machine** is a computer with one tape file, infinite in both directions, and one memory cell. The tape file is read and written at the same time, and the symbol which is written and the contents of the memory cell depend on the symbol which is read and the previous contents of the memory cell. A **Turing machine** is a sequential machine with the added feature that it can read and write either forward or backward. Whether it moves forward, backward, or not at all, and whether it writes or not, depends on the symbol which is read (either forward or backward) and on the previous contents of the memory cell. In both the sequential machine and the Turing machine, the single memory cell is called the **state** of the machine; this corresponds to our notion of state (if the file is neglected). An **automaton,** as used by several authors, is a sequential machine in which the written symbols are neglected. Rabin and Scott have also studied **two-tape automata,** in which both decisions (to move one tape or the other, or both, and which direction to move them) are determined by the previous state and the two symbols which have been read.

Appendix A

TEXTBOOK MACHINE LANGUAGE

The machine language described below is used throughout the book to illustrate various facets of machine language programming. If the student has access to a computer, he should learn the machine language of that computer from the start; if he is assigned any machine language programming problems (after the first two chapters), these should be done preferably in that machine language, rather than in Textbook Machine Language.

This machine language is designed for a computer with several index registers and at least two arithmetic registers (an accumulator and a Q register). The other characteristics of the computer, however, such as representation of negative integers, word length, instruction word format, memory size, and floating point format, are left unspecified. For the purposes of this book, it is possible to express the operation codes of Textbook Machine Language as macros on any one of a wide variety of decimal and binary computers. Even if the given computer has only one index register, as the SDS 930, or no accumulators, as the IBM 1401, these may be simulated by macros.

The operation codes are as follows:

LD (Load)—Loads the accumulator from the memory word given by the effective address.

AD (Add)—Adds the memory word given by the effective address to the accumulator, and leaves the result in the accumulator.

SU (Subtract)—Subtracts the memory word given by the effective address from the accumulator, and leaves the result in the accumulator.

MU (Multiply)—Multiplies the memory word given by the effective address by the accumulator, and leaves the result in the accumulator.

DI (Divide)—Divides the accumulator by the memory word given by the effective address, and leaves the result in the accumulator.

ST (Store)—Stores the accumulator in the memory word given by the effective address.

LX (Load index)—Loads an index register from the memory word given by the effective address.

SX (Store index)—Stores an index register in the memory word given by the effective address.

LDI (Load immediate)—Loads the accumulator with the actual effective address.

ADI (Add immediate)—Adds the actual effective address to the accumulator, and leaves the result in the accumulator.

SUI (Subtract immediate)—Subtracts the actual effective address from the accumulator, and leaves the result in the accumulator.

LXI (Load index, immediate)—Loads an index register with the actual effective address.

AX (Add to index)—Adds the memory word given by the effective address to an index register and leaves the result in the index register.

AXI (Add to index, immediate)—Adds the actual effective address to an index register and leaves the result in the index register.

FA (Floating add)—Adds the memory word given by the effective address to the accumulator, using floating point arithmetic, and leaves the floating point result in the accumulator.

FS (Floating subtract)—Subtracts the memory word given by the effective address from the accumulator, using floating point arithmetic, and leaves the floating point result in the accumulator.

FM (Floating multiply)—Multiplies the memory word given by the effective address by the accumulator, using floating point arithmetic, and leaves the floating point result in the accumulator.

FD (Floating divide)—Divides the accumulator by the memory word given by the effective address, using floating point arithmetic, and leaves the floating point result in the accumulator.

TR (Transfer)—Transfers to the location given by the effective address.

TZ (Transfer on zero)—Transfers to the location given by the effective address if the accumulator is zero; otherwise continues.

TNZ (Transfer on non-zero)—Transfers to the location given by the effective address if the accumulator is not zero; otherwise continues.

TP (Transfer on positive)—Transfers to the location given by the effective address if the accumulator is positive; otherwise continues.

TN (Transfer on negative)—Transfers to the location given by the effective address if the accumulator is negative; otherwise continues.

SA (Store address)—Stores the address field of the accumulator in the address field of the instruction word given by the effective address.

TO (Transfer on overflow)—Transfers to the location given by the effective address if the overflow indicator is on, showing that overflow has occurred, and turns off this indicator; otherwise continues.

LQ (Load Q register)—Loads the Q register from the memory word given by the effective address.

SQ (Store Q register)—Stores the Q register in the memory word given by the effective address.

CA (Call subroutine)—Calls a subroutine whose location is given by the effective address.

RT (Return from subroutine)—Returns from the current subroutine.

LSL (Left shift, logical)—Shifts the accumulator left by the number of places given in the effective address; bits at the right are filled with zeros and bits at the left are lost.

RSL (Right shift, logical)—Shifts the accumulator right by the number of places given in the effective address; bits at the left are filled with zeros and bits at the right are lost.

LSA (Left shift, arithmetic)—Multiplies the accumulator by 2^n, where n is the number given in the effective address.

RSA (Right shift, arithmetic)—Divides the accumulator by 2^n, where n is the number given in the effective address.

LSC (Left shift, circular)—Rotates the accumulator to the left by the number of places given in the effective address.

RSC (Right shift, circular)—Rotates the accumulator to the right by the number of places given in the effective address.

LDL (Left double shift, logical)—Shifts the double register formed by the accumulator and the Q register to the left, by the number of places given in the effective address; bits at the right of the Q register are filled with zeros, bits at the left of the Q register enter the accumulator, and bits at the left of the accumulator are lost.

RDL (Right double shift, logical)—Shifts the double register formed by the accumulator and the Q register to the right, by the number of places given in the effective address; bits at the left of the accumulator are filled with zeros, bits at the right of the accumulator enter the Q register, and bits at the right of the Q register are lost.

LDA (Left double shift, arithmetic)—Multiplies the double precision integer in the accumulator and Q register by 2^n, where n is the number given in the effective address.

RDA (Right double shift, arithmetic)—Divides the double precision integer in the accumulator and Q register by 2^n, where n is the number given in the effective address.

LDC (Left double shift, circular)—Shifts the accumulator and the Q register circularly to the left by the number of places given in the effective address; bits from the left of each register enter at the right of the other.

RDC (Right double shift, circular)—Shifts the accumulator and the Q register circularly to the right by the number of places given in the effective address; bits from the right of each register enter at the left of the other.

AND (Logical AND)—Forms the logical product of the accumulator and the memory word given by the effective address, leaving the result in the accumulator.

OR (Logical OR)—Forms the logical sum of the accumulator and the memory word given by the effective address, leaving the result in the accumulator.

XOR (Logical exclusive OR)—Forms the logical difference of the accumulator and the memory word given by the effective address, leaving the result in the accumulator.

ICT (Increment, compare, and transfer)—ICT X,I,M,A will increment index register X by I, and transfer to A if index register X is now less than or equal to M.

DCT (Decrement, compare, and transfer)—DCT X,I,M,A will decrement index register X by I, and transfer to A if index register X is now greater than M.

TE (Test equal)—Skips the next instruction if the memory word given by the effective address is equal to the accumulator.

TU (Test unequal)—Skips the next instruction if the memory word given by the effective address is unequal to the accumulator.

TG (Test greater)—Skips the next instruction if the memory word given by the effective address is greater than the accumulator.

TL (Test less)—Skips the next instruction if the memory word given by the effective address is less than the accumulator.

ZT (Zero test)—Skips the next instruction if the memory word given by the effective address is zero.

NZT (Non-zero test)—Skips the next instruction if the memory word given by the effective address is not zero.

PT (Positive test)—Skips the next instruction if the memory word given by the effective address is positive.

NT (Negative test)—Skips the next instruction if the memory word given by the effective address is negative.

LAN (Load accumulator, negative)—Loads the accumulator with the negative of the word given by the effective address.

LQN (Load Q register, negative)—Loads the Q register with the negative of the word given by the effective address.

DIV (Divide)—Divides the accumulator by the memory word given in the effective address, leaving the quotient in the Q register and the remainder in the accumulator.

The pseudo-operation codes are as follows:

ORG (Origin)—The next instruction or data word has an address equal to the expression in the variable field.

END—The last statement in any assembly language program.

EQU—The symbol in the label field is set equal to the symbol in the variable field.

RE (Reserve)—A block of storage, of size equal to the expression in the variable field, is reserved.

CO (Constant)—A data word is set up containing a constant, whose value is given by the expression in the variable field.

Other conventions associated with Textbook Machine Language are as follows. There are three fields of a statement. The label field, which is optional, contains a symbol whose value is assumed to be equal to the location of this instruction word or data word (except as specified otherwise by the operation). The operation code field gives the operation or pseudo-operation. The variable field contains an expression, whose value is calculated according to the usual rules of arithmetic. The value of a symbol is derived from its definition in the label field of some instruction or data statement or EQU statement; the value of a number is itself, unless it contains a decimal point, in which case it is assumed to be floating point. The variable field may also contain an index register number, which is separated from the above expression by a comma. The operation code may be followed by an asterisk to denote indirect addressing. The effective address is calculated as follows: if indirect addressing applies, then the effective address is taken from the contents of the word whose address is given in the variable field; if there is an index register number, the contents of this index register are added to the address given by the variable field to form the effective address.

Appendix B

FORTRAN

The reader of this book is presumed to be familiar with some algebraic language, such as AED, ALGOL, FORTRAN, JOVIAL, MAD, NELIAC, or PL-I. However, some of the examples use FORTRAN specifically. This Appendix is an introduction to those features peculiar to FORTRAN which are necessary in order to understand these examples. Of the various versions or "dialects" of FORTRAN, we make specific reference to FORTRAN II and FORTRAN IV.

(1) *Assignment.* A statement such as

$$H = P + Q + R$$

calculates the value of the expression on the right and treats this value as the new value of the variable on the left. The ordinary equal sign ($=$) is used in FORTRAN, rather than the assignment symbol ($:=$) used in ALGOL. Also, unlike most algebraic languages, FORTRAN does not require assignment statements to end with a semicolon or other special sign. The general form of an assignment statement is

$$<\text{variable}> = <\text{expression}>$$

(2) *Real numbers and integers.* In ALGOL and JOVIAL it is necessary to declare each real variable and each integer variable as such. In FORTRAN, however, any variable whose name begins with I, J, K, L, M, or N is presumed to be an integer, and any other variable is presumed to be a real number. In FORTRAN IV one may also declare integers and real numbers whose names violate this rule.

(3) *Statement numbers.* FORTRAN is one of the few algebraic languages which use statement *numbers,* rather than statement names. Any statement may have a number; if the statement is contained on a card, the number must be in card columns 1–5. It is not followed by a period,

colon, or any other special sign. Because of this rule, and because of the fact that statements are not followed by semicolons, only one FORTRAN statement may be given on any one card.

(4) *Transfer of control.* The GO TO statement in FORTRAN is the equivalent of GOTO in ALGOL or TRANSFER TO in MAD; most other algebraic languages use the words GO TO. It is followed by a statement number. Thus GO TO 325 directs the computer to start a new sequence of calculations at statement number 325. In PL-I, for example, the statement would have had a name, such as L325, and the transfer statement would have been GO TO L325, followed by a semicolon. There are two other types of GO TO statements in FORTRAN. One has the general form

$$\text{GO TO } k, \ (x_1, \ x_2, \ \ldots, \ x_n)$$

where k is a variable and the x_i are statement numbers; this transfers control to whichever statement number of the x_i has last been assigned to the variable k in an ASSIGN x TO k statement. The other type has the general form

$$\text{GO TO } (x_1, \ x_2, \ \ldots, \ x_n), \ k$$

Again k is a variable and the x_i are statement numbers. This statement transfers control to x_i when the value of the variable k is i. Thus k is used as a switch, whose values range from 1 to n. In algebraic languages which use statement names rather than statement numbers, both of these features are replaced by the statement label variable feature. Thus, in PL-I, instead of saying ASSIGN x TO k, we would simply say $k = x$, where k is a statement label variable and x is a statement label (constant); the first GO TO statement above would then simply be GO TO k. A statement label may also be subscripted, and the second GO TO statement above would be replaced in many algebraic languages by GO TO $X(I)$, where the values of the statement label array X were in some way declared beforehand.

(5) *Subscripted variables.* All the algebraic languages mentioned above allow some form of subscripted variable. The notation A(I) in FORTRAN denotes the I-th element of the array A; in some other algebraic languages, this would be A[I] or A(I). The total number of elements in the array A must be declared in FORTRAN; this may be done in various ways. For a single array, that is, an array whose elements are each given by a single subscript, the declaration reads DIMENSION <variable> (<constant>) , where the constant is the number of elements in this array. For multiple arrays, there must be one constant maximum subscript at each position, and these subscripts are given within

the parentheses, separated by commas. The word DIMENSION may be replaced by REAL, INTEGER, or COMMON if the array is simultaneously to be declared real or integer (in FORTRAN IV) or common; and several dimension statements may be given, separated by commas, without repeating the word DIMENSION. Thus:

DIMENSION Z(20), Y(5, 5) declares Z to be a single array of 20 floating point numbers, since Z is not I, J, K, L, M, or N; and Y to be a double array of 25 floating point numbers from Y(1, 1) to Y(5, 5), which might, for example, be the entries of a floating point matrix.

INTEGER A(3, 10, 20) declares A to be a triple array of 600 integers.

REAL I(100), J(100) declares I and J to be single arrays of 100 floating point numbers each.

(6) *Iteration.* The statement which in many algebraic languages is known as the *for* statement—such as FOR I : = 1 STEP 1 UNTIL 100 DO C(I) : = A(I) + B(I)—is called in FORTRAN the DO statement. Its general form is

$$\text{DO} <\text{statement number}> <\text{variable}> = n_1, n_2, n_3$$

where n_3 is optional; if it is missing, n_3 is taken equal to 1. The statement number in the DO statement is the statement number of the *last* statement of the loop. The variable in the DO statement initially assumes the value n_1, and is increased by n_3 after each execution of the loop until the increased value becomes greater than n_2. Thus the loop

```
      DO 371 I = 1, 5, 2
      C(I) = A(I) + B(I)
371   C(I+1) = A(I) - B(I)
```

is equivalent to the sequence of statements

```
      C(1) = A(1) + B(1)
      C(2) = A(1) - B(1)
      C(3) = A(3) + B(3)
      C(4) = A(3) - B(3)
      C(5) = A(5) + B(5)
      C(6) = A(5) - B(5)
```

A DO loop is always executed at least once.

(7) *Conditional statements.* The IF statement in FORTRAN is the analogue of the WHENEVER statement in MAD, or the IF statement in most other algebraic languages. There are two basic types of IF statements in FORTRAN. The "FORTRAN II type" IF statement has the general form

$$\text{IF } (\ <\text{expression}> \ ) \ n_1, \ n_2, \ n_3$$

where the n_i are statement numbers. The expression is evaluated; transfer is made to statement number n_1, n_2, or n_3, according as the expression is negative, zero, or positive, respectively. Thus to transfer to statement number 400 if X is equal to Y, we would write

```
        IF (Y−X) 375, 400, 375
  375     (next statement)
```

The "FORTRAN IV type" IF statement has the general form

$$\text{IF } (\ <\text{relation}> \ ) \ <\text{statement}>$$

where the relation expresses some true or false statement such as X.EQ.Y (meaning "X equals Y") and the statement, which may or may not be a GO TO statement, is executed if and only if the statement is true.

(8) *Subroutines and functions.* A subroutine is called with a CALL statement, which is the analogue of EXECUTE in MAD. Unlike some algebraic languages, FORTRAN requires that the word CALL must always be present. If parameters are given, they follow the name of the subroutine, separated by commas and enclosed in parentheses. Again unlike some languages, FORTRAN makes no syntactical distinction between parameters to a subroutine and subscripts. Thus the statement

```
      CALL MATMPY(A, B, C)
```

transfers control to the subroutine MATMPY and makes the parameters A, B, and C, and the return address, available to this subroutine. The parameters are treated as names, and they may be either used or returned by the subroutine, or both; there is no separation of used and returned parameters as there is in JOVIAL. In the ALGOL terminology every parameter is called by value unless it consists of a single variable, in which case it is called by name.*

A *function* is a subroutine which returns a value; the function name, with parameters appended, is then considered to have this value. All the algebraic languages which we have discussed have this feature, which was initially introduced to handle mathematical functions such as SIN(X). In FORTRAN, any name followed by a parameter list enclosed in parentheses is treated as a function unless it has been declared to be a subscripted variable, as by a DIMENSION statement.

When a subroutine or a function is being programmed, the first state-

* The FORTRAN treatment of parameters which are *single subscripted* variables does not correspond to anything in ALGOL: the subscripts are evaluated, but the resulting parameter, with each subscript replaced by its value, is now treated as if it were being called by name.

ment must be a SUBROUTINE or FUNCTION statement, respectively. The word SUBROUTINE or FUNCTION is followed by the name of the routine, and then the dummy argument (formal parameter) list enclosed in parentheses. Logical flow of a subroutine ends with a RETURN statement; logical flow of a main program ends with a STOP statement, or, in some versions of FORTRAN, with CALL EXIT, where EXIT is a special library subroutine which handles program termination. Any FORTRAN program, whether a main program, subroutine, or function, ends with the statement END.

(9) *Input-output.* Actual input-output statements differ from one FORTRAN compiler to another, and may be READ, WRITE, PRINT, PUNCH, READ INPUT TAPE, WRITE OUTPUT TAPE, READ TAPE, WRITE TAPE, ACCEPT, etc. However, the FORMAT statement is common to all FORTRAN compilers. This statement allows integers, real numbers, and any other data types which a given FORTRAN compiler will accept, to be written on any output medium, or read from any input medium, in a very general format. The complete description of this statement is lengthy, and one example will suffice to illustrate the idea of formatting. The statement

```
WRITE (6, 201) I, U, V, K1, K2, L
```

will cause the values of the variables I, U, V, K1, K2, and L to be written on "unit number 6" (which may be tape 6, the printer, or some other unit) according to format number 201. Suppose that this format is given by

```
201    FORMAT(I5,F12.6/E13.6,3(5X,I4))
```

with the format number 201 appearing as if it were a statement number. Let us further suppose that the values of the variables to be written are as follows:

$$I = 5 \quad U = 7.884 \quad V = 1/3 \quad K1 = 3000 \quad K2 = 49 \quad L = 0$$

Then the output unit would receive the following two lines:

```
bbbb5bbbb7.884000
b0.333333E+00bbbbb3000bbbbbbb49bbbbbbbbb0
```

where the lower case "b" denotes blank. The format is interpreted as follows:

(a) I5 means an integer with five digits. The integer I has only one digit (leading zeros are never printed in I-format) and so the first five positions on this line are blank, blank, blank, blank, 5.

(b) F12.6 means a floating point number taking up 12 places total, of which 6 are decimal places (884000 in this example). The 7 and the decimal point constitute two more places, leaving four extra places, which become leading blanks.

(c) Slash (/) means "start a new line," or, on input, read a new record.

(d) E13.6 means a floating point number written in the exponent format, in which $E+nn$ means "times 10^{nn}" and $E-nn$ means "times 10^{-nn}," taking up a total of 13 places of which 6 are decimal places. Since 4 places are used for the exponent, one for the leading zero and one for the decimal point, one place remains, which becomes a leading blank.

(e) The 3 followed by a parenthesized expression means that this format, (5X,I4), is to be repeated three times and applied to the next three variables, K1, K2, and L.

(f) 5X means "insert five blanks."

(g) I4 means an integer with four digits. Leading blanks are inserted as in (a) above; the integer zero is presumed to have one significant digit.

Appendix C

THE BINARY NUMBER SYSTEM

A *number system* is a way of expressing integers in terms of digits. In the *decimal number system,* there are ten digits, 0, 1, 2, 3, 4, 5, 6, 7, 8, and 9. Any integer larger than 9 is expressed as a sequence of digits according to the following rule: if m is any integer, and n is any digit, then the integer obtained by writing m followed by n has the value $10m + n$. For example:

$$m = 5, n = 3 \qquad 53 = 10(5) + 3 = 50 + 3$$
$$m = 37, n = 9 \qquad 379 = 10(37) + 9 = 370 + 9$$
$$m = 1638, n = 4 \qquad 16384 = 10(1638) + 4 = 16380 + 4$$

Any other number system is obtained from the decimal number system by substituting some other number for ten in the above rules. Thus, in the *binary number system,* there are two digits, 0 and 1. Any integer larger than 1 is expressed as a sequence of zeros and ones according to the rule that if m is any such sequence and n is either zero or one, then the binary integer obtained by writing m followed by n has the value $2m + n$.

The first ten binary numbers and their decimal equivalents are as follows:

0	0	101	5
1	1	110	6
10	2	111	7
11	3	1000	8
100	4	1001	9

Addition, subtraction, multiplication, and division of binary numbers are performed in the same way as they would be for decimal numbers, keeping in mind that in the binary number system $1 + 1 = 10$ (carrying 1) and $10 - 1 = 1$ (borrowing 1). Thus:

```
  110100101        10010011        101101001                    10001
+  10011100      -  110010      *        101       1011001 10111101111
 ─────────       ─────────      ─────────                   1011001
 1001000001       1100001        101101001                  ───────
                                101101001                    1011111
                                ─────────                    1011001
                                11100001101                  ───────
                                                                 110
```

These results may be checked: $421 + 156 = 577$; $147 - 50 = 97$; $361 *$
$5 = 1805$; and $1519 \div 89 = 17$, with remainder 6.

Any binary number may be converted to decimal by numbering its
binary digits according to the powers of two. Thus for the binary number
1100010111 we write

$$
\begin{array}{cccccccccc}
512 & 256 & 128 & 64 & 32 & 16 & 8 & 4 & 2 & 1 \\
1 & 1 & 0 & 0 & 0 & 1 & 0 & 1 & 1 & 1
\end{array}
$$

where the powers of two are written from right to left above the digits.
Now we simply add those powers of two which correspond to ones in the
binary number: $512 + 256 + 16 + 4 + 2 + 1 = 791$.

Any decimal number may be converted to binary with the aid of a
table of powers of 10 and their binary equivalents, such as the following:

1	1	10	1010	100	1100100	1000	1111101000
2	10	20	10100	200	11001000	2000	11111010000
3	11	30	11110	300	100101100	3000	101110111000
4	100	40	101000	400	110010000	4000	111110100000
5	101	50	110010	500	111110100	5000	1001110001000
6	110	60	111100	600	1001011000	6000	1011101110000
7	111	70	1000110	700	1010111100	7000	1101101011000
8	1000	80	1010000	800	1100100000	8000	1111101000000
9	1001	90	1011010	900	1110000100	9000	10001100101000

Thus, to calculate the binary equivalent of 9276, we write

$$
\begin{array}{rcl}
9000 & = & 10001100101000 \\
200 & = & 11001000 \\
70 & = & 1000110 \\
6 & = & 110 \\
\hline
9276 & = & 10010000111100
\end{array}
$$

In the absence of a table such as the one above, a decimal number may
be converted to binary using the iterative scheme illustrated below:

9276	1084	1084	1084	60	60	60	60	60	28	12	4	0	0
−8192	−4096	−2048	−1024	−512	−256	−128	−64	−32	−16	−8	−4	−2	−1
1084	neg	neg	60	neg	neg	neg	neg	28	12	4	0	0	0
8192	4096	2048	1024	512	256	128	64	32	16	8	4	2	1
1	0	0	1	0	0	0	0	1	1	1	1	0	0

The powers of two are written from right to left, as before, ending with the largest power of two which is smaller than the given number. The subtractions are carried out from left to right. Each negative result is discarded; each non-negative result becomes the next quantity from which to subtract a power of two. The bit obtained after each subtraction is zero for a negative result and one for a positive, non-zero result. The calculation may be stopped when a zero result is obtained, since the bit obtained thereby and all succeeding bits will now be zero.

The number of digits in any number system is called its *base*. Thus the decimal system has base 10; the binary system has base 2. Other number systems which are found in computing include *octal* (base 8) and *hexadecimal* (base 16). These number systems are used primarily as a "shorthand" to stand for binary, since large binary numbers are cumbersome to work with. They may be used in this way because conversion between binary and octal, or between binary and hexadecimal, may be performed digit by digit. In fact, this is always true for two bases, one of which is a power of the other. To convert binary numbers to octal we use the table

0	000	2	010	4	100	6	110
1	001	3	011	5	101	7	111

applied to the individual groups of three binary digits, or *bits*. Thus 101100010010000110111100 is converted to octal by writing

101	100	010	010	000	110	111	100
5	4	2	2	0	6	7	4

and the octal number 54220674 is converted back to binary in exactly the same way.

If the base is larger than 10, extra digits are needed. Any symbols may be used, but in computing it is conventional to use letters, starting with A and proceeding through the alphabet; this takes care of number systems up to and including base 36. Thus the hexadecimal digits are 0, 1, 2, 3, 4, 5, 6, 7, 8, 9, A, B, C, D, E, and F, in that order. Conversion between binary and "hex," or hexadecimal, is performed by groups of four bits instead of three. Thus the binary number illustrated above is converted to hexadecimal by writing

1011	0001	0010	0001	1011	1100
B	1	2	1	B	C

and the hexadecimal number B121BC is converted to binary in the same way.

The choice of octal or hexadecimal as a shorthand for the binary words in a binary computer is made by convention for each particular computer. The IBM 360 uses hexadecimal because its words divide naturally into groups which are a multiple of 4 bits in length, such as 8, 16, 32, or 64 bits. Most other binary computers use octal, both because it is easy to use and because their instruction words have fields which are multiples of 3 bits in length.

Appendix D

CHECKOUT

The term **checkout** refers to the finding and removing of errors from a program. More informally, such errors are called **bugs,** and checkout is called **debugging.**

Debugging a small program is often a matter of finding mistakes by hand. The programmer simply analyzes his program listing very thoroughly and finds as many errors as he can in this way; this is called **desk checking.** The easiest errors to find and remove are assembly or compilation errors—those found by the assembler or the compiler. These are always flagged and in many cases fully explained in comments on the listing made by the assembler or compiler. Most assemblers have "error flags" which are single letters standing for various errors, such as U for undefined symbol; these are always fully explained in the assembler manual.

Errors which are not found by desk checking may turn up in test runs of the program. The program may go into an endless loop; or it may print out nothing at all; or an error message produced by a subroutine may appear on the listing; or it may print out data which is obviously wrong, such as all zeros; or it may print out data which is not obviously wrong, but which proves to be inconsistent with other data. Debugging is an art, rather than a science, and the types of errors that occur most frequently depend highly on both the computer and the language involved, but there are certain programming errors which recur in almost all systems. Forgetting to initialize or to reset a variable is one of these. Skip instructions should be checked to make sure they are not "the wrong way around"; the use of a test equal instead of a test unequal, or vice versa, among similar errors, is very common. If the program is in an endless loop, the instruction which initializes the index should be checked (in machine language); beginners often put it inside the loop instead of before the loop, a procedure which always leads to endless loops.

There are several types of errors which are not, strictly speaking, *programming* errors, but which cause the same types of problems in computer runs as programming errors. Among these are the following:

(1) **Keypunch errors.** If a card has been mispunched, an error of some type will occur. In machine language, keypunch errors are almost always caught by the assembler, since every symbol must be defined; a keypunch error will be accepted by the assembler only if what is typed is actually legal in machine language. In an algebraic language, keypunch errors are more common; misspelling the name of a symbol simply causes a new symbol to be set up erroneously. In some algebraic languages, however, such as ALGOL, every symbol must be defined.

(2) **Transmission errors.** The data on the cards may be transmitted incorrectly from cards to tape or from tape to memory; the output data may be transmitted incorrectly from memory to tape or from tape to the printer. These are especially difficult errors to find, although if the cards and the listing do not agree, there has probably been a transmission error. However, transmission errors are almost never repeated; simply running the program again will resolve the error.

(3) **Data errors.** The input data, if there is any, may have been given incorrectly or (more commonly) given in the wrong format.

(4) **Control card errors.** The assembler or compiler, and also the monitor or executive system, will have a control card format. If the control cards are in error, the program will probably not run properly even if it is correct.

(5) **Design errors.** Sometimes several test runs are required on a program before the programmer discovers that it is designed incorrectly. This happens more frequently on longer programs, where the flow of control is complex. In this case, the entire program may have to be reprogrammed.

(6) **Hardware errors.** Very infrequently, a program may not work because the computer itself is not working properly. In this case, complaint should be made to the customer engineers who maintain the computer. This, however, should be done only when the fault is determined to be the computer's beyond the shadow of a doubt. A good example of such proof is a program which runs consistently on one computer and fails consistently on another one with the same characteristics.

There are many ways in which errors are found. One simple method is to insert print operations in the program every so often to see that it is proceeding properly. At the point at which the printouts stop producing correct results, there has probably been an error. If this error is not immediately apparent, another run can be made with more such print operations.

Most operating systems have **debugging aids,** or routines which help the programmer in debugging. A **dump routine** is a subroutine, called either during the program (**snapshot dump**) or after the program is finished (**post mortem dump**), which produces a listing of the contents of memory, known as a **dump** or a **core dump,** and which can be in one of various formats: instruction words, data words in octal, decimal, binary, hexadecimal, or floating point, or character codes. Sometimes only the contents of memory between two given addresses are printed, or dumped. A listing of the contents of a file is also called a **tape dump, disk dump,** etc., depending on the file medium. Dumping takes a certain amount of computer time, but is very useful provided that the address limits are kept reasonable and an effort is made to find more than one error by studying a single dump.

A **trace** is a program which follows the operation of the program being debugged and prints out various information about its progress. One type of trace interprets and executes the instructions in a program one by one; this is exceedingly slow. Some computers have a method of interrupting the program and transferring to the trace routine whenever a transfer is made in the debugged program; this permits a slightly faster trace.

An **interactive debugging system** is a program that allows the user to run all of his program or any part of it under his control. Unless the computer has a time-sharing system, interactive debugging wastes huge amounts of computer time, since the computer cannot be used by anyone else during the debugging process; these systems are generally found only in very small computers with typewriters and in time-sharing systems. Input statements given to the system by the programmer sitting at his typewriter or other console cause the program to proceed from one point to another, for information to be typed, errors changed, and various other operations.

Once an error is found, it may be corrected in any of several ways, some of which are more expensive than others. One way of correcting errors in machine language programs which was formerly used very commonly and which is still encountered sometimes today is the use of correctors. A **corrector** is a card giving an address and the contents of this address; this card is inserted in an object deck just before the last card, and the object deck is rerun. A single corrector, in some systems, may contain more than one octal word. To make a corrector, the instruction word or data word involved is calculated by hand, and the address is determined from the assembly listing. If an instruction word is to be deleted, it is replaced by a NOP or by a transfer to the next instruction word. If several instruction words are to be deleted, the first such word is replaced by a transfer around the deleted instructions. If instruction words are to be inserted before instruction word X, then X is replaced by a transfer to an area of core not used by the program; the inserted instructions, followed by instruction X, followed by a transfer to the next instruction after X, are now placed in this area of core. This process is known as **patching.**

Usually the only alternative to the use of correctors is reassembling the program. On some machines assemblies take very large amounts of time and correctors are used extensively. The correctors, however, are themselves subject to errors, especially so because the contents of instruction and data words must be calculated by hand. When the insertion of correctors fails to correct an error, the most likely possibility is that the correctors are wrong.

INDEX